Global Reordering

Series editor
André Broome
University of Warwick
Coventry, UK

Shaun Breslin
PAIS
University of Warwick
Coventry, UK

How is the global order changing, and why? The contemporary dynamics of the global political economy and global security in the twenty-first century are experiencing a series of fundamental transitions, which are challenging and transforming the existing global order. These dynamics are reshaping relations between and within different categories of actors such as states, club forums, international organizations, transnational policy communities, private sector agencies and corporations, and civil society organizations. At the same time, processes of global reordering have led to the emergence of new issue areas and policy problems that the existing landscape of national, regional, and global governance is struggling to effectively address. The Centre for the Study of Globalisation and Regionalisation (CSGR) at the University of Warwick has been home, since 2011, to a major EU funded research project on Global Reordering. With 16 partners from across the world, the project has focussed on how European interests, objectives, and modes of governance might influence the way in which a post-unipolar global order takes shape. Global Reordering seeks to build on this research agenda, and also expand it by moving beyond just a European focus towards a truly global perspective. Global Reordering invites manuscript submissions based on innovative empirical research that is theoretically-informed and is relevant for contemporary policy debates. The series welcomes proposals for authored monographs, edited volumes and short length Pivots. Key areas include: changing modes of global governance and multipolarity; global public policy networks; emerging powers and multipolar alternatives; regions and regionalism; as well as regional and global leadership.

More information about this series at
http://www.palgrave.com/gp/series/15015

Helge Blakkisrud • Elana Wilson Rowe
Editors

Russia's Turn to the East

Domestic Policymaking and Regional Cooperation

Editors
Helge Blakkisrud
Norwegian Institute of International
Affairs (NUPI)
Oslo, Norway

Elana Wilson Rowe
Norwegian Institute of International
Affairs (NUPI)
Oslo, Norway

Global Reordering
ISBN 978-3-319-69789-5   ISBN 978-3-319-69790-1   (eBook)
https://doi.org/10.1007/978-3-319-69790-1

Library of Congress Control Number: 2017960774

© The Editor(s) (if applicable) and The Author(s) 2018 This book is an open access publication
Open Access This book is licensed under the terms of the Creative Commons Attribution 4.0 International License (http://creativecommons.org/licenses/by/4.0/), which permits use, sharing, adaptation, distribution and reproduction in any medium or format, as long as you give appropriate credit to the original author(s) and the source, provide a link to the Creative Commons license and indicate if changes were made.
The images or other third party material in this book are included in the book's Creative Commons license, unless indicated otherwise in a credit line to the material. If material is not included in the book's Creative Commons license and your intended use is not permitted by statutory regulation or exceeds the permitted use, you will need to obtain permission directly from the copyright holder.
The use of general descriptive names, registered names, trademarks, service marks, etc. in this publication does not imply, even in the absence of a specific statement, that such names are exempt from the relevant protective laws and regulations and therefore free for general use.
The publisher, the authors and the editors are safe to assume that the advice and information in this book are believed to be true and accurate at the date of publication. Neither the publisher nor the authors or the editors give a warranty, express or implied, with respect to the material contained herein or for any errors or omissions that may have been made. The publisher remains neutral with regard to jurisdictional claims in published maps and institutional affiliations.

Cover illustration: Modern building window © saulgranda/Getty

Printed on acid-free paper

This Palgrave Pivot imprint is published by Springer Nature
The registered company is Springer International Publishing AG
The registered company address is: Gewerbestrasse 11, 6330 Cham, Switzerland

Preface

Pictures can sometimes be more revealing than words. If you ever sit down and look at a night-time satellite picture of the Earth, you will find that there are still huge areas on our planet that are not lit up by human activities and cities.

One of the largest 'dark spots' in the Northern Hemisphere is found in the Russian Far East or Pacific Russia. Here are enormous territories rich in natural resources like petroleum, minerals, forests and water—but these vast reaches are sparsely populated and lack connective infrastructure. A closer look at the satellite image will reveal a tiny thread of light, almost like an umbilical cord, linking the Far Eastern part of Russia with the European part. This is the Trans-Siberian Railway that connects the Eastern and Western parts of Russia.

The same satellite picture shows few traces of networking with the territories of the immediate neighbourhood—the brightly lit, heavily populated, urbanized and dynamic Asian economies of China, Japan and the Republic of Korea. It is hardly surprising that Russia has intensified its efforts at closer integration with these Asian neighbours, economically and politically. For Russia, this pivot to Asia represents huge opportunities, but it also entails significant economic, administrative, technological, cultural and strategic challenges.

The contributors to this book examine the nature, speed and direction of the long-term structural shift. Rather than taking the declared 'pivot' as a fact and exploring the likely consequences, the authors ask whether there has in fact been such a new pivot—or if what we see today is a continuation of longer-duration trends, concerns and ambitions.

The authors explore the relationship between integration and disintegration, examining whether Russia's turn to the East has intensified or changed in nature—domestically and internationally—since the onset of the current crisis in relations with the West. In turning to the East, is Russia also turning away from the West?

This project is a result of collaboration involving scholars from Norway, Russia, Korea and the UK, and has been supported financially by the Korea Foundation and the Norwegian Ministry of Foreign Affairs.

Oslo, Norway   Ulf Sverdrup
                                                                                        NUPI

Seoul, Republic of Korea   Jae-Young Lee
                                                                                        KIEP

May 2017

Contents

1 Gateway or Garrison? Border Regions in Times
   of Geopolitical Crisis   1
   Helge Blakkisrud and Elana Wilson Rowe

2 An Asian Pivot Starts at Home: The Russian Far East
   in Russian Regional Policy   11
   Helge Blakkisrud

3 Primorskii Krai and Russia's 'Turn to the East':
   A Regional View   31
   Tamara Troyakova

4 Promoting New Growth: 'Advanced Special Economic
   Zones' in the Russian Far East   51
   Jiyoung Min and Boogyun Kang

5 The Russian Far East and Russian Security Policy
   in the Asia-Pacific Region   75
   Malin Østevik and Natasha Kuhrt

6 Did China Bankroll Russia's Annexation of Crimea?
   The Role of Sino-Russian Energy Relations   95
   Indra Overland and Gulaikhan Kubayeva

7 Russia, China and the Shanghai Cooperation Organization:
   Diverging Security Interests and the 'Crimea Effect'   119
   Marc Lanteigne

8 Russia's New Asian Tilt: How Much Does Economy
   Matter?   139
   Roman Vakulchuk

9 Afterword: 6400 Kilometres Away—But Not a Policy
   World Apart   159
   Elana Wilson Rowe and Helge Blakkisrud

Index   165

List of Contributors

Helge Blakkisrud Research Group on Russia, Eurasia and the Arctic, Norwegian Institute of International Affairs (NUPI), Oslo, Norway

Boogyun Kang Russia and Eurasia Team, Department of Europe, Americas and Eurasia, Korea Institute for International Economic Policy (KIEP), Sejong, Republic of Korea

Gulaikhan Kubayeva Research Group on Russia, Eurasia and the Arctic, Norwegian Institute of International Affairs (NUPI), Oslo, Norway

Natasha Kuhrt Department of War Studies, King's College London, London, UK

Marc Lanteigne Centre for Defence and Security Studies, Massey University, Auckland, New Zealand

Jae-Young Lee Department of Europe, Americas and Eurasia, Korea Institute for International Economic Policy (KIEP), Sejong, Republic of Korea

Jiyoung Min Russia and Eurasia Team, Department of Europe, Americas and Eurasia, Korea Institute for International Economic Policy (KIEP), Sejong, Republic of Korea

Malin Østevik Research Group on Russia, Eurasia and the Arctic, Norwegian Institute of International Affairs (NUPI), Oslo, Norway

Indra Overland Energy Programme, Norwegian Institute of International Affairs (NUPI), Oslo, Norway

Elana Wilson Rowe Research Group on Emerging Powers and International Development, Norwegian Institute of International Affairs (NUPI), Oslo Norway

Ulf Sverdrup Norwegian Institute of International Affairs (NUPI), Oslo, Norway

Tamara Troyakova School of Regional and International Studies, Far Eastern Federal University, Vladivostok, Russia

Roman Vakulchuk Research Group on Russia, Eurasia and the Arctic, Norwegian Institute of International Affairs (NUPI), Oslo, Norway

List of Figures

Fig. 4.1	Industrial composition of the economy of the Russian Far East, 2014 (in per cent) (Source: Federal'naia sluzhba gosudarstvennoi statistiki 2016)	55
Fig. 6.1	Chinese oil imports, by country of origin, main suppliers (Sources: Observatory of Economic Complexity 2014; Workman 2016)	96
Fig. 6.2	Loans of Russian non-bank entities from China, million USD (Source: Calculated based on data from the Central Bank of Russia, available at http://www.cbr.ru/eng/statistics/?PrtId=svs. Accessed on 26 March 2017)	100
Fig. 6.3	FDI from China to Russia, million USD (Source: Calculated based on data from the Central Bank of Russia, available at https://www.cbr.ru/statistics/credit_statistics/inv_in-country.xlsx. Accessed on 26 March 2017)	100
Fig. 6.4	Russian income from the export of oil, gas and coal to China, million USD (Source: Based on data on import of 'coal, coke and briquettes', 'petroleum, petroleum products and related materials', 'gas, natural and manufactured' from Russia to China, retrieved from https://comtrade.un.org/data. Accessed on 10 October 2016)	101
Fig. 8.1	Imports to the Russian Far East from main Asian and non-Asian trade partners (million USD) (Source: Federal State Statistics Service 2016)	146
Fig. 8.2	Exports from the Russian Far East to main Asian and non-Asian trade partners (million USD) (Source: Federal State Statistics Service 2016)	147
Fig. 8.3	FDI in the Russian Far East by main Asian and non-Asian partners (million USD) (Federal State Statistics Service 2016)	148

LIST OF TABLES

Table 2.1	Russian ministries responsible for regional policy	14
Table 3.1	Projects under the ASEZ regime realized in Primorskii Krai	38
Table 4.1	Macroeconomic indicators of the Russian Federation (RF) and the Far East (FE) (in per cent of previous year)	54
Table 4.2	Production index of the manufacturing sector (in per cent of previous year)	55
Table 4.3	Population (1000 persons/per cent of previous year)	57
Table 4.4	Labour market (per cent of total)	57
Table 4.5	Average monthly income (in rubles, December each year)	58
Table 4.6	Cost of goods and services of fixed basket (in rubles, December each year)	58
Table 4.7	Key features of ASEZs	63
Table 4.8	Comparison of characteristics of SEZs in Asia-Pacific countries	65
Table 4.9	Designated ASEZs	67
Table 6.1	Main EU and US economic sanctions against Russia	98
Table 6.2	Timeline of Sino-Russian cooperation on ESPO pipeline	103
Table 6.3	Timeline of Sino-Russian cooperation on Power of Siberia	105
Table 6.4	Timeline of Sino-Russian cooperation on Yamal LNG	107
Table 6.5	Timeline of Sino-Russian cooperation on Vankor field	108
Table 6.6	Sino-Russian energy deals and developments	110
Table 7.1	From the Shanghai Five to the SCO	123

CHAPTER 1

Gateway or Garrison? Border Regions in Times of Geopolitical Crisis

Helge Blakkisrud and Elana Wilson Rowe

Abstract Russia's border regions have had moments as open 'gateways' to cooperation. More often, however, the border has been viewed as a 'garrison': an outpost of state power. This chapter places the Russian Far East in the broader context of Russia's pursuit of economic development and security concerns, noting that Russian foreign policy is not necessarily uniform: there are elements of compartmentalization/disaggregation along geographical vectors. The chapter broaches the question that informs all case studies in this volume: has Russia intensified its diplomatic and economic outreach to its eastern border areas and beyond because of the recent breakdown in relations with the West—or would such a shift have taken place anyway, given the economic pull of the Asia-Pacific region?

Keywords Russia • Russian Far East • Policymaking • Asia-Pacific region • Geography of foreign policy

---

H. Blakkisrud (✉)
Research Group on Russia, Eurasia and the Arctic, Norwegian Institute of International Affairs, Oslo, Norway

E. Wilson Rowe
Research Group on Emerging Powers and Global Development, Norwegian Institute of International Affairs, Oslo, Norway

© The Author(s) 2018
H. Blakkisrud, E. Wilson Rowe (eds.), *Russia's Turn to the East*,
Global Reordering, https://doi.org/10.1007/978-3-319-69790-1_1

Russia's border regions have had moments as open 'gateways' to cooperation, as seen in the development of cross-border cooperation and trade across the Russian–Norwegian border after the end of the Cold War. More often, however, the border has been viewed as a 'garrison': an outpost of state power, rather than a gateway for trade and interaction.

In many ways, the Russian Far Eastern city of Vladivostok exemplifies the broader regional dynamics, opportunities and challenges that this book seeks to explore. For centuries, the territory where Vladivostok now stands was under Chinese control—a remote source of ginseng and sea cucumbers. In the mid-nineteenth century, the Russian Empire began asserting its presence in the region. From the founding of Vladivostok in 1860 up until 1909, the city was subject to a free port regime, attracting people not only from the European part of the Empire but also a substantial colony of foreigners: in the late 1800s, nearly half of the city's population hailed from outside Russia. After the 1917 Revolution, Vladivostok was one of the last strongholds of the White Army and part of the semi-independent, short-lived Far Eastern Republic. With the establishment of Soviet power in 1922, however, the formerly internationally-oriented city was gradually closed off from the outside world, culminating with the 1951 decision to ban the entry of foreigners (a regulation in force until the end of the Soviet period). Starting with Nikita Khrushchev's visit to the region in the late 1950s, Moscow began investing in urban and port facility development in Vladivostok. However, the city remained a closed naval base. With the breakup of the Soviet Union in 1991, local residents and external observers alike predicted a new boom for the city, with a transformation from a closed garrison to an open gateway to the Asia-Pacific. More than a quarter of a century later, these high hopes for Vladivostok, as well as the wider Russian Far East, are still far from met.

Russia's Far Eastern Federal Okrug consists of nine federal subjects: three ethnic autonomies (the Sakha Republic, the Jewish Autonomous Oblast and Chukotka Autonomous Okrug) and six 'regular' regions (Amur, Kamchatka, Khabarovsk, Magadan, Primorye and Sakhalin). With its 6,169,300 km^2, it is the by far biggest federal okrug in terms of territory: in fact, the Far Eastern Federal Okrug makes up one-third of the total territory of the Russian Federation. However, with only 6.2 million inhabitants, it has the smallest population among the okrugs. The Far East's post-Soviet history thus far has been primarily one of severe economic dislocation, dramatic population decline (since 1991, the overall population has dropped by more than 20 per cent—but the Chukotka region, for instance, has lost almost 70 per cent) and rampant crime and corruption. And yet, the Russian Far East is a land of economic promise: vast natural resources and close proximity to major markets.

The need to develop the Far Eastern part of the country has been long recognized as an important issue for Russian authorities (see Stephan 1994; Kotkin and Wolff 1995; Thornton and Ziegler 2002; Lee and Lukin 2016). This recognition has been linked to the economic potential and untapped resources of the region, as well as to concerns that an underdeveloped and sparsely populated region could, in the long term, fall victim of Chinese expansionism (Lukin 2007). Over the last few years, developing the Russian Far East has become a growing political priority, with the clear objective of enabling Russia to benefit from closer cooperation with the fast-expanding East Asian economies (see, for example, Baklanov 2012; Karaganov 2012; Hill and Lo 2013; Bordachev and Kanaev 2014; Karaganov 2014; Lo 2014). To this end, Moscow has adopted a range of political strategies and investment plans aimed at developing infrastructure and generating growth in the Siberian and Far Eastern federal okrugs. Through developing the eastern regions, Russian authorities seek to tie the western part of the country closer to the Asia-Pacific, thereby facilitating a 'turn to the East' (Jeh 2015; Jeh et al. 2015).

With the crisis in Russian–European/North American relations precipitated by Russia's annexation of Crimea in 2014 and subsequent involvement in eastern Ukraine, Moscow has, with increasing urgency, been pushing the idea of turning the Russian Far East into a new gateway (see Kaczmarski 2015; Lukin 2015; Lukyanov 2015; Trenin 2015). However, little systematic, empirically based research has been done on Moscow's 'post-Crimea' emphasis on the Russian Far East and the development of relations with East Asia. This volume seeks to address this gap by exploring the scope and practical consequences of Russia's 'turn to the East', as well as the extent to which such a reorientation has been driven by its worsened relations with the West.

We present seven case studies that analyse post-2014 change at two geographical levels: the internal dimension, with the dynamics of Russian Far East political and socioeconomic development (Chaps. 2, 3, 4 and 5); and the external dimension of patterns of regional political relations and commerce in the East Asian neighbourhood (Chaps. 6, 7 and 8). These two geographical levels are not always easy to separate, but the approach allows us to examine how Moscow's political, economic and security-related policy initiatives are received not only by the region itself but also by Russia's key partners in East Asia.

In Chap. 2, Helge Blakkisrud shows how the Russian authorities have struggled to come up with a viable model for organizing centre–region relations in general and interaction with the Far East in particular. To achieve the ambitious goals the Kremlin has set for itself as regards turning the Far East into Russia's gateway to the Asia-Pacific, a new ministry was introduced in 2012—a hybrid reflecting Moscow's centralized take on policy formulation, as well as the difficulties of micro-managing politics in a distant region. Blakkisrud's chapter analyses the preliminary experiences with the work of the new Ministry for the Development of the Far East and its interactions with the rest of the institutional set-up (including other sectoral ministries, the office of the Presidential Plenipotentiary to the Far Eastern Federal Okrug and the regional governors). In this way, the chapter explores the broader issues of centre–periphery power relations and the challenges faced by Moscow in attempting to enact policy over a great distance. Blakkisrud finds that, over the past few years, the new development model for the Russian Far East has become institutionally anchored. The question remains, however, as to whether the model Moscow has produced will prove capable of dealing with the fundamental problems facing the Russian Far East.

Chapter 3 picks up on these questions from a regional perspective. Tamara Troyakova explores how the political and economic 'turn to the East' has manifested itself in specific politics and policies in Primorskii Krai, the federal subject that is home to the city of Vladivostok. Ever since the breakup of the Soviet Union, the entire Russian Far East has been struggling to attract investments and to stem the outflow of people. Troyakova examines how the authorities have attempted to meet these challenges by developing new institutions and initiatives. In particular, she focuses on local experiences of introducing special economic zones (Russkii Island, established in 2010), advanced special economic zones (ASEZs) (two in 2015, one in 2016) and the Free Port of Vladivostok (2015). Her chapter discusses the gap between formal declarations and the actual implementation of the various development mechanisms. According to Troyakova, progress has been sluggish because of a combination of factors: lack of coordination among various branches of the government and the new institutions they have set up, continued rampant corruption and an unattractive investment climate.

In Chap. 4, Jiyoung Min and Boogyun Kang explore Moscow's efforts to turn the Russian Far East into a new 'economic bridge' between Europe and Asia. They survey key milestones thus far, such as the establishment of the Ministry for the Development of the Far East in 2012, the adoption of a state programme for 'Socioeconomic Development of the Far East and the Baikal Region until 2025' in 2013 and the approval of the federal law 'On Advanced Special Economic Zones in the Russian Federation' in 2014. Ever since 2013, the Far Eastern Federal Okrug has been suffering from a downward economic cycle. Min and Kang compare the performance of this federal okrug against the seven other macro-regions in the Russian Federation, and ask whether the introduction of ASEZs could help to turn the negative trend. The chapter provides a detailed analysis of the implementation of the new development strategy, with a discussion of the pros and cons of ASEZs as an investment platform for cultivating export-oriented industry. Min and Kang conclude that the success of the ASEZs will hinge on their ability to attract extensive inflows of capital—domestic and foreign, and that in a short time-perspective, given current financial constraints, it is difficult to be optimistic regarding Far Eastern development.

Next, in Chap. 5, Malin Østevik and Natasha Kuhrt examine the place of the Russian Far East in Moscow's security-policy deliberations. They start by surveying Russian security policy since the onset of the current 'pivot' to the East—which, they hold, commenced around 2012—before going on to investigate any changes since 2014. Østevik and Kuhrt take a broad approach to security, taking into consideration local, national and international factors as well as economic security. Their chapter analyses various security-policy influences, ranging from the deployment of Russian armed forces in the Far East, to bilateral and multilateral engagements in the Asia-Pacific region and Russian–Chinese attempts at coordination in global politics. The authors find that factors local to the Russian Far East are particularly salient for understanding Russian security policy in the Asia-Pacific. Despite all the official statements on the primacy of the Russo-Chinese strategic partnership and the growing centrality of the Asia-Pacific region in world affairs, security concerns related to the social and economic underdevelopment of the Russian Far East have prevented the 'pivot' from being grounded in broad regional engagement. Further, Østevik and Kuhrt find that current security-policy trends are rooted in the period before the 2014 crisis with the West, and cannot automatically be attributed to the deteriorating relationship between Western countries and Russia.

The final three chapters place these findings about the depth and nature of the Russian 'turn to the East' in an East Asian neighbourhood context. In Chap. 6, Indra Overland and Gulaikhan Kubayeva analyse the consequences of Russia's turn to Asia for energy relations between Russia and China. The backdrop is several major breakthroughs in Russian–Chinese energy cooperation in the immediate aftermath of the introduction of the Western post-Crimea sanctions regime. In addition, China has been held to be discreetly providing financial backing to a cash-strapped Russian energy sector after the latter was cut off from receiving Western credits due to the same sanctions. Further, Overland and Kubayeva provide case studies of the major existing and potential Russian–Chinese energy projects: Transneft's Eastern Siberia–Pacific Ocean (ESPO) oil pipeline, Gazprom's Power of Siberia gas pipeline, Novatek's Yamal LNG plant and Rosneft's Vankor oil and gas field. They find a mixed picture; in the Vankor development, for example, the Chinese were eventually replaced by other investors. The chapter concludes that, in general, deals made from 2014 onwards are in line with trends that originated well before the annexation of Crimea and subsequent crisis in Russia's relations with the West and that the scale of Chinese financial contributions to the sector is not as large as often argued.

In Chap. 7, Marc Lanteigne also looks for strategic convergence between Russia and China, but here in the field of security—specifically, within the Shanghai Cooperation Organization (SCO). His chapter explains the origins and initial policies of the SCO as it made the transition from the informal 'Shanghai Five' grouping to a more structured security community. Lanteigne analyses the internal and external factors shaping the SCO's distinct security agenda and the divergence between Russian and Chinese visions about the future direction of the organization: while Russia wants to strengthen cooperation within hard security, China has been pushing an economic agenda. He also surveys the reactions of the SCO and its individual members to the annexation of Crimea and the conflict in eastern Ukraine. Lanteigne concludes that the case of the SCO underscores Beijing's interests in retaining Russia as a valuable strategic partner while also maintaining a discreet 'agree to disagree' stance on Moscow's post-Crimea strategic policies. Moreover, given the differing power trajectories of Moscow and Beijing, and their divergent views on regional and global security priorities, he finds slim prospects for a formal alliance between the two.

Concluding the case-study chapters, in Chap. 8, Roman Vakulchuk takes the reader back to the broader scale, and examines Russia's trade relations with a wide range of countries in East Asia. The chapter seeks to grasp the scope of Russia's participation (or lack thereof) in the growing Asian markets. It provides an overview of the East Asian dimension of Russia's external economic relations covering the 2010–16 period and assesses the dynamics of investment, trade and infrastructure development before and after Crimea. Vakulchuk finds that exports, imports and FDI between the Far Eastern Federal Okrug and its major Asian partners declined significantly in 2015—and this negative trend continued into 2016. His analysis nevertheless indicates that, while the overall investment climate in the Far Eastern Federal Okrug has not improved significantly since 2014, the region has become more diversified and some new infrastructure has been put in place. In a longer-term perspective, these developments might contribute to attracting new investors.

The in-depth analysis of the internal and external dimensions of Russia's 'turn to the East'—and the interactions between the two and Russia's neighbours and partners in the Asia-Pacific—provides additional evidence of how Russia's foreign policy is not uniform, but varies according to geographical vectors. The compartmentalized/disaggregated nature of Russian foreign policy is a consideration we have explored previously in connection with Russia's approach to Arctic cooperation (Wilson Rowe and Blakkisrud 2014). The current volume explores both disaggregation and interconnectedness. Diplomatic and policy thinking may indeed be shaped by differing opportunity and threat perceptions unique to a specific border region, but there are also practical and strategic interconnections between the differing compass directions of foreign and security policies. When the going gets tough with Europe, does Russia react by intensifying its diplomatic and economic outreach to its eastern border areas and beyond? Did the sanctions regime provide an impetus for a pivot and a window of opportunity for the Russian Far East? These are the underlying questions that inform all the case-study chapters presented here, and to which we return in the concluding chapter.

REFERENCES

Baklanov, Petr, ed. 2012. *Tikhookeanskaia Rossiia: stranitsy proshlogo, nastoiashego, budushchego* [*Pacific Russia: pages of the past, present and future*]. Vladivostok: Dal'nauka.
Bordachev, Timofey and Yevgeniy Kanaev. 2014. 'Russia's new strategy in Asia', *Russia in Global Affairs*, 3. http://eng.globalaffairs.ru/numbers/118. Accessed on 30 March 2017.
Hill, Fiona and Bobo Lo. 2013. 'Putin's pivot: why Russia is looking East', *Foreign Affairs*, 31 July. www.foreignaffairs.com/articles/russian-federation/2013-07-31/putins-pivot. Accessed on 30 March 2017.
Jeh, Sung Hoon. 2015. 'Russia's Far East development and directions for improvement in Korean–Russian cooperation: Korea's perspective', in *International cooperation in the development of Russia's Far East and Siberia*, edited by Jing Huang and Alexander Korolev, 144–63. Basingstoke: Palgrave Macmillan.
Jeh, Sung Hoon, Jiyoung Min, Boogyun Kang and Sergey Lukonin. 2015. 'Recent development in the Russian Far East–Baikal region and its implication', *World Economy Update*, 5(17). http://papers.ssrn.com/sol3/papers.cfm?abstract_id=2771045. Accessed on 30 March 2017.
Kaczmarski, Marcin. 2015. *Russia–China relations in the post-crisis international order*. Abingdon: Routledge.
Karaganov, Sergei, ed. 2012. 'Toward the Great Ocean, or the new globalization of Russia', *Valdai Discussion Club Analytical Report*. http://vid-1.rian.ru/ig/valdai/Toward_great_ocean_eng_short.pdf. Accessed on 30 March 2017.
Karaganov, Sergei, ed. 2014. 'Toward the Great Ocean-2, or Russia's breakthrough to Asia', *Valdai Discussion Club Report*. http://vid-1.rian.ru/ig/valdai/Twd_Great_Ocean_2_Eng.pdf. Accessed on 5 May 2017.
Kotkin, Stephen and David Wolff. 1995. *Rediscovering Russia in Asia: Siberia and the Russian Far East*. Armonk, NY: ME Sharpe.
Lee, Rensselaer and Artyom Lukin. 2016. *Russia's Far East: new dynamics in Asia Pacific and beyond*. Boulder, CO: Lynne Rienner.
Lo, Bobo. 2014. *Russia's Eastern direction – distinguishing the real from the virtual*. Paris: IFRI.
Lukin, Aleksandr. 2007. *Medved' nabliudaet za drakonom: obraz Kitaia v Rossii v XVII–XXI vekakh* [*The bear watches the dragon: the image of China in Russia in 17th–21st centuries*]. Moscow: Vostok–Zapad.
Lukin, Aleksandr. 2015. 'Konsolidatsiia nezapadnogo mira na fone ukrainskogo krizisa: Rossiia i Kitai, ShOS i BRIKS' [The consolidation of the non-Western world against the background of the Ukraine crisis: Russia and China, Shanghai Cooperation Organization and BRICS], *Mezhdunarodnaia zhizn'* 2: 72–91.
Lukyanov, Fyodor. 2015. 'Russia must exploit its pivot east', *The Moscow Times*, 25 June.

Stephan, John J. 1994. *The Russian Far East: a history.* Redwood City, CA: Stanford University Press.
Thornton, Judith and Charles E. Ziegler, eds. 2002. *Russia's Far East: a region at risk.* Washington, DC: National Bureau of Asian Research.
Trenin, Dmitri. 2015. *From Greater Europe to Greater Asia? The Sino-Russian entente.* Moscow: Carnegie Moscow Center. http://carnegie.ru/2015/04/09/from-greater-europe-to-greater-asia-sino-russian-entente-pub-59728. Accessed on 30 March 2017.
Wilson Rowe, Elana and Helge Blakkisrud. 2014. 'Great power, Arctic power: Russia's northern engagement', *Geopolitics* 19(1): 66–85.

Open Access   This chapter is licensed under the terms of the Creative Commons Attribution 4.0 International License (http://creativecommons.org/licenses/by/4.0/), which permits use, sharing, adaptation, distribution and reproduction in any medium or format, as long as you give appropriate credit to the original author(s) and the source, provide a link to the Creative Commons license and indicate if changes were made.

The images or other third party material in this book are included in the book's Creative Commons license, unless indicated otherwise in a credit line to the material. If material is not included in the book's Creative Commons license and your intended use is not permitted by statutory regulation or exceeds the permitted use, you will need to obtain permission directly from the copyright holder.

CHAPTER 2

An Asian Pivot Starts at Home: The Russian Far East in Russian Regional Policy

Helge Blakkisrud

Abstract To realize its ambitious goals of turning the Far East into Russia's gateway to the Asia-Pacific, the Kremlin in 2012 established the Ministry for the Development of the Far East. Structurally, this ministry is a hybrid, with offices at the federal and the regional levels, reflecting both Moscow's centralized take on policy formulation and the difficulties of micro-managing politics in a region distant in time and space. Analysing whether the new ministry has been a success, the author concludes that, while Moscow's primary goal has been to open a Far Eastern gateway, a side-effect might be that the Far East will become better integrated with the rest of the country, providing for more balanced development throughout the Federation.

Keywords Russian Far East • Ministry for the Development of the Far East • Policymaking • Centre–periphery relations • Regional development

---

H. Blakkisrud (✉)
Research Group on Russia, Eurasia and the Arctic, Norwegian Institute of International Affairs, Oslo, Norway

© The Author(s) 2018
H. Blakkisrud, E. Wilson Rowe (eds.), *Russia's Turn to the East*, Global Reordering, https://doi.org/10.1007/978-3-319-69790-1_2

Russia's pivot to Asia starts at home. While the turn towards Asia is fuelled by expectations of reaping benefits from integrating with the fast-growing markets of Northeast Asia, undertaking such a geo-economic reorientation is not possible without a viable springboard, or gateway, in the Russian Far East. For all the talk about Asia-Pacific markets, a key component of the pivot is therefore developing Russia's own Far Eastern region, a territory 'uniquely endowed, but perennially troubled' (Lee and Lukin 2016, p.7), an underdeveloped, crises-ridden backwater that currently constitutes a 'double periphery'—in relation to Moscow and to the Asia-Pacific (Kuhrt 2012). The dire socioeconomic conditions—and the need to take action—have been acknowledged by the Kremlin. In 2013, Vladimir Putin in his annual address to Federal Assembly even declared the development (*pod''em*, lit. 'lifting up') of the Far East a 'national priority for the entire twenty-first century' (Putin 2013).

Making the Russian Far East a viable gateway to the East will require sustained and coordinated efforts. As Putin expressed it: 'The tasks to be solved are unprecedented in scale, and therefore also our steps must be non-standard' (Putin 2013). To realize its ambitious plans, Moscow came up with an institutional innovation: a new ministry, operating partly in Moscow as a regular part of the federal government, partly as a decentralized structure based in the Far Eastern Federal Okrug.

In general, Russian politics is informed by a long tradition of implementing top-down development models. This is not something that originated with the Soviet five-year plans: also in Tsarist Russia, the state took a lead in modernization and economic development, not least in the Russian Far East. In the post-Soviet period, this 'urge to plan' manifests itself in the belief that the state can organize itself out of problems through strategic planning, bureaucratic reorganization and targeted state programmes (Cooper 2012, p.1; Monaghan 2013). Unsurprisingly, the policymaking behind the 'turn to the East' also exhibits a strong continued commitment to strategic planning (Fortescue 2016, p.423).

At the same time, this top-down approach coexists with a fair amount of hands-on management, or 'manual control' (*ruchnoe upravlenie*). The authorities frequently have to resort to the latter due to the failure of the bureaucracy to implement plans or to tackle inter-ministerial/inter-agency rivalries (Monaghan 2013). Thus, the leadership and top officials 'are required to become involved in regional, even local issues, micromanaging, rather than focusing on strategic matters' (ibid., p.1235).

The hybrid solution presented by the introduction of the Ministry for the Development of the Far East reflects an attempt to combine Moscow's traditionally centralized approach to policy formulation with bold acknowledgement of the difficulties of micro-managing policy implementation in a region extraordinarily distant both in time and space.[1] This chapter traces the role and function of the new Ministry for the Development of the Far East. How does this body interact with the other parts of the executive branch that also oversee Far Eastern policy portfolios (other branch ministries, the Presidential Plenipotentiary to the Far Eastern Federal Okrug and the regional heads)? Do we find traces of an impact of the post-Crimea breakdown of Russo-Western relations in how Moscow has approached the internal dimension of the pivot? And to what extent can this institutional innovation be characterized as a success?

Backdrop: Post-1991 Management of Centre–Region Relations

Since the break-up of the Soviet Union, the Kremlin has struggled to produce a viable model for organizing centre–region relations. In 1990, Boris Yeltsin famously encouraged the regions to 'Take as much sovereignty as you can swallow.' This ushered in a decade of ad hoc decentralization and federalization of the Russian state—partly a desired development, and partly because of Moscow's greatly reduced capacities and resultant failure to fulfil its obligations vis-à-vis the regional level (Blakkisrud 2003). From the turn of the millennium, however, political priorities shifted. The transfer of power and responsibilities to the regional level was first halted, then replaced by far-reaching re-centralization (Ross 2002, 2010; Blakkisrud 2015).

The shifting priorities in centre–region relations are reflected in the way the federal government has sought to organize this administratively. The portfolio of regional policies has had a tumultuous history, at times coordinated by a separate body, at other times divided across various ministries. After the turn of the millennium, regional policy as a separate domain fell victim to Putin's centralization drive, and the ministry was abolished (see Table 2.1). However, during Putin's second term, as part of a concerted push towards strengthening state institutions, the Ministry of Regional Development was re-introduced. This heralded a relative stabilization of the institutional framework: for the next ten years, this ministry oversaw the implementation of regional policy within Russia's increasingly emasculated federalism.

Table 2.1 Russian ministries responsible for regional policy

Name	Years in operation
State Committee on Federal Affairs and Nationalities	1993–1994
Ministry on Nationality Affairs and Regional Policy	1994–1996
Ministry on Nationality Affairs and Federal Relations	1996–1998
Ministry on Regional and Nationalities Policy	1998
Ministry on Regional Policy (nationality policy as separate ministry)	1998–1999
Ministry on Federal Affairs and Nationalities	1999–2000
Ministry on Federal Affairs, Nationalities and Migration Policy (Goskomsever and migration service added)	2000–2001
No separate ministry (portfolio divided between Ministry of Internal Affairs and Ministry of Economic Development)	2001–2004
Ministry of Regional Development	2004–2014
No separate ministry, but ministries for the Far East (2012–), North Caucasus (2014–) and Crimea (2014–2015)	2014–

Source: *RIA Novosti* (2011); author's compilation

The Russian Far East

Regarding the Russian Far East, centre–region relations in the 1990s revolved around issues of regional autonomy, control over natural resources and federal tax policy (Lee and Lukin 2016, p.9). China was also a recurrent topic, with regional leaders in the Far East often less enthusiastic than Moscow politicians about the benefits to be gained from developing relations with neighbouring Chinese provinces (see, for example, Burles 1999, pp.43–47).

Most federal subjects in the Russian Far East are net recipients of transfers over the federal budget, heavily dependent on Moscow's subsidizing the local economy. During the economic upheaval of the 1990s, the gut reaction of regional leaders was to lobby Moscow for greater support rather than to seek to develop the region's comparative advantages in the wider Asia-Pacific region. However, with the economic crisis and empty state coffers, Moscow had little to offer but promises. In 1996 the federal government adopted a targeted programme for the development of the Russian Far East, but most plans never materialized. The reason was, according to Stephen Fortescue, a combination of lack of genuine commitment and lack of adequate resource allocation (Fortescue 2016, p.425).

New attempts to revive the Far Eastern provinces were undertaken through new targeted programmes adopted in 2002 (focusing on exploitation of natural resources) and 2006 (living standards and social welfare) (Fortescue 2016, p.425). As the state finances gradually improved in the early 2000s, the problem of underfinancing became less acute. Especially with the adoption of the 2006 revision, the state began investing massively in the socioeconomic development of the Far East. Ambitious goals were set for economic growth, job creation, and renovation and expansion of existing infrastructure (Lee and Lukin 2016, p.9).

Another breakthrough came in 2009 when, in the midst of a new economic crisis, the government adopted a revised long-term development agenda for the Russian Far East: the 'Strategy for the Socioeconomic Development of the Far East and the Baikal Region for the Period until 2025' (Pravitel'stvo 2009). The Strategy highlighted the potential for regional economic development through integration with the Asia-Pacific region, by supplying countries like China, Japan and South Korea with energy and natural resources.

Based on an understanding that only the state and state-owned corporations had the economic muscle necessary for implementing such a grand project, the idea of setting up a special state corporation for the development of Eastern Siberia and the Russian Far East was floated in the run-up to Putin's third presidential term.[2] This corporation would be responsible for ensuring efficient exploitation of the region's natural resources and be under direct presidential oversight (Mel'nikov et al. 2012). It would enjoy wide powers: federal legislation would partly be set aside, to be replaced by a special economic regime for 16 federal subjects in the Far East and Eastern Siberia (encompassing about 60 per cent of all the territory of the Russian Federation).

However, the idea was controversial—among the general public and within the government. It drew criticism for attempting to introduce something akin to a 'state within the state' (Mel'nikov et al. 2012) and, through its emphasis on state-managed resource extraction, for reminding the local population about the region's status as an 'exploited semicolonial periphery' (Lee and Lukin 2016, p.84). A draft law for establishing such a corporation was shelved, and in its place came the Ministry for the Development of the Far East.

The Ministry for the Development of the Far East

The new ministry was established in June 2012. For the first two years of its existence, it functioned in parallel to the Ministry of Regional Development. The rationale for lifting the Far Eastern portfolio out of regular regional development policy was the belief in top-down implementation of development: that a separate bureaucratic structure would offer the most efficient way of addressing the socioeconomic challenges of the Russian Far East. This new ministry was tasked with coordinating and monitoring the implementation of existing policies, as well as elaborating a new set of mechanisms for stimulating economic and social development in the Far East. To give additional clout to the new minister, it was also decided that the minister should double in the position as Presidential Plenipotentiary to the Far Eastern Federal Okrug.

The most innovative aspect of the new ministry was its partially decentralized structure, with the ministry physically being set up in Moscow and Khabarovsk and the minister dividing his time between the two branches. In fact, the initial plan had been to make the Khabarovsk branch the main one, with 200 out of a total staff of 240 being located there (Netreba 2012). The rationale was obvious: the Russian Far East, in itself spanning four time-zones (Yakutsk, Vladivostok, Magadan and Kamchatka), was simply too far away from Moscow to be micro-managed from the capital. Setting up a decentralized structure that ensured a regional presence was intended to make the new ministry better positioned to follow up implementation of state priorities and programmes in the field, as well as get a better grasp of regional challenges and potentials. And since Khabarovsk was the seat of the Presidential Plenipotentiary, the natural choice was to co-locate the ministry there.

The first Minister of Far Eastern Development was Viktor Ishaev, a local political heavyweight who had served as governor of Khabarovsk Krai from 1991 to 2009, when he was made Presidential Plenipotentiary to the Far Eastern Federal Okrug. Now he would combine the two jobs: as minister of the federal government and the president's special representative to the Far East. The recruitment of a minister with more than 20 years of first-hand experience from the regional executive branch seemed to signal that Moscow was now ready to allow room for regional inputs.

Within a few months, however, Ishaev fell out of favour with Putin for his failure to move forward in implementing the government's Far Eastern policy (Zav'ialova 2012; Fortescue 2016, p.443). In August 2013 he was replaced, both as minister and as presidential plenipotentiary, and the two positions were then split. The new minister was Aleksandr Galushka, recruited from Putin's All-Russian National Front, where he had been co-chair. Unlike Ishaev, Galushka was a Muscovite with no experience from the Far East beyond having served for a year in the State Commission for the Socioeconomic Development of the Far East (2011–2012). As we will see below, the position of plenipotentiary went to Iurii Trutnev, a long-term Minister of Natural Resources (2004–2012).

In parallel, the ministry itself underwent structural reorganization, with an additional branch being set up in Vladivostok. In the process, staffing at the Khabarovsk branch, Ishaev's old stronghold, was cut back from more than 200 to a mere 28, while the new branch in Vladivostok was assigned 129 (compared to Moscow's 120) (*Deita* 2014). In December 2016, the organizational structure was further tempered by the decision to open a small 'mobile' office in Petropavlovsk-Kamchatskii (*RIA Novosti* 2016).

At the time, the ministry hinted that in future all nine federal subjects in the Far Eastern Federal Okrug might get their own branches of the ministry. This could have implications for the way the ministry functions. Today, the Khabarovsk and Vladivostok offices are officially equal in status to the Moscow one, although, with the shift from Ishaev to Galushka, the minister seems to be spending more time in Moscow. Within the ministry there is no clear branch specialization whereby a separate portfolio is allocated exclusively to Khabarovsk or Vladivostok: instead, there is regional representation to facilitate the flow of information and decisions between the capital and the federal subjects.[3]

Portfolio

According to the website of the Ministry for the Development of the Far East, it is responsible for the implementation of state programmes and federal targeted programmes in the Far Eastern Federal Okrug, the management of federal property and monitoring the work of the regional executive branch.[4]

The main focus of the ministry is reflected in its organizational structure. Besides departments for administration and control, it includes the following divisions, as of March 2017:[5]

- Department for Complex Macro-Regional Development, Attracting Budget Financing and Public Investment
- Department for Attracting Private Investment
- Department for Infrastructure Development
- Department for Advanced Special Economic Zones (ASEZs) and the Free Port of Vladivostok
- Department for Development of Human Capital and Territorial Development.

Within the portfolio of the ministry are also the following agencies:

- the Far East Human Capital Development Agency, established in September 2015 with offices in Moscow, Khabarovsk and Vladivostok, and tasked with attracting labour force to the Russian Far East and facilitating positive migration dynamics;[6]
- the Far East Investment and Export Agency, established in September 2015 with an office in Moscow, responsible for marketing the region and working with potential national and international investors, including potential residents of the ASEZs;
- the joint stock company Far East Development Corporation, established in April 2015 with offices in Moscow and Vladivostok, handling the operation of the ASEZs and development of the Free Port of Vladivostok regime.[7]

On the whole, this is a watered-down portfolio, as compared to the lofty plans for a state corporation. Not only has the territory falling under the purview of the ministry been nearly halved (when Eastern Siberia was excluded, the figure fell from some 60 per cent of Russia's territory to 36 per cent), the powers and prerogatives were also cut back to something more resembling a regular ministry: its current portfolio is more about oversight and facilitating development than being directly involved in running Far Eastern businesses. Nataliia Zubarevich, one of Russia's leading experts on centre–region relations, thus argues that the ministry proved more akin to a Soviet *sovnarkhoz* (quoted in Polunin 2012)[8] than the kind of super-ministry some people initially had speculated that it might become (Netreba 2012).

Plans and Implementation

While the powers of the ministry were reduced as compared to what key actors behind the idea of a state corporation had envisioned, what the new ministry initially *did* enjoy was impressive economic muscle. In March 2013, during Ishaev's stint as minister, an ambitious new state programme with a total budget more than 10 trillion rubles, of which the government was to contribute 3.8 trillion, was adopted (Gorshkova 2013). For the period up until 2025, the state was to spend lavishly on realizing what Stephen Fortescue has called a 'resource-oriented monster' by implementing 'a huge catalog of projects, many of which had been bandied around and included in funding wish lists since Soviet times' (Fortescue 2016, p.431).[9]

Economic realities soon kicked in, however. With the change in leadership in the ministry, the plans were overhauled and ambitions were cut back. Prime Minister Dmitrii Medvedev openly admitted that the previous development models had failed:

> We must admit frankly that all approaches, all the models that we have used in recent years, in order to change the development of the Far East radically, have not been unequivocally successful, they have not yet brought the results we expected, they have not produced economic effects. (*Government. ru* 2013)

In April 2014, when a revised version of the programme was adopted, the state funding for the period up to 2020 had been reduced to 346 billion rubles (*Government.ru* 2014)—to less than a tenth of what the government had pledged the previous year. Gone were the extravagant state-funded investment projects pushed by Ishaev; the focus was now on attracting *private* investment—national and foreign—to accelerate the economic development in the Russian Far East. In the course of the next year, several new mechanisms were introduced to facilitate the influx of capital—both financial and human—into the Far Eastern Federal Okrug. Three key initiatives deserve to be highlighted in this respect.

First, there is the establishment of *advanced special economic zones* (ASEZs), introduced in March 2015.[10] The ASEZs are based on deregulation and tax breaks working as incentives for attracting private investment. The idea is for these specialized zones to serve as growth engines for the wider region (Turovskii 2016). The ASEZs are nominated by the ministry and operated by the Far East Development Corporation (see Min and Kang, Chap. 4, this volume, for a detailed discussion).

Second, there is the *Free Port of Vladivostok*, which was signed into law in 2015, turning 15 municipalities in the southern part of Primorskii Krai into a special economic zone. The Free Port regime encompasses 28,400 km^2 and 1.4 million people. Like the ASEZs, it involves tax and customs benefits and simplified regulations—in this case, also potentially a special simplified visa regime. The Free Port is, however, far more ambitious in scale and complexity. The plans involve creating 85,000 new workplaces by 2021 and more than doubling the GRP of Primorskii Krai by 2025.[11] As with the ASEZs, the regime is operated by the Far East Development Corporation.

Third, there is the *Far Eastern hectare* initiative, introduced in 2016 to counteract the negative migration balance. The population of the Russian Far East has dropped year on year ever since the break-up of the Soviet Union. By offering land for free, the authorities hope to attract settlers to move to the more fertile southern parts of the federal okrug. Since 1990 the area of cultivated arable land in the Russian Far East has decreased by a factor of 2.3 (Lee and Lukin 2016, p.48). To recover this land, increase regional self-sufficiency in food production as well as boost the population, prospective farmers will get one hectare for free, on the condition that they begin to cultivate the land within five years.[12] The mechanism is administered by the Far East Human Capital Development Agency and was initially reserved for locals, but from 1 February 2017 has been open to all citizens of the Russian Federation.[13]

The ministry has thus come up with a set of mechanisms aimed at improving the local investment climate, hoping to give the regional economy the boost it so desperately needs if the Far East is to function as a gateway to the Asia-Pacific. Due to sequestration and changing priorities, state spending earmarked for Far Eastern development has been slashed several times over the last few years,[14] making such private contributions even more crucial.

Institutional Environment

The Ministry for the Development of the Far East is responsible for coordinating state policies for economic and sociodemographic development of the Far Eastern Federal Okrug, but it operates in an institutional landscape within the executive branch that involves a series of other actors with partially overlapping portfolios—if not always fully overlapping interests. The most important of these actors are as follows: other federal ministries as well as the deputy prime minister coordinating Far Eastern policy, the Office of the Presidential Plenipotentiary to the Far Eastern Federal Okrug, the State Commission on the Socioeconomic Development of the Far East and—at the regional level—the governors.

Intra-Ministerial Competition and Rivalries

Most immediately, the Ministry for the Development of the Far East faces intra-ministerial competition within the federal government. Until the Ministry of Regional Development was abolished in 2014, there was a potential tension between priorities in regional development as such and specific prioritization of the Russian Far East. In November 2012, President Putin, at a meeting of the Presidium of the State Council devoted to the development of the Far East, castigated the two ministries for their failure to implement the transfer of relevant federal programmes, which, he went on to say, had resulted in 'blurred responsibilities', lack of progress in the work, and the Ministry for the Development of the Far East 'still not justifying its existence' (*Kremlin.ru* 2012).[15]

However, even with the Ministry of Regional Development gone, there remain other real and potential overlaps—for example, with the priorities of the Ministry of Natural Resources or the Ministry of Economic Development. The latter, which coordinates Russia's special economic zones (SEZs), has questioned the efficiency of the new ASEZ regime, arguing that the new workplaces created come with a price tag of 6 million rubles, money that could be spent more efficiently on creating 'regular' jobs (Lossan 2014). Economic development is also the portfolio of First Deputy Prime Minister Igor Shuvalov, who has taken a keen interest in the development of the Russian Far East—whereas, as we will see below, since 2013 the Far East has been represented in the government by a separate Deputy Prime Minister, Iurii Trutnev.

Not surprisingly, there have also been repeated clashes with the Ministry of Finance over funding. For example, the latter was seen as attempting to torpedo Ishaev's ambitious but costly plans for the development of the Russian Far East, with Minister of Finance Anton Siluanov arguing that the proposed state contribution 'was 14 times more than his ministry considered realistic' (Fortescue 2016, p.432). Over time, the Ministry of Finance has tightened the purse-strings considerably, most recently with an almost 50 per cent cut in spending on the state targeted programme in 2017 as compared to the previous year (*PrimaMedia* 2016). According to Galushka, it was only the direct intervention of Putin that prevented even deeper cuts at this stage (*TASS* 2016).

Oversight Versus Overlap: The Role of the Presidential Plenipotentiary

Ishaev combined being Minister for the Development of the Far East with serving as the personal representative of the Russian President to the Far Eastern Federal Okrug. The task of the presidential plenipotentiary is to monitor implementation of Moscow's policies in the subjects within the federal okrug in question. In case of the Far Eastern Federal Okrug, the territorial area of responsibility of the plenipotentiary overlaps with that of the Ministry for the Development of the Far East. In other words, Ishaev was responsible for monitoring the work of his own ministry.

When in 2014 Ishaev was replaced by Trutnev, checks and balances were only partially restored: while Trutnev was not given charge of the ministry itself, he was made Deputy Prime Minister with responsibility for the Russian Far East. Trutnev would thus ensure the coordination of the interests of the presidential administration and the government. Besides enjoying direct access to the President, Trutnev holds a more senior position in the cabinet than Galushka: as Deputy Prime Minister he can issue directives regarding his portfolio to any federal minister. Thus, Galushka has been relegated to a more subordinate position when it came to setting the priorities for Far Eastern development. Increasingly, Trutnev and his staff seem to be taking the lead in developing new initiatives here.

Bureaucratization and Duplication

In order to facilitate coordination of state policies on the Far East, in June 2012, in parallel to the establishment of the ministry, a separate state commission for the socioeconomic development of the Far East, Buryatia, Zabaikal Krai and Irkutsk Oblast was introduced under the chairmanship of First Deputy Prime Minister Shuvalov. In September 2013, the commission was revamped, and the territorial delimitation changed so as to coincide fully with that of the portfolio of the Ministry for the Development of the Far East. In its new incarnation, the commission is chaired by Prime Minister Medvedev himself, and includes relevant ministers, regional heads from the Far East and fairly broad participation of major business actors (Gazprom, Mechel, RusHydro, Rosneft, Transneft, Sberbank and others).[16]

The State Commission on the Socioeconomic Development of the Far East meets at least once every six months to discuss draft strategies, programmes and policies for the socioeconomic development of the Russian Far East, as well as to determine priorities for investment projects (*Rossiiskaia gazeta* 2013). As such, it serves to anchor the priorities in a wider group of key actors beyond the government—but this arrangement may also slow down the decision-making process, as plans and priorities of the Ministry for the Development of the Far East must be approved here before the ministry can move forward. The personal involvement of Putin in Far Eastern politics (Fortescue 2016, p.441) serves as a guarantee against Moscow slipping back into its traditional relative political and economic neglect of the Russian Far East. However, with Prime Minister Medvedev taking a lead in, for example, the improvement of the Far Eastern investment climate (Wegren et al. 2015), Deputy Prime Minister Trutnev carrying overall responsibility for coordinating Far Eastern development and Galushka being in charge of the relevant ministry, there is a risk of duplication, inefficient resource management and a certain marginalization of the ministry itself.

The Regional Executive

At the regional level, the most important counterparts to the Ministry for the Development of the Far East are the regional heads of executive power, the governors and—in the case of Sakha—the head of the republic. Under the administrative-institutional reforms of the 1990s, the regional executive branch became the centre of political power at the federal subject level. Towards the end of the decade, the regional heads were likened to 'the boyars of the old, apparently insulated from the writ of federal laws and the constitution', turning their federal subjects into 'separate fiefdoms' (Sakwa 2002, p.16). One of the most glaring examples of such wilful regional rulers was Governor Evgenii Nazdratenko of Primorskii Krai (1993–2001), the *bête noire* of Russian regional politics in the 1990s, who repeatedly challenged the Kremlin's right to intervene in regional power politics.

With the onset of Putin's presidency, however, the Kremlin started pushing back the concessions the regional heads had won during the previous decade, a process that culminated with the 2004 decision to reintroduce presidentially appointed governors (Blakkisrud 2015). In 2012, the Kremlin again decided to slacken the reins, allowing a return to direct elections. In practice, however, the presidential administration has continued to control gubernatorial turnover, with elections serving more as referenda over the Kremlin's choice of candidates.

Deprived of a strong independent power-base, today the power and influence of the regional heads are largely a function of their connections and lobbying potential in Moscow. However, while formally an integrated part of the 'executive vertical', this does not prevent ambitious regional heads from launching their own projects that may compete, overlap with or duplicate the work of the Ministry for the Development of the Far East.[17] The ministry has also been criticized for not consulting sufficiently with regional actors, for example, when designating new ASEZs (see Troyakova, Chap. 3, this volume). It thus appears that bringing the ministry closer to the regions by maintaining a decentralized structure has not shielded it from criticism for failing to take local conditions and input into consideration in the planning process.

MINISTRY FOR THE DEVELOPMENT OF THE FAR EAST: SUCCESSES AND PITFALLS

The Putin-era approach to the Russian Far East has 'marked a significant departure from the traditional posture of selective inattention or even outright neglect by the central government' (Lee and Lukin 2016, p.9). However, the post-Crimea crisis in relations with the West has not been the primary driver, although it may have added a sense of greater urgency to the pivot. As we have seen, concerted efforts to accelerate socioeconomic development, as well as to open up the region as a gateway for exports to the Asia-Pacific, predated the introduction of Western sanctions. Already by the summer of 2012, the main institutional framework for the internal dimension of the turn to Asia was in place, with the establishment of the Ministry for the Development of the Far East. And, whereas specific mechanisms for attracting private investment and people to the Far Eastern Federal Okrug have been established only in the last couple of years, the marching orders had been given far before the Crimean situation developed. In fact, if we look at fiscal investment in this endeavour, the post-Crimea period has been marked by a steady decline in state involvement.

Peaking with the adoption of Ishaev's grandiose state programme in 2013, state funding and promises have been cut back, year after year. Even if the federal budget is currently under strong pressure, this certainly gives rise to some questions about Moscow's long-term commitment to the pivot.

What *has* been achieved over the past few years is that the new development model for the Russian Far East has been institutionally anchored. Uncertainty remains, however, as to whether the institutional model devised by the Kremlin will prove capable of dealing with the fundamental problems facing the Russian Far East. The process is still characterized by Moscow's firm penchant for strategic planning and pursuing state-sponsored, top-down development models—even the (partially) decentralized Ministry for the Development of the Far East seems to be sliding back to the traditional Moscow-centred model. In parallel, the bureaucracy has multiplied, while political ownership of the processes has become diffused.

It could also be argued that most of the new mechanisms introduced have already been tried and tested. The most basic problems that the Ministry for the Development of the Far East is struggling with are essentially the same as those that have plagued the Russian Far East ever since the territory fell under Russian control—as are the basic tenets of the solutions that have been proposed. In 1909, for example, Prime Minister Petr Stolypin introduced a Committee on Resettlement to the Far East and, in the 1920s, the Soviets established a Far Eastern Migration Department. Similarly, Vladivostok was under a free port regime from 1861 to 1909.

Will the Ministry for the Development of the Far East succeed where others have failed, and manage to lift the Far East to same level of socio-economic development as the rest of the Russian Federation? Although local observers complain that they have still not seen any economic effects of the new development mechanisms in the form of the creation of new jobs or increased tax revenues (see Troyakova, Chap. 3, this volume), it might not be fair to attempt to draw firm conclusions at this stage—as of this writing, the main mechanisms of the new development model have been in place for less than two years. While Vladivostok is hardly likely to become a future capital of Russia—as was suggested by Sergei Karaganov, a key conceptual strategist behind Russia's pivot (Karaganov 2012), the new interest in turning the Russian Far East into an Asia-Pacific gateway may still have the side-effect of integrating the Far Eastern federal subjects more closely with the rest of the country, providing for more balanced development throughout the Federation. But both tracks—the internal and the external dimension of the pivot—will need long-term commitment from Moscow if they are to yield results.

Notes

1. The vast territory of the Far East is located from six to nine time-zones ahead of Moscow; the distance from Moscow to Petropavlovsk-Kamchatskii, the capital of Kamchatka Krai, is about 6780 kilometres. For comparison, the distance between Moscow and Quebec is not much greater: 6840 kilometres.
2. The main sponsor of this idea was Sergei Shoigu, Minister of Emergency Situations, who was seen as a potential head of the corporation (*Gazeta.ru* 2012). Instead, Shoigu was made governor of Moscow Oblast and later that same year promoted to Minister of Defence.
3. The observations in this paragraph are based on informal conversations with Russian experts on the Russian Far East from Moscow and Vladivostok.
4. See http://minvr.ru/about/ministry.php. Accessed on 10 March 2017.
5. For more details on the organizational structure, see http://minvr.ru/about/struct.php?SECTION_ID=182. Accessed on 10 March 2017.
6. For a full description, see the agency website, http://hcfe.ru/about/general-information. Accessed 10 March 2017.
7. See the company's website at http://erdc.ru/. Accessed on 10 March 2017.
8. The sovnarkhozes, or regional economic soviets, were introduced by Nikita Khrushchev in 1957 in an attempt to counteract the centralization and departmentalization of union ministries. Each sovnarkhoz had planning and operational responsibility in a given region. The sovnarkhozes were abolished in 1965.
9. For an overview of the various sub-programmes see http://government.ru/en/docs/1158. Accessed on 14 March 2017.
10. Officially these zones are designated as *territoriia operezhaiushchego sotsial'no-ekonomicheskogo razvitiia*, or 'territories for advanced socioeconomic development'.
11. For information on the free port regime, see the webpages of the Eastern Economic Forum at https://forumvostok.ru/en/mesto/about-freeport. Accessed on 15 March 2017.
12. The initiative extends to the whole of the Far Eastern Federal Okrug. Land use is not limited to agriculture: the prospective owner may pursue other business models, such as construction or tourism.

13. The application process and selection of the desired plot are done online and can be completed in a few clicks, see link to the Far Eastern hectare on http://minvr.ru. Accessed on 14 March 2017.
14. See *PrimaMedia* 2016 for more detail on the numerous cuts in state funding.
15. According to Deputy Prime Minister Iurii Trutnev, the transfer of powers and competencies to the Ministry for the Development of the Far East encountered resistance from other branch ministries (Gabuev and Mel'nikov 2014).
16. For the most recent composition of the commission, see http://government.ru/info/25386. Accessed on 16 March 2017.
17. See, for example, the mission statement of the Primorskii Krai Investment Agency at https://pkia.ru/ob_agentstve/missia_celi_zadachi/?lang=ru-RU. Accessed on 20 March 2017. The agency was established by Governor Vladimir Miklushevskii in 2012.

References

Blakkisrud, Helge. 2003. 'The rise and fall of the Russian governor: institutional design vs. elite bargaining as explanatory factors in Russian politics', in *Elites and democratic development in Russia*, edited by Anton Steen and Vladimir Gel'man, 71–91. London: Routledge.

Blakkisrud, Helge. 2015. *The governor's last stand: federal bargaining in Russia's transition to appointed regional heads, 2005–2009*. Oslo: University of Oslo.

Burles, Mark. 1999. *Chinese policy toward Russia and the Central Asian republics*. Santa Monica, CA: RAND.

Cooper, Julian. 2012. *Reviewing Russian strategic planning: the emergence of Strategy 2020*. Rome: NATO Defense College.

Deita. 2014. 'Samoe krupnoe podrazdelenie Minvostokrazvitiia razmestiat vo Vladivostoke' [The biggest subdivision of the Ministry for the Development of the Far East to be located in Vladivostok], 21 February. http://deita.ru/news/politics/21.02.2014/4652297-krupneyshee-podrazdelenie-minvostokrazvitiya-poyavitsya-vo-vladivostoke. Accessed on 7 February 2017.

Fortescue, Stephen. 2016. 'Russia's "turn to the east": a study in policy-making', *Post-Soviet Affairs* 32(5): 423–54.

Gabuev, Aleksandr and Kirill Mel'nikov. 2014. 'Blizhaishaia zadacha – eto peredacha polnomochii' [The most immediate task is a transfer of power], *Kommersant* 17 February. http://kommersant.ru/doc/2410187. Accessed on 7 February 2017.

Gazeta.ru. 2012. 'Goskorporatsiia podoshla k granitse' [The state corporation approaches the border], 21 January. https://www.gazeta.ru/business/2012/01/21/kz_3970553.shtml. Accessed on 10 March 2017.
Gorshkova, Olga. 2013. 'Who will pay to develop the Russian Far East?' *Russia Beyond the Headlines*, 3 April. http://rbth.com/business/2013/04/03/who_will_pay_to_develop_the_russian_far_east_24583.html. Accessed on 14 March 2017.
Government.ru. 2013. 'Pravitel'stvennaia komissiia po voprosam sotsial'no-ekonomicheskogo razvitiia Dal'nego Vostoka' [State Commission on the Socioeconomic Development of the Far East], 24 October. http://government.ru/news/7718. Accessed on 21 March 2017.
Government.ru. 2014. 'Ob utverzhdenii novoi redaktsii gosudarstvennoi programmy "Sotsial'no-ekomicheskoe razvitie Dal'nego Vostoka i Baikal'skogo regiona"' [On the approval of a new version of the state programme 'On the Socioeconomic Development of the Far East and the Baikal region'], 15 April. http://government.ru/docs/11959. Accessed on 19 December 2016.
Karaganov, Sergei. 2012. 'Rossiia nuzhna eshche odna stolitsa – sibirskaia' [Russia needs another capital – a Siberian one], *Rossiiskaia gazeta*, 17 May. https://rg.ru/2012/05/16/stolica-site.html. Accessed on 21 March 2017.
Kremlin.ru. 2012. 'Zasedanie prezidiuma Gossoveta' [Meeting of the presidium of the State Council], 29 November. http://kremlin.ru/events/president/news/16990. Accessed on 9 November 2017.
Kuhrt, Natasha. 2012. 'The Russian Far East in Russia's Asia policy: dual integration or double periphery? *Europe-Asia Studies*, 64(3): 471–93.
Lee, Rensselaer and Artyom Lukin. 2016. *Russia's Far East: new dynamics in Asia Pacific and beyond*. Boulder, CO: Lynne Rienner.
Lossan, Alexei. 2014. 'Seven large foreign investors are to come to Russian Far East', *Russia Beyond the Headlines*, 20 September. http://rbth.com/business/2014/09/20/seven_large_foreign_investors_are_to_come_to_russian_far_east_39979.html. Accessed on 20 February 2017.
Mel'nikov, Kirill, Aleksandr Gudkov and Aleksandr Panchenko. 2012. 'Vsia vlast' Sibiri' [All power to Siberia], *Kommersant*, 20 April. http://www.kommersant.ru/doc/1919404. Accessed on 7 February 2017.
Monaghan, Andrew. 2013. 'Putin's Russia: shaping a "grand strategy"?' *International Affairs*, 89(5): 1221–36.
Netreba, Petr. 2012. 'Dal'nevostochnaia konfederatsiia' [The Far Eastern Confederation], *Kommersant*, 4 June. http://www.kommersant.ru/doc/1950814. Accessed on 7 March 2017.
Polunin, Andrei. 2012. 'N. Zubarevich: Minvostokrazvitiia – eto novyi sovnakhoz' [N. Zubarevich: The Ministry for the Development of the Far is a new sovnarkhoz], *Svobodnaia pressa*, 4 June. http://svpressa.ru/society/article/55906/. Accessed on 10 March 2017.

Pravitel'stvo Rossiiskoi Federatsii. 2009. 'Strategiia sotsial'no-ekonomicheskogo razvitiia Dal'nego Vostoka i Baikal'skoga regiona na priod do 2025' [Strategy for the Socioeconomic Development of the Far East and the Baikal Region for the Period until 2025], 28 December. http://old.sakha.gov.ru/node/68499. Accessed on 7 March 2017.

PrimaMedia. 2016. 'Net effektivnosti, net deneg: Minvostok ne smog otstoiat' sredstva na razvitie regiona' [There is no efficiency, no money: Minvostok could not defend funds for the development of the region], 18 November. http://primamedia.ru/news/548538. Accessed on 8 March 2017.

Putin, Vladimir. 2013. 'Poslanie Prezidenta Federal'nomu Sobraniiu' [The President's address to the Federal Assembly], *Kremlin.ru*, 12 December. http://kremlin.ru/events/president/news/19825. Accessed on 2 February 2017.

RIA Novosti. 2011. 'Istoriia ministerstv po delam natsional'nostei v SSSR i RF' [History of ministries on nationalities in the USSR and the Russian Federation], 15 December. https://ria.ru/spravka/20111215/517534894.html. Accessed on 5 March 2017.

RIA Novosti. 2016. 'Minvostokrazvitiia otkroet podrazdelenie na Kamchatke' [Ministry for the Development of the Far East opens subdivision in Kamchatka], 23 December. https://ria.ru/politics/20161223/1484496251.html. Accessed on 7 February 2017.

Ross, Cameron. 2002. *Federalism and democratisation in Russia*. Manchester: Manchester University Press

Ross, Cameron. 2010. 'Federalism and inter-governmental relations in Russia', *Journal of Communist and Transition Politics* 26(2): 165–87.

Rossiiskaia gazeta. 2013. 'O Pravitel'stvennoi komissii po voprosam sotsial'no-ekonomicheskogo razvitiia Dal'nego Vostoka' [On the State Commission on the Socioeconomic Development of the Far East], 19 September. https://rg.ru/2013/09/19/dv-komissia-site-dok.html. Accessed on 3 January 2017.

Sakwa, Richard. 2002. 'Federalism, sovereignty and democracy', in *Regional politics in Russia*, edited by Cameron Ross, 1–22. Manchester: Manchester University Press.

TASS. 2016. 'Aleksandr Galushka: gosprogramma razvitiia Dal'nego Vostoka budet realizovana polnost'iu' [Aleksandr Galushka: the state programme for the Far East will be fully implemented], 24 October. http://tass.ru/opinions/interviews/3728408. Accessed on 15 March 2017.

Turovskii, Rostislav. 2016. 'Dal'nii Vostok: prioritet Rossiiskoi Federatsii' [The Far East: a priority of the Russian Federation], *EastRussia*, 27 December. http://www.eastrussia.ru/material/dalniy-vostok-strategicheskiy-prioritet-rossiyskogo-gosudarstva. Accessed on 10 February 2017.

Wegren, Stephen K., Alexander M. Nikulin and Irina Trotsuk. 2015. 'Russia's tilt to Asia and implications for agriculture in the Far East', *Eurasian Geography and Economics*, 56(2): 127–49.

Zav'ialova, Kseniia. 2012. 'Vladimir Putin raskritikoval rabotu Minvostokrazvitiia' [Vladimir Putin criticized the work of the Ministry for the Development of the Far East], *Kommersant*, 29 November. http://kommersant.ru/doc/2078790. Accessed on 7 March 2017.

Open Access   This chapter is licensed under the terms of the Creative Commons Attribution 4.0 International License (http://creativecommons.org/licenses/by/4.0/), which permits use, sharing, adaptation, distribution and reproduction in any medium or format, as long as you give appropriate credit to the original author(s) and the source, provide a link to the Creative Commons license and indicate if changes were made.

The images or other third party material in this book are included in the book's Creative Commons license, unless indicated otherwise in a credit line to the material. If material is not included in the book's Creative Commons license and your intended use is not permitted by statutory regulation or exceeds the permitted use, you will need to obtain permission directly from the copyright holder.

CHAPTER 3

Primorskii Krai and Russia's 'Turn to the East': A Regional View

Tamara Troyakova

Abstract This chapter surveys the plans for making Primorskii Krai a key actor in Moscow's efforts to expand political and economic ties with the countries of Northeast Asia. After a review of key budgetary, administrative, legislative and policy changes accompanying Russia's 'turn to the East', the author examines several specific tools mandated by these changes to see how they have performed in practice in Primorskii Krai: special economic zones of various stripes, a land giveaway programme, transport infrastructure development and efforts to make the region attractive for investors. While the 'turn to the East' has brought intensified cooperation with China in the Russian Far East, it seems questionable whether these initiatives have entailed substantial changes in the socioeconomic conditions of the region.

Keywords Primorskii Krai • Russian regional politics • Regional economic development • China • Advanced special economic zones

T. Troyakova (✉)
Department of International Relations, Far Eastern Federal University, Vladivostok, Russia

Seen from Moscow, the Russian Far East is a remote periphery and a strategic area for developing international cooperation, primarily with the Northeast Asian states. However, from the Far Easterners' viewpoint, Primorye has its own political, economic and social dynamics. For two centuries the local population has been engaged in cross-border relations.

Thanks to its location, Primorskii Krai can function as Russia's interface with the countries of East Asia. As John Stephan put it: 'simultaneously comprising the northern periphery of East Asia and eastern periphery of the Russian Republic, [the region] has an elasticity inherent in the Russian term Dalnii Vostok, which can refer to anything from a province to half the world' (Stephan 1994, p.7). Deteriorating relations with the West in the context of the Russia–Ukraine crisis and Western economic sanctions have made Russia's 'turn to the East' a vital necessity. However, such a turn to the East is easier said than done. This chapter describes the plans—and challenging realities—for turning Primorskii Krai and the Far Eastern Federal Okrug more broadly into key players in Moscow's efforts to expand political and economic ties with the countries of Northeast Asia.

I begin by reviewing the key budgetary, administrative, legislative and policy changes accompanying Russia's 'turn to the East', as manifested in the region itself, before turning to several specific tools mandated by these changes to see how they have performed in practice. These include the establishment of special economic zones (SEZs) of various stripes, a land giveaway programme, transport infrastructure development and efforts to make Primorye attractive for investors. I conclude by noting that the turn to Asia has indeed resulted in intensified cooperation with China in the Russian Far East, but question whether these initiatives have brought actual substantial change in the socioeconomic conditions of the region.

Budgetary, Administrative, Legislative and Policy Changes

Since the break-up of the Soviet Union, two different approaches have emerged as regards developing the Russian Far East. In the 1990s, the Far East was left to survive mainly on its own, developing cross-border relations and integrating in global trade, while Moscow retained the functions of protecting the borders and preventing secessionism. During this period, business activity in the Russian Far East was closely linked to international trade, primarily within the Asia-Pacific region (Troyakova 2007).

After the turn of the millennium, Moscow changed its approach, taking an active role in the socioeconomic development of the region. A key element in this has been the internal redistribution of budget revenues, which have benefitted the Far Eastern Federal Okrug immensely. However, Moscow's increased transfers have been accompanied by stricter control over the Far Eastern 'gateway to the global world', and a reorientation of the regional economy towards Moscow. Nevertheless, some experts hold that federal support is integral to expanding economic relations in the Far East. According to Anton Kireev, 'existing cross-border cooperation mechanisms in the Far Eastern regions (…) are highly dependent on government support, they operate on a local scale, are primarily trade-oriented and largely incapable of attracting foreign technology and investment' (Kireev 2012, p.63).

These changes have taken place in parallel to key shifts in the overall dynamics of centre–periphery relations. In the 1990s, most Far Eastern governors represented the local elite and were able to play an independent role. For example, in the mid-1990s Primorye Governor Evgenii Nazdratenko (1993–2001) repeatedly spoke out against the demarcation of the Russian–Chinese border (Troyakova 2000). However, with the consolidation of the federal government that commenced with the Putin presidency, local politicians were gradually replaced with appointees from Moscow. Under the new conditions, governors lost their independent power base and position and could readily be removed. In the run-up to the 2012 APEC summit in Vladivostok, Governor Sergei Darkin (2001–12) was replaced, at Moscow's behest. An extraordinary session of the Legislative Assembly of Primorskii Krai voted for Moscow's gubernatorial candidate, rector of the Far Eastern Federal University Vladimir Miklushevskii, a former Russian Deputy Minister of Education and Science who had arrived in the region only two years prior.

Also the ways Moscow organizes government functions for the 'periphery' have changed. In May 2012, President Putin signed an executive order establishing the Ministry for the Development of the Far East (see Blakkisrud, Chap. 2, this volume). A local, Viktor Ishaev, former Khabarovsk governor (1991–2009), now Presidential Plenipotentiary to the Far Eastern Federal Okrug (2009–13), was appointed minister. However, already the following year, in August 2013, Ishaev was dismissed. He was replaced as minister by an activist from the All-Russian People's Front, Aleksandr Galushka, while Iurii Trutnev, who had been serving as a presidential aide since May 2012 and as Minister of Natural

Resources (2004–12), became Presidential Plenipotentiary to the Far Eastern Federal Okrug.

The 'turn to the East' has been supported by a suite of new legislation, programmes and strategy documents. In 2008, in relation to the decision to organize the 2012 Asia-Pacific Economic Cooperation (APEC) Summit in Vladivostok, the 'Development of Vladivostok as a centre for international cooperation in the Asia–Pacific region 2008–2012' was adopted as a sub-programme within the federal targeted programme for the development of the Far East (*FTsP* 2013). Moreover, in December 2009, a 'Strategy for the Socioeconomic Development of the Far East and the Baikal Region until 2025' was adopted. The extensive list of regional policy objectives listed in the preamble to the strategy can be reduced to three political objectives. First, the Far Eastern Federal Okrug must have sufficient permanent population to stave off any claims of foreign powers to the area. Second, the standard of living in the Far East must be improved. Third, infrastructure and industrial capabilities must be created to exploit the natural resources of the Russian Far East for the benefit of the entire nation. This strategy was operationalized through several rounds of revisions of the associated federal targeted programme, the most important of which took place in March 2013 (Ishaev's programme) and April 2014 (Galushka and Trutnev's revision).

The latest major revision was adopted in June 2016. The current version envisages implementation of five sub-programmes: 'Creating conditions for advanced social and economic development of the Far Eastern Federal Okrug', 'Support for the implementation of investment projects in the Far Eastern Federal Okrug', 'Support for the implementation of investment projects planned for implementation in the Baikal region', 'Improving the investment attractiveness of the Far East' and 'Ensuring implementation of the State Programme and other measures in the field of balanced spatial development' (Minvostokrazvitiia Rossii 2016a).[1]

A major challenge in relation to realizing these ambitious programmes is to attract private investment and, to this end, Moscow has introduced a range of new institutions. The Far East Development Corporation develops infrastructure for investors and represents them vis-à-vis the regulatory authorities. The Far East Human Capital Development Agency provides investors with labour resources. The Far East Development Fund offers long-term low-interest project funding. And the Far East Investment and Export Agency is tasked with working with potential investors, interfacing with residents in the advanced special economic zones (ASEZs; see below) and promoting exports.

A further key challenge related to the future development of the region is depopulation. With its 1.9 million inhabitants (2017), Primorye is the most populous region of the otherwise sparsely populated Far Eastern Federal Okrug. However, over the past 25 years, Primorskii Krai has lost about 360,000 residents, and the trend continuous to be negative. According to the Primorye statistics department, in 2016 there were 23,600 births (4 per cent less than in 2015) and 26,200 deaths in Primorye: thus, the number of deaths was 11 per cent higher than the number of births. Also the migration balance has been negative: between January and November 2016, 19,400 people from other parts of Russia and 11,300 from abroad migrated to the region, whereas 23,300 people left for other Russian regions and 9700 moved abroad during the same period (*ZRpress.ru* 2017a).

In January 2017, the Ministry for the Development of the Far East submitted a concept for the demographic development of the Far East to Prime Minister Dmitrii Medvedev (Minvostokrazvitiia Rossii 2017). According to this document, the plan is to increase the population of the Far Eastern Federal Okrug from the current 6.2 million to 7 million by 2030 by attracting people from other regions (Avdeev 2017). Reaching this target will require ensuring good living conditions for the current inhabitants of the Far East so as to stop outmigration—and this again will hinge on the realization of the socioeconomic ambitions outlined in many of the recent strategic documents and laws summarized above.

Economic Development Zones in Primorskii Krai

If effectively implemented, SEZs may become one such tool to promote satisfactory living conditions and a competitive labour market. In Russia, the first SEZ was instituted in 2005. The SEZ on Russkii Island in Vladivostok was announced in March 2010. Primorye authorities hoped to attract investment into the development of the region's tourism potential and utilize the infrastructure developed for the 2012 APEC Summit (Shevtsov 2016).

The Russkii Island SEZ was to focus on wellness, nautical tourism, and eco- and adventure tourism. However, ever since it was established, there have been unresolved issues regarding the free transfer of lands from the Ministry of Defence and the federal government to Primorskii Krai.

Numerous difficulties in competing regulations between federal and regional authorities hampered the project (federal land transfer in particular). As a result, many potential investors pulled out. In 2014, the Ministry of Economic Development proposed to close the SEZ. A year later, it was decided that the project for developing a special regime on Russkii Island would be continued, at the expense of Primorskii Krai alone. However, the region had no funds to conduct such an independent effort. In September 2016, the federal government decided to close down the tourism and recreation SEZ on Russkii Island.

The Ministry for the Development of the Far East took over the project and proposed developing it in a new format: as an ASEZ. The new plan envisages the island as an area for research, education, innovation, and tourism and recreation, with the Far Eastern Federal University and Primorskii Aquarium as the major hubs of these activities. At the 2016 Eastern Economic Forum, President Putin instructed the government to complete a development strategy for Russkii Island by June 2017; the Moscow-based Strelka design company, owned by billionaire Aleksandr Mamut, was contracted to develop a master plan (*Primamedia.ru* 2017b).

Here it could be noted that the construction of the Primorskii Aquarium on Russkii Island is a clear example of the mismatch between lofty declarations and the implementation of Far Eastern policy. The aquarium was scheduled to open in September 2012, in advance of the APEC summit, but the official opening came four years later. In addition to the lengthy delay, misuse of public funds during construction resulted in a protracted court case (*Primamedia.ru* 2016d).

The establishment of a special gambling zone, introduced by a governmental decree in August 2009, has been more successful, with several projects currently under way. The Primorye Entertainment Zone is being developed by the Primorskii Krai Development Corporation, established in 2013 and wholly owned by the Primorskii Krai administration. Among foreign investors in the zone are companies from Macao, Malaysia, South Korea and elsewhere. In August 2016, Hong Kong-based Summit Ascent Holdings, which owns the Tigre de Cristal Casino—the only casino to have opened in the designated zone thus far—signed a memorandum of understanding with Kangwon Land, South Korea's largest gambling operator, on the potential involvement of the latter in the development of a phase two of Tigre de Cristal. In November 2016, Cambodian NagaCorp Ltd started building a new hotel with a casino and a waterpark, Maiak, scheduled to open in 2019 (*Primamedia.ru* 2016b). And in December

2016, representatives of the China Overseas Development Association (CODA) met with Primorye Governor Miklushevskii to discuss construction of an international exhibition and convention centre in the Primorye Entertainment Zone (*Moskovskii Komsomolets* 2016).

By 2016, Tigre de Cristal has become the largest casino in Russia, with more than 200,000 visitors, mostly from China, South Korea and Japan. Citizens of South Korea may visit Russia without a visa. There are also simplified entry procedures for Chinese citizens travelling to Russia in organized tourist groups. With the plans for a visa-free regime within the Free Port of Vladivostok (see below) came expectations of an increased influx of tourists from other countries to the casino as well. However, the simplified visa regime has not yet been implemented.

Advanced Special Economic Zones

The ASEZ regime is based on deregulation and large-scale tax incentives (see Min and Kang, Chap. 4, this volume, for an extensive discussion). On 30 April 2015, the Russian government adopted a resolution handing over responsibility for managing the ASEZs in the Far Eastern Federal Okrug to the Far East Development Corporation. In Primorskii Krai, the corporation works together with the Primorskii Krai administration to establish the necessary infrastructure. To date, three ASEZs have been established in Primorye: Nadezhdinskaia, Mikhailovskii and Bolshoi Kamen (see Table 3.1).

A few other prospective ASEZs are currently under consideration. For example, there are plans to establish a petrochemical and refining ASEZ, Neftekhimicheskii, on the premises of the Far East Petrochemical Company (FEPCO), located near the sea terminal in Vostok Bay, Nakhodka. FEPCO is a subsidiary of Rosneft, and in 2016 Rosneft and the China National Chemical Corporation (ChemChina) agreed to establish a joint venture to implement the FEPCO project.

However, it is difficult to foresee successful business development within the ASEZs as long as these are designated by the Ministry for the Development of the Far East without much consultation with the local business community. The number of potential investors remains limited, and it is not always clear how infrastructure development will be funded. In addition, interconnections with the broader Asia-Pacific market are largely absent—as yet, none of the current residents in the local ASEZs aim to go international with an innovative product.

Table 3.1 Projects under the ASEZ regime realized in Primorskii Krai

Name	ASEZ profile	Initiated	Major investors (country)
Nadezhdinskaia	Light and food industry Transport and logistics	25 June 2015	Evroplast (Russia) Inkom DV (Russia) Primorskii Konditer (Russia) Nevada-Vostok (Russia) Kirei Chemical (Japan) Sewon Group (South Korea) Domostroitelnyi Kombinat Primorye (Russia)
Mikhailovskii	Agrobusiness (pig farming with associated feed production) Food processing and storage	21 August 2015	Mercy Trade (Russia) Primorskii Bacon (Russia) RusAgro-Primorye (Russia) Chernigovskii Agroholding Company (Russia) Yug Rusi (Russia)
Bolshoi Kamen	Shipbuilding Construction of logistics centres for storage and shipping of fish Residential construction	28 January 2016	Zvezda Shipbuilding Complex (Russia)

Source: Investsionnyi portal Primorskogo kraia (2017a)

Free Port of Vladivostok

The Far East Development Corporation is also responsible for developing the Free Port of Vladivostok, one of the most promising investment projects in Primorye. The law introducing the Free Port of Vladivostok was signed by President Putin in July 2015 and came into effect in October 2015. The free port regime includes a preferential tax system, the status of a free trade zone and a visa-free travel regime. The free port includes altogether 15 municipalities in the south of Primorskii Krai—from the port of Vostochnyi to the port of Zarubino close to the border with China and North Korea.

Several foreign companies have expressed interest. In December 2016, the Japanese engineering company JGC Corporation announced its plans to invest in the development of medical services in Russia, opening an outpatient care centre in the Free Port of Vladivostok (Shatina 2016). The establishment of the free port has also been a major driver for South Korean interest in developing contacts and establishing or expanding the activities of Korean-owned companies in Primorye. In 2015, for example, Ssang Mun Co announced its plans for building a fish and seafood processing facility on the territory the free port.

Most active of all are the Chinese investors. In December 2016, UBO-Sumotori signed an agreement to set up facilities in the free port. This company is a joint Russian–Chinese project between the Sumotori Group, which specializes in the sale and maintenance of cars and lorries, and the Chinese state-owned automotive manufacturing company FAW Group; it will assemble and produce Chinese trucks. And in spring 2017, the Chinese Zhunda Timber Company will launch production at a new zero-waste wood-processing facility in Ussuriisk to manufacture modern construction materials.

This free port project has mostly progressed according to plan, but there have been some challenges related to introducing a simplified visa regime. This regime was originally scheduled to enter into force on 1 January 2016, then 1 July 2016, and was then postponed to the end of the year due to lack of regulatory approval. In December 2016, the Government Commission on Legislative Activity approved a draft law on a simplified visa regime for the Free Port of Vladivostok (*EastRussia* 2016). In connection with the State Duma's first reading of this draft in January 2017, Deputy Minister for the Development of the Far East Pavel Volkov stated: 'We hope the law will be passed by the end of March and the investors coming to the 3rd Eastern Economic Forum will be able to utilize this mechanism' (*ZRpress.ru* 2017b). At the same time, he emphasized that 'the draft law is only a part of a larger process which needs to be implemented to ensure simplified visa entry'.

Since the Free Port of Vladivostok regime entered into effect and up until late 2016, the Far East Development Corporation received 197 applications for 256.7 billion rubles worth of investment projects with the potential for creating more than 27,000 new jobs (*DV Kapital* 2016). As of this time of writing (March 2017), the free port already has 150 resident companies.[2] Not all companies are staying, however. In late December 2016, the agricultural company Mentor, one of the free port's first residents, announced that it was leaving. According to General Director Dmitrii Panarin,

The incentives turned out to be unprofitable for us and, in my opinion, they are not of much help to small businesses overall. And, if we go back to what was promised to businesses when they just started talking about the free port, and look at the current law, we'll see two very different things. (*Primpress.ru* 2016)

In December 2016, the *Zolotoi Rog* business newspaper interviewed local entrepreneurs about the Free Port of Vladivostok. According to Andrei Michulis, a partner in Tiger Consulting, 'Asian investors taking steps to establish businesses in Russia is a qualitative indicator of an improving investment climate... The deficiencies of the legal framework for the state programmes remain the weak spot' (*ZRpress.ru* 2016a). Andrei Golotin, director of the Primorye branch of MOSP MSP–Opora, an association of small- and medium-sized construction enterprises, put it this way:

We have yet to feel a positive impact of the free port on business... We do not register any substantial interest in Primorye from investors. I am sure this interest will appear if investors become more confident about the Russian government being serious about attracting investment, that our country has serious intentions and that the rules of the game will not change (*ZRpress.ru* 2016b).

Far Eastern Hectare

To address the demographic challenges of the Russian Far East, the Russian government in 2016 launched the 'Far Eastern Hectare' programme, allocating land for free to people interested in settling in the Far East. The idea was first brokered in late 2015, and, being pushed by Presidential Plenipotentiary to the Far Eastern Federal Okrug Trutnev, relevant legislation was adopted unusually swiftly.

The programme is administered by the Far East Human Capital Development Agency. Interested individuals can log onto the agency's website and select a land plot up to one hectare from throughout the entire Far Eastern Federal Okrug. The website also offers users business project ideas to pursue—ranging from growing strawberries to sheep farming.

Initially, in an attempt to retain the population already living in the region, the application process was open only to the Far Easterners. Between June and mid-November 2016, almost 2400 applications were filed for a free hectare in Primorskii Krai of which 440 were approved. From 1 February 2017, all citizens of the Russian Federation are eligible to participate. At a meeting of the Primorskii Krai administration in February 2017, Governor Miklushevskii announced that since the programme was introduced, there had been 17,860 applications from Russian citizens wishing to obtain a free hectare in Primorye. This means that Primorye ranks first among Far Eastern regions by number of applications (Veka 2017).

However, throughout the process, there have been numerous complaints about people being denied land, as well as problems with land plots with unmapped boundaries, unclear third-party rights and lack of registration in the cadastre system. The eventual success of the programme will depend on many factors—and many questions remain. To take but one: the land giveaway is focused more on immediate action than on long-term solutions. If the new owners do not put the land to use within five years, the government will reclaim it. But how can new business models be financed by individual land-holders if their land cannot be pledged as collateral? Successful implementation of the programme will require the establishment of a system of incentives, subsidized mortgages, taxation, infrastructure and the like. For the time being, however, officials prefer to highlight the number of applications for land, while they keep silent about the associated challenges and measures needed to create real, new possibilities for the freshly minted landowners.

Developing Infrastructure

In the end of December 2016, Presidential Plenipotentiary to the Far Eastern Federal Okrug, Deputy Prime Minister Trutnev, and Deputy Prime Minister Arkadii Dvorkovich approved the development concept for the international transport corridors Primorye-1 and Primorye-2, linking China's northeast with the ports of the Russian Far East (*Government. ru* 2016). According to international expert assessments, 45 million tons of grain and containerized cargo will be shipped through Primorye-1 and Primorye-2 by 2030, generating an additional 91 billion rubles in annual revenues for the local ports and transport companies (Minvostokrazvitiia Rossii 2016c). Both Russia and China are predicted to benefit from the development of these transport corridors. During the construction phase, at least 3000 jobs will be created, followed by about 4000 new jobs at new infrastructure facilities once the transport corridors are in place.

The focus on international transport corridors is nothing new; the idea first came to the fore in Primorye in the mid-1990s when various initiatives were put forward for using the ports of Nakhodka, Vladivostok and Posyet as transit points for freight from Northeast China. However, despite the clear geographic potential, freight volumes on these routes have been modest; as of today, they lose in competition with alternative routes, in terms of cost and time.

South Korean actors are also interested in developing transport infrastructure in Primorye. In March 2015, the Korean International Trade Association (KITA) and the Primorskii Krai administration agreed to establish a council for logistics cooperation and to facilitate joint investment in developing the port of Zarubino. By the end of May 2015, a regular container shipping line connecting Hunchun (China), Zarubino (Russia) and Pusan (South Korea) was launched. A new project, the Big Port of Zarubino, to be developed in the Troitsa Bay by Russian port operator Summa Group, envisages development of rail, road and energy infrastructure between Zarubino and Hunchun. The plan is for the port to serve as a transit point for shipping freight from Northeast China to Southern China as well as for Russian grain exports. Investment is estimated to be upwards of 200 billion rubles.

The Free Port of Vladivostok regime can play a decisive role in further development of transit corridors in Primorye. Through the Free Port law, various new measures aimed at removing administrative barriers for the movement of goods, including from China to the ports of Primorye, entered into force from 1 October 2016. These include such measures as round-the-clock checkpoints, a 'single window' for border control, preliminary e-declarations and a 'green channel' for foreign trade.

It should be noted that these international transport corridors will be operational without substantial additional investment, once the new administrative regulations are in place. For example, the infrastructure related to the Primorye-1 corridor and the ports of Nakhodka and Vladivostok is already sufficient to handle several million tons of cargo. To manage these levels of cargo, the main updates needed involve expanding the existing border checkpoint, upgrading the Grodekovo railway station (the first station east of the Sino-Russian border) and renovating the road between Pogranichnyi and Ussuriisk. These measures can be implemented in the foreseeable future and will require no more than an estimated 10 billion rubles worth of investment. However, more extensive work is needed for the Primorye-2 corridor, including laying railway tracks, constructing a road and port infrastructure. An estimated 170 billion rubles worth of infrastructure investment is needed. The cargo flow through this corridor could be up to 38 million tons of grain and containers. Tentatively, the Primorye-2 project is scheduled for launch in 2020.

Primorye's Regional Economic Diplomacy

Various challenges are facing the region in connection with attracting foreign direct investment. One is the overlapping and sometimes competitive or confusing jurisdictions of federal and regional authorities. Russian regional policy, with its heavy focus on bureaucratic regulation, has resulted in the establishment of many administrative entities which often duplicate each other. However, the regional authorities in Primorskii Krai and the city of Vladivostok have sought to attract investors and create a positive image of the region's investment potential. The Primorye Investment Portal contains detailed information about local development institutions: the Primorskii Krai Investment Agency, Primorskii Krai Guarantee Fund, Primorskii Krai Development Corporation and Primorskii Krai Export Development Centre (Investsionnyi portal Primorskogo kraia 2017b). A total of 184 projects are currently listed in the Investment Project Register (Investsionnyi portal Primorskogo kraia 2017c).

Vladivostok, with its 7 consulates-general and 16 honorary consulates as well numerous representative offices of international companies, constitutes the diplomatic capital and international gateway of the Russian Far East. The city regularly hosts large international events attracting, among others, heads of Asian states. Recently, a special focus on economic diplomacy has become evident. In the autumn of 2015, an annual Eastern Economic Forum was launched in Vladivostok to attract investors in the context of the 'turn to the East' policy. The first forum, held in September 2015, resulted in signing of more than 80 large investment contracts (*Primamedia.ru* 2016a). At the 2016 forum, the authorities and businesses signed 216 agreements. The number of forum participants had more than doubled: from 2000 to 4600—and it included three heads of state/government: from Russia, Japan and South Korea. Similarly, at the end of September 2016, Vladivostok hosted the Fifth International Economic Business-Congress. This event, initiated by the Dialogues business club, targets owners and executives of companies in the Far Eastern Federal Okrug and the Asia-Pacific region (Minvostokrazvitiia Rossii 2016b).

A key target of these efforts is China, whose engagement in the region outstrips other countries. Out of 1 trillion rubles invested in ASEZs and the Free Port of Vladivostok, some 160 billion are of Chinese origin. The relationship attracts high-level attention, also at the federal level. In late December 2016, Presidential Plenipotentiary Trutnev was appointed Russian co-chair of the Bilateral Russian–Chinese Commission on Cooperation and Development of Russia's Far East and Baikal Region and Northeast China. This Commission will deal with Russian–Chinese cooperation projects in Russia's Far Eastern Federal Okrug and Baikal region, as well as in the Chinese provinces of Heilongjiang, Liaoning and Jilin and the Inner Mongolia Autonomous Region.

However, the Russian Far East is also looking beyond China, courting investors from the rest of East Asia. An important milestone in this respect was the acquisition of Vladivostok International Airport in 2017 by an international consortium comprising Singapore's Changi Airports International, Basic Element and the Russian Direct Investment Fund (RDIF). At the 2016 Eastern Economic Forum, the delegation of the Republic of Korea, headed by President Park Geun-hye, presented investment proposals for more than 2.6 billion rubles, now under review with the Far East Development Corporation. Korean investors are ready to develop an electronic fare payment system for public transport in Vladivostok and to build a plant for the production of polyurethane and household chemicals in Primorye.

Improving Russian–Japanese relations also offer hope for the development of cooperation between Primorskii Krai and Japan. It has already been announced that Japanese Prime Minister Shinzo Abe will attend the 2017 Eastern Economic Forum. And at the end of November 2016, Governor Miklushevskii visited Japan with a group of entrepreneurs to mark the 25th anniversary of friendly relations between Primorskii Krai and the Japanese prefectures of Tottori and Shimane.

Concluding Remarks

Recent years have seen massive government investment in the Russian Far East. Indeed, if divided among the 6.2 million Far Easterners, it could make each regional resident a rich individual. However, putting this money to work in the service of broader, long-term aims has proven challenging.

Implementation of Russia's regional policy has been hampered by sluggish economic performance and by the attempts of Western powers to reprimand Russia, politically and economically. Unsurprisingly, the recent fall in GDP led to a reduction in the federal government's capacities for investing in regional development. In November 2016, substantial funding cuts to the federal targeted programme for the socioeconomic development of the Far East and Baikal region were announced (*Primamedia.ru* 2016c, 2017a). Besides budget constraints, another reason for reducing the funding to the Far East has been the alleged low effectiveness of programme implementation. Both the Ministry of Finance and the State Duma Committee on Regional Policy and the Problems of the North and the Far East have assessed the effectiveness of implementation of this state programme as unsatisfactory (*Primamedia.ru* 2016c).

Key causes for this lack of progress are the lack of coordination among various branches of the government and the new institutions they have set up, problems of corruption and an unsatisfactory investment climate. Instead of deregulation, bureaucracy has proliferated. New entities for managing development projects are established, spending project budgets on developing new governance methods, performance indicators and the like—without bearing any responsibility for the effectiveness of the end product. High levels of corruption still plague major government projects in Primorye. At present, the development forecast for Primorskii Krai can hardly be called optimistic. However, thanks to the implementation of several projects, some moderate growth can be expected. Moreover, if Moscow will continue to keep the Far Eastern periphery in focus, that should help to prevent further economic and demographic decline. One can also hope for greater interest from Russian and foreign entrepreneurs in the new mechanisms that have been introduced to stimulate socioeconomic development.

If the federal and regional authorities can work together and coordinate their efforts, and if the authorities and business can cooperate, the goal of improving the investment attractiveness of Primorye may be achieved. Growth centres, such as the ASEZs, the Free Port of Vladivostok and international transport corridors, have already been established, but much work remains to be done to ensure that these mechanisms will live up to expectations. In sum, there remains a substantial discrepancy between the declarations of making Primorskii Krai the frontrunner in Russia's 'turn to the East' and actual achievements.

NOTES

1. For an overview of the numerous revisions, see the governmental webpage listing federal targeted programmes, at http://fcp.economy.gov.ru/cgi-bin/cis/fcp.cgi/Fcp/ViewFcp/View/2013/136/. Accessed on 23 March 2017.
2. An overview is available on the webpages of the Far East Development Corporation, http://erdc.ru/upload/iblock/8cb/8cb9bffd1262c2ced54 86f9fb14f4850.pdf. Accessed on 23 March 2017.

REFERENCES

Avdeev, Iurii. 2017. 'Uezhat' uzhe nekomu. I nekomu rabotat'' [There is no one to leave. And no one to work], *Primamedia.ru*, 27 January. http://primamedia.ru/news/565028/. Accessed on 23 February 2017.

DV Kapital. 2016. 'Rossiisko-kitaiskii proekt po vypusku gruzovikov realizuet vo Vladivostoke GK Sumotori' [Sumotori implements Russian–Chinese truck project in Vladivostok], 8 December. http://dvkapital.ru/regionnow/primor skij-kraj_08.12.2016_9174_rossijsko-kitajskij-proekt-po-vypusku-gruzovikov-realizuet-vo-vladivostoke-gk-sumotori.html. Accessed on 23 February 2017.

EastRussia. 2016. 'Zakonoproekt ob uproshchennom vizovom poriadke v Svobodnom portu Vladivostok odobren Pravkomissiei' [Government commission approves draft law on simplified visa regime in Free Port of Vladivostok], 20 December. http://www.eastrussia.ru/news/zakonoproekt-ob-uproshchennom-vizovom-poryadke-v-svobodnom-portu-vladivostok-odobren-pravkomissiey-/. Accessed on 23 February 2017.

FTsP. 2013. 'Razvitie goroda Vladivostoka kak tsentra mezhdunarodnogo sotrudnichestva v Aziatsko-Tikhookeanskom regione' [Development of Vladivostok city as a centre for international cooperation in the Asia-Pacific region]. http://fcp.economy.gov.ru/cgi-bin/cis/fcp.cgi/Fcp/FcpList/Full/2013/. Accessed on 23 February 2017.

Government.ru. 2016. 'Ob utverzhdenii Kontseptsii razvitiia mezhdunarodnykh transportnykh koridorov "Primor'e-1" i "Primor'e-2"' [On the approval of development concept for international transport corridors 'Primorye-1' and 'Primorye-2'], 30 December. http://government.ru/news/25953/. Accessed on 23 February 2017.

Investsionnyi portal Primorskogo kraia. 2017a. 'Special economic regimes'. https://invest.primorsky.ru/investicionnyj_klimat/osobye_jekonomicheskie_rezhimy/?lang=en-US. Accessed on 5 March 2017.

Investsionnyi portal Primorskogo kraia. 2017b. 'Instituty razvitiia v Primorskom krae' [Development institutes in Primorskii Krai]. https://invest.primorsky.ru/instituty_razvitiya/?lang=ru-RU. Accessed on 23 February 2017.

Investsionnyi portal Primorskogo kraia. 2017c. 'Katalog investitsionnykh proektov' [Catalogue of investment projects]. https://invest.primorsky.ru/investicionnyj_klimat/reestr_investicionnyh_proektov/?lang=ru-RU. Accessed on 23 February 2017.

Kireev, Anton. 2012. 'Evropeiskaia i dal'nevostochnaia granitsy Rossii: dve modeli upravleniia?' [Russia's European and Far Eastern borders: two governance models?], *Oikumena* 2: 60–69. http://ojkum.ru/arc/2012_02/index.html#2012_02_10. Accessed on 23 February 2017.

Minvostokrazvitiia Rossii. 2016a. 'Artur Niiazmetov: Programmy razvitiia Dal'nego Vostoka podderzhany v Federal'nom Sobranii Rossiiskoi Federatsii' [Artur Niiazmetov: Far East development programmes supported by the Federal Assembly of the Russian Federation], 19 May. http://www.minvostokrazvitia.ru/press-center/news_minvostok/?ELEMENT_ID=4264&sphrase_id=36242. Accessed on 20 March 2017.

Minvostokrazvitiia Rossii. 2016b. 'Perspektivy razvitiia Dal'nego Vostoka v usloviiakh dvustoronnikh otnoshenii "Rossiia–strany Aziatsko-Tikhookeanskogo regiona" obsudili uchastniki MBEK' [Participants of IEBC discuss Far East development potential in the context of Russia–Asia-Pacific relations], 23 September. http://www.minvostokrazvitia.ru/press-center/news_minvostok/?ELEMENT_ID=4652. Accessed on 23 February 2017.

Minvostokrazvitiia Rossii. 2016c. 'Pravitel'stvo Rossii utverdilo kontseptsiiu razvitiia mezhdunarodnykh transportnykh korridorov "Primor'e-1" i "Primor'e-2"' [Russian government approves development concept for international transport corridors Primorye-1 and Primorye-2], 30 December. http://www.minvostokrazvitia.ru/press-center/news_minvostok/?ELEMENT_ID=4937. Accessed on 23 February 2017.

Minvostokrazvitiia Rossii. 2017. 'Stenogramma vystupleniia Aleksandra Galushki v ramkakh "pravitel'stvennogo chasa" v Gosudarstvennoi Dume Federal'nogo Sobraniia Rossiiskoi Federatsii' [Aleksandr Galushka at the "Government's hour" in the State Duma of the Federal Assembly of the Russian Federation. Verbatim report], 12 January. http://www.minvr.ru/press-center/news_minvostok/?ELEMENT_ID=4948. Accessed on 23 February 2017.

Moskovskii Komsomolets. 2016. 'Kitaiskie investory planiruiut postroit' ploshchadku dlia forumov vo Vladivostoke' [Chinese investors to build a convention centre in Vladivostok], 21 December. http://vlad.mk.ru/articles/2016/12/21/kitayskie-investory-postroyat-v-primore-ploshhadku-dlya-forumov.html. Accessed on 23 February 2017.

Primamedia.ru. 2016a. 'Glavnye ekonomicheskie sobytiia 2015 goda v Primor'e' [Economic highlights of 2015 in Primorye], 7 January. http://primamedia.ru/news/482330/. Accessed on 23 February 2017.

Primamedia.ru. 2016b. 'Gostinichnyi kompleks s kazino i akvaparkom nachnut stroit' v IRZ "Primor'e" v noiabre' [Construction of hotel with casino and aqua park in Primorye gambling zone to begin in November], 18 October. http://primamedia.ru/news/539134/. Accessed on 23 February 2017.

Primamedia.ru. 2016c. 'Net effektivnosti, net i deneg: Minvostok ne smog otstoiat' sredstva na razvitie regiona' [There is no efficiency, no money: Minsvostok could not defend funds for the development of the region], 18 November. http://primamedia.ru/news/548538/. Accessed on 23 February 2017.

Primamedia.ru. 2016d. 'Eks-kurator i eks-stroitel' Primorskogo okeanariuma skhlestnulis' v sude' [Ex-supervisor and ex-builder of Primorskii Aquarium clash in court], 1 December. http://primamedia.ru/news/553154/. Accessed on 23 February 2017.

Primamedia.ru. 2017a. 'Ekonomika Primor'ia v 2016 godu: "bumazhnye" investitsii, stagnatsiia i nadezhdu na budushchee' [Primorye's economy in 2016: 'paper' investment, stagnation and future hopes], 3 January. http://primamedia.ru/news/559483/. Accessed on 23 February 2017.

Primamedia.ru. 2017b. 'Poluchitsia li u KB "Strelka" gorod budushchego na ostrove Russkom' [Will Strelka manage to create a city of future on Russkii Island?], 3 February. http://primamedia.ru/news/565705/. Accessed on 23 February 2017.

Primpress.ru. 2016. 'Svobodnyi port Vladivostok poterial rezidenta' [Free port of Vladivostok lost a resident], 28 December. http://primpress.ru/index.php?cont=article&id=9801. Accessed on 23 February 2017.

Shatina, Iuliia. 2016. 'Iaponskie investory postroiat meditsinskii tsentr v Primor'e' [Japanese investors build medical centre in Primorye], *Ofitsial'nyi sait Administratsii Primorskogo kraia*, 2 December. http://www.primorsky.ru/news/121190. Accessed on 23 February 2017.

Shevtsov, Andrei. 2016. 'Viktor Ishaev: Esli by polpredstvo sozdavali segodnia, ono bylo by vo Vladivostoke' [Viktor Ishaev: If plenipotentiary representation were set up now, it would be in Vladivostok], *Primamedia*.ru, 4 May. http://primamedia.ru/news/503752. Accessed on 23 February 2017.

Stephan, John J. 1994. *The Russian Far East: a history*. Stanford, CA: Stanford University Press.

Troyakova, Tamara. 2000. 'A view from the Russian Far East', in *Rapprochement or rivalry? Russia–China relations in a changing Asia*, edited by Sherman W. Garnett, 203–25. Washington, DC: Carnegie Endowment for International Peace.

Troyakova, Tamara. 2007. 'The Russian Far East: integration or isolation?' *Problems of Post-Communism* 54(2): 61–71.

Veka, Ekaterina. 2017. 'Pochti 18 tysiach zaiavlenii postupilo ot zhelaiushchikh poluchit' gektar v Primor'e' [Nearly 18 thousand applications received from those wanting to have a hectare in Primorye], *Ofitsial'nyi sait Administratsii Primorskogo kraia*, 9 February. http://www.primorsky.ru/news/123787/. Accessed on 23 February 2017.

ZRpress.ru. 2016a. 'Andrei Michulis, partner kompanii Tiger Consulting: Kachestvennym pokazatelem uluchsheniia investklimata stali deistviia so storony aziatskikh investorov po sozdaniiu biznesa v Rossii' [Andrei Michulis, partner of the company Tiger Consulting: an indicator of the improved investment climate was the actions taken by the Asian investors to develop business in Russia], 30 December. http://zrpress.ru/business/primorje_30.12.2016_81646_andrej-michulis-partner-kompanii-tiger-consulting-kachestvennym-pokazatelem-uluchshenija-investklimata-stali-dejstvija-so-storony-aziatskikh-investorov-po-sozdaniju-biznesa-v-rossii.html. Accessed on 23 February 2017.

ZRpress.ru. 2016b. 'Andrei Golotin, direktor primorskogo filiala NP SRO "MOSP MSP–OPORA": Polozhitel'nogo vliianiia svobodnogo porta na biznes my eshche ne pochuvstvovali' [Andrei Golotin, director of the Primorye branch of MOSP MSP–OPORA: We have not yet felt positive effects of the free port on business], 31 December. http://zrpress.ru/business/primorje_31.12.2016_81671_andrej-golotin-direktor-primorskogo-filiala-np-sro-mosp-msp--opora-polozhitelnogo-vlijanija-svobodnogo-porta-na-biznes-my-esche-ne-pochuvstvovali.html. Accessed on 23 February 2017.

ZRpress.ru. 2017a. 'Ekonomika Primor'ia ser'ezno prosela' [Primorye's economy in serious decline], 8 February. http://zrpress.ru/business/primorje_08.02.2017_82092_ekonomika-primorja-serjezno-prosela.html. Accessed on 23 February 2017.

ZRpress.ru. 2017b. 'Vladivostoku svetit bezviz' [Visa-free promise for Vladivostok], 28 January. http://www.zrpress.ru/society/primorje_28.01.2017_81948_vladivostoku-svetit-bezviz.html. Accessed on 23 February 2017.

Open Access This chapter is licensed under the terms of the Creative Commons Attribution 4.0 International License (http://creativecommons.org/licenses/by/4.0/), which permits use, sharing, adaptation, distribution and reproduction in any medium or format, as long as you give appropriate credit to the original author(s) and the source, provide a link to the Creative Commons license and indicate if changes were made.

The images or other third party material in this book are included in the book's Creative Commons license, unless indicated otherwise in a credit line to the material. If material is not included in the book's Creative Commons license and your intended use is not permitted by statutory regulation or exceeds the permitted use, you will need to obtain permission directly from the copyright holder.

CHAPTER 4

Promoting New Growth: 'Advanced Special Economic Zones' in the Russian Far East

Jiyoung Min and Boogyun Kang

Abstract To become a major manufacturing hub for East Asia, the Russian Far East must overcome various socioeconomic challenges, including an imbalanced economic structure, decreasing population, and a poor investment climate. To address these challenges, the Russian authorities in 2014 adopted a new development mechanism, 'advanced special economic zones' (ASEZs). This chapter discusses pros and cons of introducing ASEZs as investment platforms for cultivating export-oriented industry. Much will depend on the domestic and foreign capital inflow over the next years. If the ASEZ policy works out as planned, in the medium and long term there are possibilities for creating a new industrial value chain linking the Russian Far East with Asia-Pacific markets.

Keywords Russian Far East • Economic policy • Industrial policy • Advanced special economic zones • Foreign direct investment

J. Min (✉) • B. Kang
Department of Europe, Americas and Eurasia, Korea Institute for International Economic Policy, Sejong, Republic of Korea

At the 2014 Asia-Pacific Economic Cooperation (APEC) summit in Beijing, Vladimir Putin declared that the Russian Far East should and must develop into a major manufacturing hub for East Asia (*Kremlin.ru* 2014). Moscow envisages the Far East as a new 'economic bridge' between Europe and Asia and is currently enacting a range of investment plans and political strategies aimed at stimulating the economy and building infrastructure in Siberia and the Far Eastern Federal Okrug. Key milestones have been the 2012 establishment of the Ministry for the Development of the Far East, the 2013 adoption of a state programme for the socioeconomic development of the Far East and the Baikal region (revised in April 2014 and in August 2016), and the 2014 approval of a federal law on advanced special economic zones (ASEZs). These domestic efforts are by necessity combined with plans for stronger economic cooperation with the Asia-Pacific region. However, so far, little is known about the consequences of this increasingly urgent economic development focus on the Russian Far East. To fill some of this knowledge gap, we here carry out a close analysis of one of the key policy tools—the ASEZs. We summarize major socioeconomic challenges to the development of the Russian Far East, examine the policy itself, and evaluate implementation of the policy over time.

Major Socioeconomic Challenges in the Russian Far East

In 2015, due to a combination of plummeting oil prices and Western sanctions, Russia entered an economic recession. The economy suffered from soaring inflation and a significant reduction in investment and consumption. In 2016, the economy seemed to have adjusted to the shocks, and in 2017 it is expected to grow again. However, Russia has a long way to go before its economy is back on track. Although the economic downturn was accelerated by external factors, the fundamental problem is an internal structural one: energy dependency. The oil rents that the Russian economy obtained during the years of high oil prices were not utilized for diversifying the economy. Ever since the 1990s, the investment rate in Russia has been low compared to similar economies. Even in the 2000s the gross capital formation (as percentage of GDP) of the economy has never exceeded 26 per cent, and in 2014 it stood at 21.4—below the world average of 23.3 per cent.[1] Owing to low investment and a skewed economic structure, Russia has been experiencing economic slowdown since 2012. With the country's current economic growth model reaching its limits, structural reforms are necessary.

Basically, the Far Eastern Federal Okrug faces the same economic challenges as the broader national economy: it is characterized by economic slowdown and heavy dependence on energy revenues. In 2014, the economy of the Russian Far East accounted for 5.5 per cent (3.2 trillion rubles) of the Russian economy, making it the second smallest among the eight federal okrugs (Federal'naia sluzhba gosudarstvennoi statistiki 2016). Even though the Russian government had for several years been implementing various Far Eastern development policies, the economy still did not outpace that of other federal okrugs.

Ever since 2013 the Far Eastern Federal Okrug has been suffering from a downward economic cycle. After the completion of mega-investment projects like preparations for the September 2012 APEC summit in Vladivostok and the construction of the Eastern Siberia–Pacific Ocean 2 (ESPO 2) oil pipeline and the Ulak-Elga railroad, investments shrank considerably (Prokapalo et al. 2013, p.125). While these projects had boosted regional economic growth for a few years, they had very limited mid- and long-term economic impact (Prokapalo et al. 2014, p.113). In addition, tight credit conditions for Russian companies (few chances for borrowing in the international financial market and higher interest rate on loans in domestic banks) due to Western financial sanctions contributed to a continued reduction in investments in 2015 (Prokapalo et al. 2016, p.129).

Industrial production in the Far East stayed in the positive (see Table 4.1) thanks to the mining sector, which recorded 7.7 per cent growth in 2015. By contrast, the manufacturing sector suffered a 10 per cent reduction, linked to insufficient investment due to the higher cost of borrowing (Prokapalo et al. 2016, pp.124–25). Also in 2015, the consumer price index and producer price index stood at 112.0 and 116.5 respectively—the second year in a row that these two indices ended above the 110 mark (see Table 4.1). The main reason was the weakening of the ruble, which led to price increases on imported goods. In particular, prices on non-food items rose, since such goods could not quickly be replaced by domestic products (ibid., p.131). As a result, in 2015 retail sales in the Russian Far East turned negative—whereas the savings rate went up. This can be understood as Russian consumer behaviour shifting to a pattern of saving—not entirely a good sign, as that could further limit consumption. The decrease in consumer demand was partially reflected in imports as well.

Table 4.1 Macroeconomic indicators of the Russian Federation (RF) and the Far East (FE) (in per cent of previous year)

	2010		2011		2012		2103		2014		2015	
	RF	FE	RF	FE	RF	FE	RF	FE	RF	FE	RF	FE
G(R)DP	104.6	106.8	105.4	105.4	103.1	103.1	101.8	99.1	101.3	101.9	96.3	99.4
Industrial production	107.3	106.9	105.0	109.1	103.0	103.4	100.4	102.0	101.7	105.3	96.6	101.0
Investment on fixed capital	106.3	106.1	110.8	126.5	106.8	88.1	100.8	83.2	98.5	93.4	91.6	96.6
Consumer price index	108.8	107.7	106.1	106.8	106.6	105.9	106.5	106.6	111.4	110.7	112.9	112.0
Producer price index	116.7	110.4	112.0	117.7	105.1	108.8	103.7	101.5	105.9	110.4	110.7	116.5
Real income	105.3	102.6	105.6	105.1	105.3	107.7	104.8	106.1	99.5	102.8	95.1	99.7
Unemployment	108.3	109.2	107.3	108.6	106.5	107.4	105.5	106.7	105.5	106.5	105.2	106.4
Export	131.6	155.4	130.1	135.6	101.5	102.9	100.5	108.6	94.4	101.7	69.0	72.0
Import	136.8	155.1	133.6	119.3	103.7	114.9	99.3	116.3	91.0	87.1	63.7	55.1

Source: Federal'naia sluzhba gosudarstvennoi statistiki (2016)

The major trading partners of the Russian Far East are the three biggest economies in Northeast Asia—China, Japan and South Korea. According to the Russian customs services, these three accounted for 77 per cent of the region's total trade in 2015 (Dal'nevostochnoe tamozhennoe upravlenie 2016). As a result, trade volumes were not immediately affected strongly by the 2014 geopolitical instability. With the plunge in the oil prices, however, trade took a nosedive.

As for the labour market, the unemployment rate in the Far East remains higher than the Russian average, although it has been decreasing over time (see Table 4.1). However, this is not attributable to improved conditions on the labour market, but to a shrinking population and workforce (see discussion of demographics below).

The economy of the Russian Far East is highly dependent on the primary sector (see Fig. 4.1). The mining sector makes up 28.6 per cent of the region's economy (compared to 10.6 per cent in the Federation as a whole), whereas the manufacturing sector constitutes a mere 5.1 per cent (17.4 per cent in the Federation as a whole). The latter has been heavily affected by the economic downturn. As shown in Table 4.2, production in the manufacturing sector began to slow already from 2012, turning negative in 2015 (Prokapalo et al. 2016, p.124). Primorye and Khabarovsk were especially hard hit by the 2015 recession, as these two regions stand

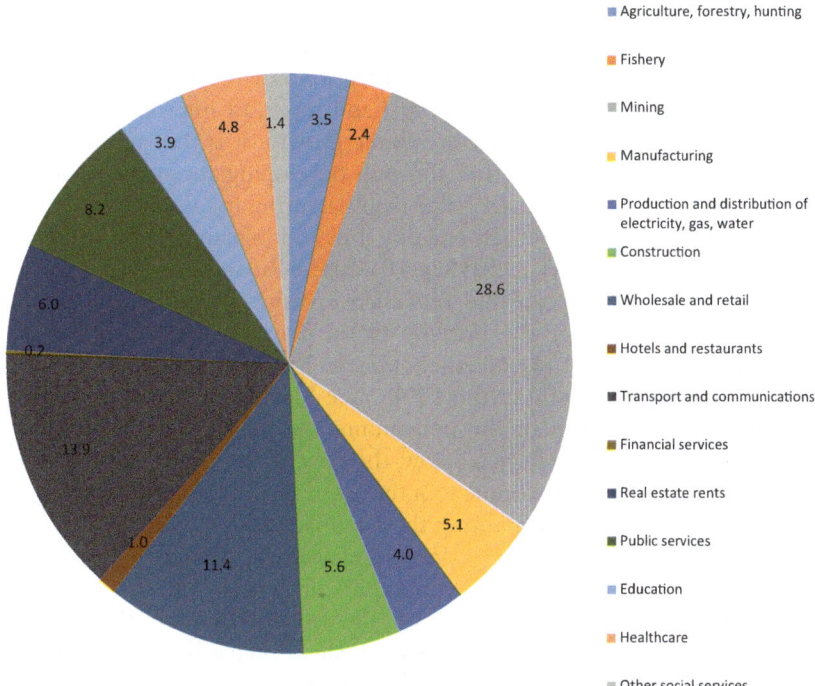

Fig. 4.1 Industrial composition of the economy of the Russian Far East, 2014 (in per cent) (Source: Federal'naia sluzhba gosudarstvennoi statistiki 2016)

Table 4.2 Production index of the manufacturing sector (in per cent of previous year)

	2010	2011	2012	2013	2014	2015
Russian Federation average	*110.6*	*108.0*	*105.1*	*100.5*	*102.1*	*94.6*
Central Federal Okrug	105.3	107.8	106.7	102.3	101.7	97.4
Northwestern Federal Okrug	112.5	113.6	104.7	100.2	96.6	94.4
Southern Federal Okrug	109.3	110.5	108.4	103.9	105.2	103.1
North Caucasus Federal Okrug	105.9	113.5	109.9	110.3	99.8	104.0
Volga Federal Okrug	114.2	114.5	106.7	102.4	103.8	96.5
Ural Federal Okrug	111.2	108.2	107.6	104.1	103.5	98.9
Siberian Federal Okrug	108.5	105.0	103.0	103.1	102.6	97.5
Far Eastern Federal Okrug	114.5	121.3	108.9	104.9	102.7	91.1

Source: Federal'naia sluzhba gosudarstvennoi statistiki (2016)

for over half of manufacturing production in the Russian Far East (car production in Primorye; airplanes and ship-building in Khabarovsk).

In general, economies heavily dependent on raw materials are particularly vulnerable to external factors, first and foremost international commodity prices. To sustain stable economic growth, it is thus necessary to diversify the economic structure through developing the manufacturing sector (Su and Yao 2016, p.13). The manufacturing industry is important in driving economic growth, by creating jobs and in many other aspects of the economy (Maniyka et al. 2012, p.18). In the Russian Far East, reforming the industrial structure has remained a major challenge (Jeh et al. 2014, p.27). Ever since the breakup of the Soviet Union, the Russian government has sought to implement policies for developing the Far East. While largely unsuccessful in the 1990s (see Blakkisrud, Chap. 2, in this volume), since the turn of the millennium there have been more concerted efforts. As will be shown below, the government's new approach to facilitating economic development in the Far East is specifically targeted at attracting investors and promoting the manufacturing sector.

In addition to the macro-economic challenges outlined above, the Russian Far East faces serious demographic problems. The vast territory of 6.2 million km^2 has a population of only some 6.2 million. While since 2010 the total population of the Russian Federation has begun to increase slightly, that trend is not evident in the Russian Far East (see Table 4.3), where the population has decreased every year since 1991. Likewise, the economically active share of the population in the Russian Far East is also decreasing year by year (see Table 4.4). This, however, is a trend that characterizes the whole of Russia. In general, population is an important factor when gauging the workforce and market size. In such a perspective, the Russian Far East is losing market size and potential for economic growth.

Low living standards due to the high cost of living and poor infrastructure are seen as major culprits in the depopulation of the Far East. In 2015, the average monthly income of the Russian Far East reached 53,862 rubles. Among Russia's eight federal okrugs, the Central Federal Okrug had the highest average income in 2015, followed by the Far Eastern Federal Okrug (see Table 4.5). However, this should not be taken to mean that people living in the Far East are relatively better off compared to other regions because the cost of living is high. To give but one example: in 2014, the average price on the primary housing market in the Far East was 62,140 rubles per square metre, higher than in the Central Federal

Table 4.3 Population (1000 persons/per cent of previous year)

	2010	2011	2012	2013	2014	2015
Russian Federation	142,865 (0.02)	143,056 (0.1)	143,347 (0.2)	143,667 (0.2)	146,267 (1.8)	146,545 (0.2)
Central Federal Okrug	38,445 (0.3)	38,538 (0.2)	38,679 (0.4)	38,820 (0.4)	38,951 (0.3)	39,104 (0.4)
Northwestern Federal Okrug	13,626 (0.2)	13,660 (0.3)	13,717 (0.4)	13,801 (0.6)	13,844 (0.3)	13,854 (0.1)
Southern Federal Okrug	13,851 (−0.02)	13,884 (0.2)	13,910 (0.2)	13,964 (0.4)	14,004 (0.3)	14,045 (0.3)
North Caucasus Federal Okrug	9,439 (0.9)	9,493 (0.6)	9,541 (0.5)	9,590 (0.5)	9,659 (0.7)	9,718 (0.6)
Volga Federal Okrug	29,880 (−0.4)	29,811 (−0.2)	29,772 (−0.1)	29,739 (−0.1)	29,715 (−0.1)	29,674 (−0.1)
Ural Federal Okrug	12,087 (−0.01)	12,143 (0.5)	12,198 (0.4)	12,234 (0.3)	12,276 (0.3)	12,308 (0.3)
Siberian Federal Okrug	19,252 (−0.2)	19,261 (0.05)	19,278 (0.1)	19,292 (0.1)	19,312 (0.1)	19,324 (0.1)
Far Eastern Federal Okrug	6,285 (−0.6)	6,266 (−0.3)	6,252 (−0.2)	6,227 (−0.4)	6,211 (−0.3)	6,195 (−0.3)

Source: Federal'naia sluzhba gosudarstvennoi statistiki (2016)

Table 4.4 Labour market (per cent of total)

	Share of economically active population						Share of population older than economically active population					
	2010	2011	2012	2013	2014	2015	2010	2011	2012	2013	2014	2015
Russian Federation average	61.5	60.9	60.1	59.3	58.4	57.4	22.3	22.6	23.1	23.5	24.0	24.6
Central Federal Okrug	61.3	60.7	60.0	59.3	58.5	57.6	24.8	25.2	25.6	25.9	26.4	26.8
Northwestern Federal Okrug	62.0	61.4	60.6	59.9	59.0	57.9	23.6	24.0	24.4	24.8	25.3	25.8
Southern Federal Okrug	60.3	59.8	59.2	58.4	57.6	56.7	23.6	24.0	24.3	24.7	25.2	25.7
North Caucasus Federal Okrug	61.0	60.7	60.3	59.8	59.3	58.7	15.1	15.4	15.7	16.1	16.5	17.0
Volga Federal Okrug	61.2	60.5	59.6	58.7	57.8	56.8	22.6	23.1	23.6	24.1	24.7	25.2
Ural Federal Okrug	62.3	61.6	60.7	59.7	58.7	57.7	20.4	20.8	21.2	21.6	22.1	22.6
Siberian Federal Okrug	61.9	61.0	60.2	59.2	58.2	57.2	20.4	20.9	21.3	21.8	22.4	22.9
Far Eastern Federal Okrug	63.4	62.7	61.9	61.0	60.1	59.2	19.2	19.7	20.1	20.6	21.1	21.6

Source: Federal'naia sluzhba gosudarstvennoi statistiki (2016)

Table 4.5 Average monthly income (in rubles, December each year)

	2010	2011	2012	2013	2014	2015
Russian Federation average	28,173.2	31,568.0	35,547.9	39,758.0	40,972.0	45,139.0
Central Federal Okrug	38,841.7	44,140.4	49,455.5	51,384.0	54,302.0	61,378.0
Northwestern Federal Okrug	29,020.5	30,211.5	35,986.3	40,978.0	45,938.0	49,452.0
Southern Federal Okrug	21,299.2	23,707.7	28,329.3	31,921.0	34,232.0	37,836.0
North Caucasus Federal Okrug	21,420.1	24,640.8	27,573.5	31,250.0	33,909.0	36,644.0
Volga Federal Okrug	22,791.1	25,501.7	28,728.1	31,356.0	33,984.0	37,211.0
Ural Federal Okrug	31,240.8	35,564.0	39,502.2	42,381.0	43,020.0	45,952.0
Siberian Federal Okrug	21,911.2	24,545.2	28,598.7	31,733.0	32,348.0	34,521.0
Far Eastern Federal Okrug	32,013.8	36,148.6	41,719.8	46,875.0	49,120.0	53,862.0

Source: Federal'naia sluzhba gosudarstvennoi statistiki (2016)

Table 4.6 Cost of goods and services of fixed basket (in rubles, December each year)

	2010	2011	2012	2013	2014	2015
Russia Federation average	8,711.8	9,174.2	9,868.0	10,737.0	12,034.9	13,404.3
Central Federal Okrug	9,471.0	10,182.1	10,985.5	11,986.0	13,481.6	14,978.2
Northwestern Federal Okrug	9,227.0	9,525.6	10,220.3	11,046.6	12,537.9	14,106.0
Southern Federal Okrug	8,393.1	8,528.3	9,099.6	9,834.9	11,362.3	12,735.0
North Caucasus Federal Okrug	7,919.8	8,220.8	8,987.5	9,572.1	11,073.8	12,359.1
Volga Federal Okrug	7,766.9	8,180.7	8,874.9	9,671.5	10,959.3	12,169.5
Ural Federal Okrug	8,878.7	9,393.6	10,122.4	10,954.7	12,029.5	13,406.8
Siberian Federal Okrug	8,072.2	8,446.9	9,185.5	10,023.4	11,116.4	12,382.5
Far Eastern Federal Okrug	11,108.7	11,958.6	12,840.3	14,022.5	15,427.0	16,857.6

Source: Federal'naia sluzhba gosudarstvennoi statistiki (2016)

Okrug, and much higher than the Russian average of 51,714 rubles (Federal'naia sluzhba gosudarstvennoi statistiki 2016). The cost of the fixed basket of goods and services in the Far East is the highest among the Russian federal okrugs: thus, consumers in this federal okrug are paying more than the average Russian for the same goods and services (see Table 4.6). When the average monthly income and the cost of goods and services are taken into consideration,[2] the purchasing power of those living in the Far Eastern Federal Okrug falls to fourth place among the eight federal okrugs.

Cost levels are related to the huge distances and poorly developed transport infrastructure in the Russian Far East. For example, the proportion of paved public roads in the okrug in 2014 was 66.6 per cent, lower than Russia's average of 70.5 per cent. Likewise, railroad density per 10,000 km² in the Russian Far East was only 14 km in 2014, the lowest among all federal okrugs. The national average was 50 km per 10,000 km²—and in the Central Federal Okrug it was 262 km.[3] Transport fees in the Russian Far East are higher than elsewhere, and the weakly developed transport infrastructure discourages private investors. To improve the quality of local lives and realize industrial development, not least the promotion of export-oriented industries in the ASEZs, the transport infrastructure of the Far East has to be upgraded.

In recent years, the investment climate in Russia seems to have improved greatly. Simplified administrative procedures helped Russia to jump from being ranked 120th among 183 countries in 2011 to 40th among 190 countries in 2016 on the World Bank's Doing Business Index (World Bank 2012, p.6; 2016, p.7). However, the current economic recession and the limited availability of international financing due to Western sanctions have become major stumbling blocks for new investments, also in the Russian Far East.

The Far Eastern Federal Okrug is faced with a whole range of socioeconomic challenges—including economic slowdown, imbalanced economic structure, decreasing population, low living standards, and poor investment conditions. These challenges are partly interrelated and will need to be dealt with through long-term strategies. Cognizant of this, the Russian government has devised a new approach to Far Eastern development, to which we now turn.

Russia's New Development Strategy for the Far East

From the onset of Putin's third term, Russia has been searching for more forceful ways of accelerating development in the Far Eastern Federal Okrug. In May 2012, the government established a separate ministry—the Ministry for the Development of the Far East. This ministry oversees the development of the region and implementation of the state programme 'On the Socioeconomic Development of the Far East and the Baikal Region until 2025', adopted in March 2013 and revised in April 2014 and August 2016. Moreover, to ensure momentum, a separate commission, the Government Commission on the Socioeconomic Development of the Far East, over which Prime Minister Dmitrii Medvedev personally presides, was added in 2013 (Jeh et al. 2014, pp.124–25, see also Blakkisrud, Chap. 2, this volume).[4] At the heart of these efforts aimed at improving the situation of the Far Eastern Federal Okrug stands the plan to create 'territories of advanced socioeconomic development' (*territorii operezhaiushchego sotsial'no-ekonomicheskogo razvitiia*), commonly referred to as 'advanced special economic zones' (ASEZs).

The idea behind the ASEZs is to foster a business and investment friendly environment and to cultivate export-oriented industries targeting the Asia-Pacific region. This is to be achieved through the introduction of an institutional mechanism backed by unprecedented tax benefits, infrastructure development, and administrative support. Why has Russia taken these steps? There are two main reasons. First, ever since the breakup of the Soviet Union, Russia has continued to push forward with development projects in the Far East—without tangible results (*Government.ru* 2013a). The Russian Far East still lags far behind other federal okrugs on various indexes (quality of life, social conditions for developing the labour force, social infrastructure, etc.). As investment incentives decreased sharply after the 2012 APEC summit in Vladivostok, the Kremlin had to devise a new policy to attract private and public capital.

Second, while the Russian Far East has recorded relatively low economic growth, it has great potential for economic development linked to the Asia-Pacific region, if it can capitalize on resources, transport, and logistics advantages. The Russian government has noted that the Asia-Pacific region, including China, Japan and South Korea, has emerged as a primary supplier of global financial resources and a logistics hub. Moreover, the government hopes to mitigate workforce shortages in the Russian Far East by drawing on the labour mobility and technology development capacity of the Asia-Pacific region (Minvostokrazvitiia 2016b, p.2).

Russia has needed to set a new direction so as to transform the currently underdeveloped Far East into a new growth engine. In the following, we examine the content of this policy and the primary characteristics of the ASEZs, and discuss the future prospects and challenges for the ASEZs regime.

ASEZs: An Investment Platform to Cultivate Export-Oriented Industry

One option for the Kremlin would have been to focus on the import-substituting industry in the Far East and turn the region into an internal supply base for all of Russia. However, given the limits to growth described above, it was deemed difficult to produce swift changes with tangible results along these lines. Instead, based on an assessment of the geographical proximity to the Asia-Pacific region with its huge markets, the Russian government opted to cultivate export-oriented industries as the new development model for the Far East. As the Russian Far East has a weak manufacturing base, substantial investments would be required to implement this model. Therefore, in parallel to developing a plan for regional development, the Russian government had to design a plan for attracting investors. The answer came in the form of a new strategic development model: the ASEZs (*Government.ru* 2013a).[5]

The new development model was introduced in October 2013 by Aleksandr Galushka, Minister for the Development of the Far East, at a meeting of the Government Commission for the Socioeconomic Development of the Far East. According to Galushka, the new model would be based on

(1) increasing the export of finished goods (including services) produced in the Russian Far East to countries in the Asia-Pacific region
(2) creating a competitive investment environment, and attracting direct investments, including foreign, to revitalize businesses and help small- and medium-sized companies develop
(3) developing competitive territories of advanced development [*territorii operezhaiushchego razvitiia*], including special economic zones in the form of industrial, techno- and agro-industrial parks. (*Government.ru* 2013b)

President Putin picked up on the idea in his annual address to the Federal Assembly in December that year, emphasizing the development of the Russian Far East as the top national priority of the twenty-first century (Putin 2013). He proposed the establishment of a network of economic development zones to nurture the export-oriented manufacturing industry in the Russian Far East, thus giving further shape and momentum to the plans for introducing ASEZs.

The federal law on ASEZs was introduced with unprecedented swiftness. The basic principles for the creation and operation of the ASEZs were approved by the federal government in February 2014 (*Government.ru* 2014a). A bill was forwarded to the State Duma in October 2014, only one year after the idea was first discussed. President Putin signed the law on 29 December 2014 (*Government.ru* 2014c), and it entered into effect on 30 March 2015.

The ASEZs is a key component of the 2013 state programme 'On the Socioeconomic Development of the Far East and the Baikal Region'. When this programme was revised in April 2014, it was with the goal of accelerating the development of the Far East and improving sociodemographic conditions there (*Government.ru* 2014b). The August 2016 revisions focus on new mechanisms designed to achieve this accelerated development, including the ASEZs, the Free Port of Vladivostok and infrastructure support to major investment projects (*Government.ru* 2016). This illustrates how important the ASEZs are to current Russian Far Eastern development policies.

Content and Characteristics

What are the primary characteristics of the ASEZs? Intended as a new policy tool for enhancing the global competitiveness of the Russian Far East, the ASEZs are economic zones that enjoy a wide range of deregulations and tax benefits, while also serving as investment platforms (Minvostokrazvitiia n.d.). The federal law on the ASEZs stipulates that the zones are 'a part of Russian territory (…) in which (…) a special legal system is established for business and other activities in order to create favourable conditions for attracting investments, ensuring rapid socioeconomic development and creating comfortable living conditions for the population' (Federal'nyi zakon 2014). While the bill was originally promoted as legislation targeting the Far East and 'other special areas', it became a law covering Russia as a whole: to be implemented first in the Russian Far East, and then, in three years, to be extended to the rest of the Federation.

The new Russian Far Eastern development model focuses on the innovation of institutional mechanisms, illustrated by the establishment of an integrated governance structure composed of the Ministry for the Development of the Far East and its affiliated organizations, accompanied by the introduction of preferential laws and regulations. Table 4.7 outlines the main features of the ASEZs.

Whereas previous development policies have been pushed forward by the unilateral efforts of the Russian government and self-reliance, the new policy also relies on attracting domestic private as well as foreign investments. To facilitate this, it is considered necessary to offer tax benefits, lower administrative barriers, and create the necessary infrastructure essential to investors. In fact, this had already been attempted. When the idea of introducing ASEZs emerged, Russia had already created a number of SEZs: as of the end of 2016, there were 5 technology innovation SEZs,

Table 4.7 Key features of ASEZs

Category	Highlights		
	On Territories of Advanced Socioeconomic Development		
Governance	The Ministry for the Development of the Far East (*Minvostokrazvitiia*) and its affiliated organizations: the Far East Development Corporation (infrastructure provision and ASEZ operator); the Far East Development Fund (project financing); the Far East Investment and Export Agency (attracting investment); and the Far East Human Capital Development Agency (providing workforce)		
State-funded infrastructure	Covered by the federal budget, budgets of the federal subjects and local budgets as well as extra-budgetary sources: Installation of infrastructure like roads (but not railroads), gas, water, sewage, electricity, etc., is split 50/50 between federal and regional budgets		
Administrative benefits	- expedited permits (subject to special control system at the federal and regional government levels) - possibility to attract skilled foreign manpower in a rapid and preferential way - subject to the custom procedures regulating customs-free zones		
Tax preferences		ASEZs:	General tax rate:
	Profit tax	0% for at least the first 5 years, 10% for the next 5 years after this	20%
	Property tax	In general, 0% for at least the first 5 years, 0.5% for the next 5 years, but tax rates will differ among federal subjects	2.2%
	Land tax	0% for the first 5 years	1.5%
	Social security and payroll tax	7.6% for the first 10 years	30%, from 2017 34%
	Customs	Tax exemption (customs-free zone)	Tax imposition
	Mineral resource taxation	Discount factor: 0% for the first 2 years, 0.2% for years 3 to 4, 0.4% for years 5 to 6, 0.6% for years 7 to 8 and 0.8% for years 9 to 10	Various tax rates, ranging from minimum 3.6% (potash) to maximum 16.5% (petroleum)

Source: Compiled by the authors

8 industrial production SEZs, 15 tourism and recreational SEZs and 3 port SEZs. Three of these were located in the Russian Far East: the Vladivostok Industrial Production SEZ, the Russkii Island Tourism and Recreational SEZ and the Sovetskaia Gavan Port SEZ (the first two in Primorskii Krai and the third one in Khabarovsk) (Minekrazvitiia n.d.). Why, then, create the ASEZs in addition?

First, the Russian Far East needed to secure special means for backing up investors: a new type of investment platform. The existing SEZs fell within the portfolio of the Ministry of Economic Development. And while the industrial production and technology innovation SEZs were seen as successful, the tourism and port SEZs were not functioning as planned: they did not reflect what investors were calling for, and they were not equipped to push forward with relevant projects themselves (Byun 2014). To enhance the efficiency and implementing power of the development policy, the Russian government wanted the Ministry for the Development of the Far East to have responsibility for the economic zones in the Far East.

Second, to boost the development of the Far East, Russian authorities intended to rely partly on private investment. To attract such investment, they would have to offer more effective tax cuts than in the existing SEZs. Also other laws were amended in order to offer a wider range of benefits to those who made investments in ASEZs. Thus we find a clear difference between the SEZs and ASEZs: while the former focus on creating competitive investment environments with a minimum level of incentives, the latter are based on a concentrated effort to attract more investments through unprecedented benefits. The Ministry for the Development of the Far East emphasizes that ASEZs are fundamentally different from the existing SEZs: ASEZs provide basic infrastructure, a guarantee of an extendable 70-year operation period (with the SEZs, there is a non-extendable 49-year operation period), an extensive preferential regime (including reduced corporate tax and simplified administrative procedures) and one-stop service for residents.

Third, the ASEZs are intended to offer better business environments than elsewhere in the Asia-Pacific region, with states in the latter offering conditions more similar to those of Russia's existing SEZs. The Ministry for the Development of the Far East is convinced that the ASEZs will prove more competitive than these SEZs as a result of the additional emphasis on swift administrative procedures, tax benefits and crucial infrastructure (see Table 4.8) (Minvostokrazvitiia 2016a).

Initial Results

As of the end of 2016, a total of 14 ASEZs have been designated since the federal law went into effect in March 2015. Three zones had been selected in advance, in February 2015: Nadezhdinskaia in Primorskii Krai and

Table 4.8 Comparison of characteristics of SEZs in Asia-Pacific countries

	Korea	China	Singapore	USA	Canada	Japan	Russia	Russian ASEZs	Unit
Corporate tax	10	15	17	33	23.5	26.4	13.5	10	% on operating profits
Transportation costs	700	550	440	1,320	1,660	970	1,800	440	USD/ 20ft container
Electricity charges	7.3	7.4	13.6	6.9	7.4	17.9	11.7	6.9	cent/ 1kWh
Payroll tax	8.8	26.7	16.0	7.7	8.7	25.6	14.0	7.6	% on wages
Time needed to obtain construction permit	29	67	26	27	163	193	244	26	number of days
Connection to energy supply system	28	41	36	68	142	105	254	28	number of days
Export support policy	5	4	4	4	5	3	2	5	points
Intellectual property protection	2	3	4	5	4	5	3	5	score on IPRI ranking
Professional manpower availability	High	High	High	High	Average	High	Low	High	
Supplier availability	High	High	High	High	Average	High	Low	High	

Source: Titov (2014)

Khabarovsk and Komsomolsk in Khabarovskii Krai. Selection criteria had been the potential demand for attracting investment, the number of investors, and the plans for infrastructure construction.

After the law entered into force, another six zones were designated in August 2015: one each in the Sakha Republic, Kamchatka Krai, Chukotka Autonomous Okrug and Primorskii Krai, and two in Amur Oblast. These were followed by another five new zones in 2016: one each in Primorskii Krai, the Jewish Autonomous Oblast and the Sakha Republic, and two in Sakhalin Oblast. The only Far Eastern federal subject without an ASEZ is thus Magadan. The new ASEZs were designated according to the specialization principle, in line with the specific characteristics of each area. The individual ASEZs will specialize in fields like industry, logistics, food processing, wood processing, etc., as appropriate (see Table 4.9).

As of October 2016, a total of 194 investment applications had been submitted by Russian and foreign companies; out of these, the authorities had concluded moving-in agreements with 91 companies. The size of planned investments by these 91 businesses is more than 400 billion rubles, and the investments are expected to create a total of 20,533 new jobs. The great majority of the businesses are Russian: 81 out of 91. As to foreign companies, there are five from China, two each from Japan and Australia, and one from Lithuania.[6] An additional 16 foreign companies have applied.[7] The total planned investment of these 26 foreign companies would be 171.3 billion rubles, and they are expected to create 4778 new jobs.

Evaluation of Policy Implementation and Prospects for Development

The plan of the Russian government is to use the ASEZs as a new policy means for developing its Far Eastern backwater. In recent years, the government has been pushing forward with its development policy more briskly than ever before. The reason behind the Kremlin's new, proactive approach is not only that previous instruments failed and that Russia needed a new model for regional development: it also decided that the time had come for Russia to maximize its growth potential by connecting with the Asia-Pacific region. Today, the Russian government appears set to take all necessary steps to attract more investors; there seems to be a new approach to listening to what investors need, rather than simply expecting investors to contribute to the state's plans for development.

Since the ASEZ regime was introduced only in March 2015, it is still in a transitional, formative period. Those working on ASEZs will need clearer policy directions, budgets and operational know-how: detailed development concepts or development strategies have yet to be formulated. Although each zone specializes within a field where it is deemed competitive, there are no unique identities, concrete action plans, or synergy policies among the ASEZs—a problem seen as major hurdle (POSCO 2016).

Table 4.9 Designated ASEZs

Name (federal subject)	Designation date (adoption of government decree)	Specialization	Expected investment (billion rubles)		Job creation (number of people)
			Private capital	Government budget	
Nadezhdinskaia (Primorskii Krai)	June 2015	Light industry, food, logistics	36.0	3.9	5,800
Khabarovsk (Khabarovsk Krai)	June 2015	Industry, logistics	39.4	2.5	7,800
Komsomolsk (Khabarovsk Krai)	June 2015	Industry (aircraft manufacturing)	16.2	1.2	3,500
Mikhailovskii (Primorskii Krai)	August 2015	Agriculture and livestock, grain production	56.5	4.44	5,700
Priamurskaia (Amur Oblast)	August 2015	Industry, logistics	136.5	0	3,150
Belogorsk (Amur Oblast)	August 2015	Agriculture	10.2	0.046	1,860
Kamchatka (Kamchatka Krai)	August 2015	Industry, tourism	22.1	8.5	2,918
Beringovskii (Chukotka Autonomous Okrug)	August 2015	Mining industry	11.6	0	450
Kangalassy (Sakha Republic)	August 2015	Industry	4.28	0.2	350
Bolshoi Kamen (Primorskii Krai)	January 2016	Shipbuilding	148.5	3.2	11,000
Gornyi Vozdukh (Sakhalin Oblast)	March 2016	Tourism	9.9	10	624
Iuzhnaia (Sakhalin Oblast)	March 2016	Agriculture	10.6	1.46	2,091
Amuro-Khinganskaia (Jewish Autonomous Oblast)	August 2016	Agriculture and livestock	17.1	0	1,292
Iuzhnaia Iakutiia (Sakha Republic)	December 2016	Industry	24.7	0	2,900

Source: General Consulate of the Republic of Korea in Vladivostok (2016), *Iasia.ru* (2016), Minvostokrazvitiia (2016c)

Concerning tax benefits, the single greatest advantage offered by the ASEZs, there are competing perspectives on specificities and timelines, with the relevant agencies at odds with one another over the benefits of attracting investments versus the loss of state revenues (POSCO 2016). The period for corporate tax exemption has already been reduced from ten to five years.

When it comes to the government's decision to back infrastructure development, another key advantage of the ASEZs, the construction of such infrastructure suffers from the failure of the cash-strapped regional authorities to ensure matching funding. This is critical, since the central government and the regional authorities are equally responsible for securing funding for infrastructure construction projects (see Table 4.7 above). As it often takes several years to get proper infrastructure in place, concerns have also been raised about the considerable sunk costs that will accrue (KOTRA 2015).

Finally, as mentioned, the initial idea had been to promote the ASEZs as a special tool for developing the *Far East*. Then, with the adoption of the federal law, it became—with a delay of three years—applicable to all of Russia. From March 2018, it will be extended to other regions as well. That entails the danger of potential investors preferring to invest in other regions with more favourable geographical conditions or more well-balanced development than in the Far East. And that may weaken the original aim of attracting investment to the Far East by offering the most competitive benefits in the Asia-Pacific region (Byun 2014, p.69).

It is still too early to say whether the ASEZs will be a success. This is a long-term project; stakeholders should approach it with a macro-perspective. It has also been argued that in order to promote such specialized industries Russia should first set about developing and improving public health, education, social infrastructure and living conditions (Isaev 2016). The Russian Far East needs to attract skilled manpower—but, to achieve this, the authorities will have to improve the quality of living, offer residents and newcomers a wider range of benefits, and implement special measures to back and develop small- and medium-sized companies.

Russia's strained relations with the West after 2014 gave an impulse and further motivation to the Far Eastern development policy. However, the most important factor is to be able to accrue sufficient 'capital input'. Due to the Western economic sanctions, investors are experiencing difficulties in financing their projects in Russia. And as Russia is undergoing an economic recession and has adopted an austere fiscal regime, also from the side of the authorities, there is not much room for allocating large volumes of investment to Far Eastern development. In the August 2016 second revision of the state programme, the overall budget for Far Eastern development was cut back: whereas 3.8 trillion rubles had been allocated for the period 2014–25, the budget for 2016–25 was now adjusted to 466.52 billion rubles in federal funding (Jeh et al. 2014, pp.81–82; Eastern Economic Forum 2016). This huge cut reflects the current internal and external economic conditions that have forced the Kremlin to budget more realistically. The ASEZs can therefore be understood as a focused approach for advancing development in the Russian Far East under the recent budget constraints: The Russian government intends to continue to push for the development of the Russian Far East, despite deteriorating internal and external economic conditions.

All the same the success of the ASEZs will hinge on being able to attract huge domestic and foreign inflows of capital. In a short-term perspective, it is hard to be optimistic about the future of the Russian Far East. However, in a medium- and long-term perspective, if the ASEZs policy proves functional, there is a real possibility for the formation of new industrial value-chains linking the Russian Far East with the Asia-Pacific market. In that case, the ASEZs will not only facilitate the sustainable development in the Russian Far East but also contribute towards its integration into the economy of the wider Asia-Pacific area. But there are many challenges remaining before this vision can be realized.

Notes

1. On Russia's gross capital formation over time, see World Bank data at http://data.worldbank.org/indicator/NE.GDI.TOTL.ZS?locations=RU. Accessed on 27 February 2017.
2. The fixed basket of goods and services represents the purchases of the average consumer, and refers to a relatively fixed set of consumer products and services valued on an annual basis. This is used primarily to calculate the consumer price index or inflation of a certain market.
3. Calculated based on data from the Federal'naia sluzhba gosudarsvennoi statistiki 2016.
4. At the first meeting of the Government Commission on the Socioeconomic Development of the Far East in October 2013 Prime Minister Medvedev emphasized that this commission—besides the one on the North Caucasus—was the only such commission over which the prime minister presided in person (*Government.ru* 2013a).

5. Although various experts have long held that the Russian Far East should adopt an export-oriented industrial development model targeted at the Asia-Pacific region, their ideas failed to gain official approval. Since the breakup of the Soviet Union, the Russian government has sought to revitalize its economic relations with the global community, but as far as the Russian Far East was concerned, such an approach was seen as posing a serious threat to territorial integration. Accordingly, the Russian government paid more attention to boosting trade between the Far East and European Russia. However, given the high costs of transportation, this model could not work without government subsidies. As a result, the Russian Far East found itself in a situation where it could neither trade profitably with the rest of Russia nor foster its own export-oriented industries (Jeh et al. 2014, pp.91–92).
6. The five Chinese companies are the Amur Energy Company (oil refinery) and S Technology (cement plant) in Priamurskaia ASEZ; STK (road construction equipment) in Khabarovsk ASEZ; Sato (textiles) in Nadezhdinskaia ASEZ; and Sakha Clay Pits (building materials) in Kangalassy ASEZ. The two Japanese companies are JGC Evergreen (greenhouses) in Khabarovsk ASEZ and Sayuri (greenhouses) in Kangalassy ASEZ. The two Australian are Port Ugolnyi (modernization of coal terminal) and Beringugol (coalmine development) in Beringovskii ASEZ. Finally, the Lithuanian company is SakhaLipsnele (boilers) in Kangalassy ASEZ (General Consulate of the Republic of Korea in Vladivostok 2016, pp.6–7).
7. Eight from China, two each from South Korea, Singapore, and Italy, and one each from Kazakhstan and Israel (General Consulate of the Republic of Korea in Vladivostok 2016, p.6).

References

Byun, Hyun-Sub. 2014. '러시아 극동지역개발 전략으로서 선도경제구역 설립의 의미와 전망' [The meaning and prospects of establishing advanced development zones as Russia's Far East development strategy], *Slavic Studies* 30(4): 55–79.

Dal'nevostochnoe tamozhennoe upravlenie. 2016. 'Statisticheskaia informatsiia o vneshnei torgovle za dekabr' 2015 g' [Statistical information on foreign trade for December 2015]. http://dvtu.customs.ru/index.php?option=com_content&view=article&id=18551:-2015-&catid=63:stat-vnesh-torg-cat&Itemid=282. Accessed on 19 December 2016.

Federal'nyi zakon. 2014. 'O territoriiakh operezhaiushchego sotsial'no-ekonomicheskogo razvitiia v Rossiiskoi Federatsii' [On territories of advanced socioeconomic development in the Russian Federation], N473-FZ, 29 December. http://www.consultant.ru/document/cons_doc_LAW_172962. Accessed on 20 December 2016.

Federal'naia sluzhba gosudarstvennoi statistiki. 2016. *Regiony Rossii: sotsial'no-ekonomicheskie pokazateli* [Russia's regions: socioeconomic indicators]. http://www.gks.ru/free_doc/doc_2016/region/reg-pok16.pdf. Accessed on 12 December 2016.

Eastern Economic Forum. 2016. 'Far East to annually receive RUB 466 bln for development', 16 August. https://forumvostok.ru/en/far-east-to-annually-receive-rub-466-bln-for-development. Accessed on 19 December 2016.

General Consulate of the Republic of Korea in Vladivostok. 2016. '2016년 선도개발구역 및 블라디보스톡자유항 제도 개요' [An outline of ASEZs and the Free Port of Vladivostok in 2016]. http://rus-vladivostok.mofa.go.kr/korean/eu/rus-vladivostok/policy/market/index.jsp. Accessed on 19 December 2016.

Government.ru. 2013a. 'Pravitel'stvennaia komissiia po voprosam sotsial'no-ekonomicheskogo razvitiia Dal'nego Vostoka' [Government Commission on the Socioeconomic Development of the Far East], 24 October. http://government.ru/news/7718. Accessed on 16 December 2016.

Government.ru. 2013b. 'Resheniia po itogam zasedaniia Pravitel'stvennoi komissii po voprosam sotsial'no-ekonomicheskogo razvitiia Dal'nego Vostoka' [Conclusions of the meeting of the Government Commission on the Socioeconomic Development of the Far East], 12 November. http://government.ru/orders/selection/401/8051. Accessed on 19 December 2016.

Government.ru. 2014a. 'O resheniiakh po itogam soveshchaniia ob osnovnykh printsipakh sozdaniia i upravleniia territoriiami operezhaiushchego sotsial'no-ekomicheskogo razvitiia na Dal'nem Vostoke' [Conclusions from the meeting on the main principles of establishing and managing territories of advanced socio-economic development in the Far East], 24 February. http://government.ru/orders/selection/401/10631. Accessed on 19 December 2016.

Government.ru. 2014b. 'Ob utverzhdenii novoi redaktsii gosudarstvennoi programmy "Sotsial'no-ekomicheskoe razvitie Dal'nego Vostoka i Baikal'skogo regiona"' [On the approval of a new version of the state programme 'On the socioeconomic development of the Far East and the Baikal region'], 15 April. http://government.ru/docs/11959. Accessed on 19 December 2016.

Government.ru. 2014c. 'Prezident podpisal razrabotannyi Pravitel'stvom Federal'nyi zakon "O territoriiakh operezhaiushchego sotsial'no-ekonomicheskogo razvitiia v Rossiiskoi Federatsii' [President signed the Federal law 'On Territories of Advanced Socioeconomic Development in Russian Federation' developed by the Government], 29 December. http://government.ru/news/20176. Accessed on 19 December 2016.

Government.ru. 2016. 'Ob utverzhdenii novoi redaktsii gosudarstvennoi programmy "Sotsial'no-economicheskoe razvitie Dal'nego Vostoka i Baikal'skogo regiona"' [On the approval of a new version of the state programme 'On the Socioeconomic Development of the Far East and the Baikal Region'], 16 August. http://government.ru/docs/24166. Accessed on19 December 2016.

Iasia.ru. 2016. 'Pravitel'stvo Rossii utverdilo sozdanie TOR "Iuzhnaia Iakutiia"' [Russian government approved the establishment of the ASEZ 'Iuzhnaia Iakutiia'], 30 December. http://ysia.ru/ekonomika/pravitelstvo-rossii-utverdilo-sozdanie-tor-yuzhnaya-yakutiya. Accessed on 4 March 2017.

Isaev, Artem. 2016. 'Rossiiskii plan razvitiia Dal'nego Vostoka i ego vypolnenie' [Russia's plan for the development of the Far East and its implementation], in *Changes in the global and domestic conditions and future of the development of the Far East*, 111–17. http://www.kiep.go.kr/sub/view.do?bbsId=seminarData&nttId=189778&searchCate1=%EA%B5%AD%EC%A0%9C&pageIndex=3. Accessed on 20 December 2016.

Jeh, Sung Hoon, Jiyoung Min, Boogyun Kang and Sergey Lukonin. 2014. '러시아의 극동. 바이칼 지역 개발과 한국의 대응방안' [Russia's development of the Far East and the Baikal Region and Korea's countermeasures], *KIEP Policy Analysis* 14(23). http://www.kiep.go.kr/eng/sub/view.do?bbsId=policyAnalyses&nttId=186011. Accessed on 28 February 2017.

KOTRA. 2015. '극동러시아 개발정책의 중심에 있는 TOR' [ASEZ at the heart of the Russian Far East development policy] http://news.kotra.or.kr/user/globalAllBbs/kotranews/album/2/globalBbsDataAllView.do?dataIdx=141690&column=title&search=tor&searchAreaCd=&searchNationCd=&searchTradeCd=&searchStartDate=&searchEndDate=&searchCategoryIdxs=&searchIndustryCateIdx=&page=1&row=1. Accessed on 20 December 2016.

Kremlin.ru. 2014. 'APEC CEO summit', 10 November. http://en.kremlin.ru/events/president/news/46988. Accessed on 27 February 2017.

Maniyka, James, Jeff Sinclair, Richard Dobbs, Gernot Strube, Louis Rassey, Jan Mischke, Jaana Remes, Charles Roxburgh, Katy George, David O'Halloran and Sreenivas Ramaswamy. 2012. 'Manufacturing the future: the next era of global growth and innovation', *McKinsey Global Institute Report*. http://www.mckinsey.com/business-functions/operations/our-insights/the-future-of-manufacturing. Accessed on 15 December 2016.

Minekrazvitiia. n.d. 'Osobye ekonomicheskie zony' [Special economic zones]. http://economy.gov.ru/minec/activity/sections/sez/main. Accessed on 20 December 2016.

Minvostokrazvitiia. 2016a. 'Osnovnye rezul'taty raboty Ministerstva Rossiiskoi Federatsii po razvitiiu Dal'nego Vostoka v 2015 godu' [Main results of the work of the Russian Federation's Ministry for Development of the Far East in 2015]. http://government.ru/dep_news/22608/#tor. Accessed on 16 December 2016.

Minvostokrazvitiia. 2016b. 'Ob itogakh deiatel'nosti Ministerstva Rossiiskoi Federatsii po razvitiiu Dal'nego Vostoka v 2015 godu i zadachakh na 2016 god' [On the results of the Russian Federation's Ministry for Development of the Far East in 2015 and the plans for 2016]. http://minvr.ru/upload/itog2015.pdf. Accessed on 16 December 2016.

Minvostokrazvitiia. 2016c. 'Chetyrnadtsataia dal'nevostochnaia TOR budet sozdana v Respublike Sakha (Iakutiia)' [The fourteenth Far Eastern ASEZ to be established in the Sakha Republic (Iakutiia)], 13 October. http://www.minvostokrazvitia.ru/press-center/news_minvostok/?ELEMENT_ID=4690&sphrase_id=38165. Accessed on 4 March 2017.

Minvostokrazvitiia. n.d. 'Territorii operezhaiushchego sotsial'no-ekonomicheskogo razvitiia' [Territories of advanced socioeconomic development]. http://minvr.ru/activities/toser.php. Accessed on 20 December 2016.

POSCO. 2016. '러시아의 신극동개발정책, '선도개발구역' 활용 방안' [Russia's new development policy for the Far East: utilization of the ASEZs], *POSRI Issue Report*, 1 September. https://www.posri.re.kr/ko/board/content/14236. Accessed on 20 December 2016.

Prokapalo, Ol'ga, Artem Isaev, Denis Suslov and Marina Mazitova. 2013. 'Ekonomicheskaia kon'iunktura v Dal'nevoctochnom federal'nom okruge v 2012 g' [Economic conjunctures in the Far Eastern Federal Okrug in 2012], *Prostranstvennaia ekonomika* 2: 119–49.

Prokapalo, Ol'ga, Artem Isaev, Denis Suslov and Marina Mazitova. 2014. 'Ekonomicheskaia kon'iunktura v Dal'nevoctochnom federal'nom okruge v 2013 g' [Economic conjunctures in the Far Eastern Federal Okrug in 2013], *Prostranstvennaia ekonomika* 2: 106–40.

Prokapalo, Ol'ga, Artem Isaev and Marina Mazitova. 2016. 'Ekonomicheskaia kon'iunktura v Dal'nevoctochnom federal'nom okruge v 2015 g' [Economic conjunctures in the Far Eastern Federal Okrug in 2015], *Prostranstvennaia ekonomika* 2: 123–57.

Putin, Vladimir. 2013. 'Poslanie Prezidenta Federal'nomu Sobraniiu' [Presidential Address to the Federal Assembly], *Kremlin.ru*, 12 December. http://www.kremlin.ru/events/president/news/19825. Accessed on 19 December 2016.

Su, Dan and Yang Yao. 2016. 'Manufacturing as the key engine of economic growth for middle-income economies', *ADBI Working Paper Series* 573. https://www.adb.org/publications/manufacturing-key-engine-economic-growth-middle-income-economies. Accessed on 15 December 2016.

Titov, Sergei. 2014. 'Territorii vmesto zon' [Territories instead of zones], *Vedomosti*, 17 July. http://www.vedomosti.ru/newspaper/articles/2014/07/17/territorii-vmesto-zon. Accessed on 20 December 2016.

World Bank. 2012. *Doing Business Report 2012: Doing business in a more transparent world*. http://www.doingbusiness.org/~/media/WBG/DoingBusiness/Documents/Annual-Reports/English/DB12-FullReport.pdf. Accessed on 1 March 2017.

World Bank. 2016. *Doing Business Report 2017: Equal opportunities for all*. http://www.doingbusiness.org/reports/global-reports/doing-business-2017. Accessed on 27 February.

Open Access This chapter is licensed under the terms of the Creative Commons Attribution 4.0 International License (http://creativecommons.org/licenses/by/4.0/), which permits use, sharing, adaptation, distribution and reproduction in any medium or format, as long as you give appropriate credit to the original author(s) and the source, provide a link to the Creative Commons license and indicate if changes were made.

The images or other third party material in this book are included in the book's Creative Commons license, unless indicated otherwise in a credit line to the material. If material is not included in the book's Creative Commons license and your intended use is not permitted by statutory regulation or exceeds the permitted use, you will need to obtain permission directly from the copyright holder.

CHAPTER 5

The Russian Far East and Russian Security Policy in the Asia-Pacific Region

Malin Østevik and Natasha Kuhrt

Abstract This chapter examines the place of the Russian Far East in Moscow's security-policy deliberations. Analysing influences ranging from the deployment of Russian armed forces in the Far East to bilateral and multilateral engagements in the Asia-Pacific, and Russian–Chinese attempts at coordination in global politics, the authors find that factors local to the Russian Far East are particularly salient for understanding Russian security policy in the Asia-Pacific. The asymmetry between Russia's underdeveloped Far Eastern region and the populous and economically thriving countries of the Asia-Pacific region represents a significant vulnerability for Russia. Security concerns related to the social and economic underdevelopment of the Russian Far East have thus prevented the 'pivot' from being grounded in broad regional engagement.

Keywords Security • Russian Far East • Asia-Pacific region • Military policy • Securitization

---

M. Østevik (✉)
Research Group on Russia, Eurasia and the Arctic, Norwegian Institute of International Affairs, Oslo, Norway

N. Kuhrt
Department of War Studies, King's College, London, UK

© The Author(s) 2018
H. Blakkisrud, E. Wilson Rowe (eds.), *Russia's Turn to the East*, Global Reordering, https://doi.org/10.1007/978-3-319-69790-1_5

Security concerns are a central aspect of the Russian 'pivot to the East': Moscow's security policy towards the wider Asia-Pacific region is closely linked with the status of the Russian Far East as both a frontier and a gateway region. Since the breakdown in Russian relations with the West in the aftermath of the 2014 annexation of Crimea, steps have been taken towards integrating the Russian Far East into Asia-Pacific economic networks. The current crisis has undoubtedly added a sense of urgency to Moscow's policies of reorienting towards the Asia-Pacific region. But to just what extent can recent changes and initiatives be attributed to the deteriorating relationship between Western countries and Russia? Has a fundamental shift taken place—or is this simply an acceleration of processes already well underway before 2014?

In this chapter we survey recent developments in the Kremlin's security policy in the Russian Far East and towards the Asia-Pacific region. First, we establish a baseline by exploring the main policy tenets since the onset of Russia's current 'pivot to the East', which commenced around 2012. Here we map out issues of contention, areas of cooperation and important bilateral and multilateral relationships in the broader region. We then look for significant changes in these patterns since 2014.

The focus is on state-level security policy, but 'security' is understood here across a broad spectrum of national, international, central and local factors. Beyond hard security, we pay particular attention to economics, a field that has become increasingly securitized in Russia in recent years (Connolly 2016). We also examine various security-policy influences, ranging from the deployment of Russian armed forces in the Far East to bilateral and multilateral engagements in the Asia-Pacific region, and Russian–Chinese attempts at coordination in global politics. But first, a few words on the historical background.

HISTORICAL BACKDROP TO RUSSIA'S SECURITY POLICY IN THE ASIA-PACIFIC

With the break-up of the Soviet Union, Russia revived relations with key countries of East Asia, hereunder its three immediate neighbours in the Russian Far East: China, Japan and the Democratic People's Republic of Korea (DPRK). Already in December 1991, Russia resumed diplomatic relations with China, and these were strengthened throughout the Yeltsin presidency (Kuhrt 2007, pp.10, 45). The focus on China was due primarily to the pressing need for border demarcation, a process that had begun already in 1989. After this process was concluded in 2004, the strategic partnership between China and Russia picked up speed.

In the early 1990s, it was Japan that, due to its economic strength and Western outlook, was seen as the most important player in the Asia-Pacific. However, Russia's territorial dispute with Japan over the Kuril Islands persisted, impeding any significant improvement of Russo-Japanese relations in the 1990s and early 2000s (Kuhrt 2007, p.99).

Russia also shares a 17 km long land border with the DPRK. Soviet relations with the DPRK had started to deteriorate already during the Gorbachev presidency, and continued to worsen during the 1990s. Under Putin's presidency, relations were revived, and in 2003 Russia became a party to the Six-Party Talks on DPRK's nuclear programme. DPRK–Russian relations have since experienced peaks and low points, but the ascendancy of Kim Jong-un in 2012 brought relations to a standstill (Shin 2014, pp.133–35).

Russian Security Policy in the Asia-Pacific Region: 2012–14

Throughout history, Russia has attempted various 'pivots' to the East. The most recent one entered the public debate as 'the turn to the East' (*povorot na vostok*) in the latter part of the first decade of the new millennium (Lukianov 2010; Karaganov 2014). This 'pivot' has three main parts: a programme for the socioeconomic development of the Russian Far East, efforts towards economic integration into the Asia-Pacific region and strategic bilateral and multilateral political engagement in the region (Fortescue 2016, p.423). All three parts play into each other, but the third one is in focus here.

With its harsh climate and shortage of human capital, the Russian Far East has lagged behind European Russia, not to say its Northeast Asian neighbours, in socioeconomic development (see Vakulchuk, Chap. 8, this volume). This is seen as a national security concern. To address this, Russian authorities undertook a new political push towards developing the Russian Far East from around 2012. That year the Ministry for the Development of the Far East was set up at the federal level, headed by Viktor Ishaev, former governor of Khabarovsk Krai and, since 2009, Presidential Plenipotentiary to the Far Eastern Federal Okrug (see Blakkisrud, Chap. 2, this volume).

Before being replaced in 2013, Ishaev announced a comprehensive programme for the economic and social development of the Far East and Baikal region. While the programme was concerned primarily with the economic and social dimensions of development, the overarching context was framed in terms of security. The Russian Far East was said to occupy 'a favourable economic and geographical position in the (...) Asia-Pacific region', as 'the ratio of the major economic power centres of the world economy is changing quite rapidly in favour of the Asia–Pacific region'. Hence, the 'welfare of the whole country' depended on the government's ability to solve the 'geopolitical, strategic, economic and demographic problems' of the Russian Far East (Pravitel'stvo Rossiiskoi Federatsii 2013).

The programme thus illustrates how the economic and social development of the region was securitized and treated as inherently interlinked with regional security concerns in the Asia-Pacific region. However, such interlinkage was nothing new. While still head of Khabarovsk Krai, Ishaev had drawn attention to the plight of the region in a plan for regional development that warned of the Russian Far East becoming a double periphery, isolated from European Russia as well as from the Asia-Pacific region, should Moscow fail to develop it (see Kuhrt 2012).

The external trigger of Russian foreign policy's 'turn to the East' was the realization, demonstrated by the 2008 financial crisis in the West and the relative robustness of the Asia-Pacific region by contrast, that the latter was indeed becoming a global centre of power. While this realization concerned the increased influence of Asia-Pacific states in global economic terms specifically, it also had geopolitical and security implications. According to the 2013 Foreign Policy Concept: 'The current stage of the world development is characterized by profound changes in the geopolitical landscape largely provoked or accelerated by the global financial and economic crisis' (Ministry of Foreign Affairs 2013). With territories bordering on China, Japan and the Korean peninsula, Russia was, at least from its own perspective, in a geopolitical position to claim a more substantial role in regional Asia-Pacific affairs.

To explore the security-related aspect of Russia's 'turn to the East' prior to 2014, we begin by assessing Russia's strategic partnership with China and the Eastern border as a driver of insecurity. We then turn to military deployment in the Russian Far East, bilateral relations with Japan, the US alliance system in the Asia-Pacific and Russian multilateral engagements in the region.

Strategic Partnership with China

The Sino-Russian strategic partnership is central for understanding Moscow's security policy in Northeast Asia. In the autumn of 2004, agreement was finally reached on a treaty to demarcate the border between Russia and China (Kuhrt 2007, p.116). On the Russian side, there were some grievances concerning concessions made to the Chinese, particularly among local Russian residents, but, in general, the agreement represented significant progress and provided a basis for a maturing of state-level relations between the two countries. The settlement of territorial claims served to defuse lingering tensions, so that the two sides could move on to tackling other practical security and economic issues of a less principled character.

Joint military exercises can function as an indicator of the actual level of trust between countries, in terms of security. The first such joint exercise between Russia and China—Peace Mission-2005 (*Mirnaia missiia-2005*)—was held already in the autumn of 2005, only one year after settlement of the border dispute (Pulin 2005). These 'peace mission' exercises continued to be held, generally every second year, interchangeably as bilateral exercises between Russia and China and multilateral exercises within the framework of the Shanghai Cooperation Organization. In 2012, Russian–Chinese joint naval exercises were added to the portfolio. The exercise scenarios have mostly focused on anti-terrorism and counter-piracy, but the number of troops involved has been very high and both sides have contributed advanced equipment. The conduct of such joint exercises has thus been a way of signalling a commitment to defence cooperation (Weitz 2015).

Still, despite the improving situation, scholars have noted that the Sino-Russian strategic partnership is far from turning into an alliance (Bolt and Cross 2010; Weitz 2012). In 2008, Bobo Lo coined the term 'axis of convenience', arguing that, although the two countries cooperated on several issues, the collaboration was mostly grounded in tactical concerns and lacked a strategic underpinning. This stemmed from fundamental differences in national interests and outlook (Lo 2008). While some Western analysts and unofficial Chinese voices (Gelb and Simes 2013; Goldstein 2017; Stokes 2017) now suggest that an alliance is in the making, this seems to be an unlikely outcome (Wishnick 2017). It is true that the strategic partnership is increasingly based on a shared agenda and that there is a significant alignment. However, this is a 'soft alliance'. There is no significant military component (Gabuev 2015), and the disparity in economic status continues to be unpalatable to the Russians. Despite the Sinocentric nature of Russia's Asia policy, Russia aspires to engage other Asian partners, and an alliance with China would complicate such engagement. Moreover, China has traditionally eschewed alliances of any kind (Wishnick 2017).

The Russo-Chinese Border as a Source of Insecurity

Russia has a 4209 km long border with China. Understanding the implications of this from a symbolic and practical perspective is essential for uncovering the local- and regional-level insecurities that drive Russian security policy in the Far East. The border and its adjacent regions constitute an important source of Russian vulnerability, primarily vis-à-vis China. Cross-border trade and engagement have highlighted the asymmetry between Russia's underdeveloped and underpopulated eastern regions, and the economically thriving and densely populated Chinese territory on the other side.

The insecurity associated with the border region can easily be identified in official discourse, such as in the 2009 National Security Strategy (*Rossiiskaia gazeta* 2009). Informally, there has at times been 'widespread suspicion of Chinese activity in the Russian Far East and resentment of China's economic power' in the Russian Ministry of Foreign Affairs (Kuhrt 2012, p.477). In the public discourse, old fears of uncontrolled Chinese immigration frequently resurface (see *Lenta.ru* 2015). Such anxieties are, according to Viktor Larin, 'informed to a great extent by perceptions of illegality and fears of Chinese expansion' (Larin 2012, p.70). This was despite the fact that net Chinese immigration with the goal of permanent residence declined from 2001 to 2008 (Larin 2008, pp.148–49). According to the Federal State Statistic Service, between 2008 and 2012, fewer than 2000 Chinese immigrated to Russia yearly for permanent residence.[1] Likewise, trade asymmetries have been a concern—some regions that adjoin China, for example Amur Oblast, are reported to rely on China for nearly 90 per cent of their trade (*RIA Novosti* 2015b).

For these reasons, the high-priority issue of developing the Russian Far East has become securitized and fraught with ambivalence. However, it is also recognized that achieving this long-sought social and economic development will necessitate Chinese and other East Asian economic involvement, not least in investments and financing (*Kremlin.ru* 2013, see also Blakkisrud, Chap. 2, this volume). To mitigate the insecurity that accompanies initiatives aimed at greater investment, Russian policymakers have sought to integrate the Russian Far East into East Asian networks, while simultaneously deepening the region's integration with European Russia (Kuhrt 2012).

Deployment of Armed Forces in the Russian Far East

Security concerns associated with regional integration are also evident in the military posturing in the Eastern Military District (EMD), which includes the Pacific Fleet. The EMD was established in 2010 as part of a reform of the command structure through a merger of the Far Eastern Military District and the eastern parts of the Siberian Military District. With the merger, the entire Chinese border area, except for the short, mountainous and inaccessible stretch west of Mongolia, was covered by one military district. Indeed, a decisive factor behind the restructuring was probably the wish for more effective control over the Far Eastern border region (Hyodo 2014, p.47). Accompanying the structural reform of the Russian armed forces was the State Armament Programme 2020, likewise adopted in 2010. Although it is difficult to assess the relative prioritization of the EMD within this programme, it is clear that the EMD has seen significant improvement in firepower and equipment more broadly (see below for more detail).

Defence capacity against a possible Chinese ground-force invasion is an important factor in the dimensioning of the EMD: Whereas the three other military districts in Russia have two armies each, the EMD has four. They are all stationed along the country's perimeters, and the two stationed on the border with China are unusually large in terms of troop numbers (Carlsson et al. 2013, p.52). That the Russian armed forces are deploying on the basis of a scenario involving a potential conflict with China is hardly surprising: contingency planning is a military responsibility. Nonetheless, it is a further indication that the Sino-Russian partnership remains fraught with tensions and insecurities.

Bilateral Relations with Japan

The main feature of Russo-Japanese bilateral relations remains the border dispute over the Kuril Islands.[2] Despite increases in Russo-Japanese trade, the dispute has long obstructed the development of mutual trust at the political level. Moreover, in recent years, with the evolving regional power dynamics in the Asia-Pacific region, the military-strategic importance of the Kuril Islands appears to have grown for Moscow—as signalled by then-President Dmitrii Medvedev's visit to the islands in 2010 and the beefing-up of military infrastructure there. However, Tokyo has interpreted the increased strategic emphasis as directed primarily at balancing China; although it monitored military activity closely, Japan also seized the opportunity to build stronger military-to-military ties with the Russian armed forces (Tabata 2012; Pajon 2013).

When Putin returned to the presidency in 2012, he signalled willingness to negotiate on the border issue, should Japan be willing to compromise (Akaha 2012). In March 2013, it was agreed to reopen peace talks between the two countries, and in April that year, Shinzo Abe visited Moscow, as the first Japanese prime minister to do so for more than ten years (Chotani 2015). The two countries also agreed on a 2+2 dialogue mechanism involving the defence and foreign ministers of both states (Pajon 2013). These meetings indicated a push for improvement of Russo-Japanese relations. Significant areas of contention nonetheless remained, with Russia being particularly hostile to the development of a joint Japanese–US anti-missile system (Blank 2014).

US-led Alliances in Northeast Asia

Following the US 'pivot', or rebalancing, to Asia announced in late 2011, Washington took a more proactive stance in the Asia-Pacific region. The major objective of the US approach was 'to dissuade China from making a bid for hegemony' and to sustain its own strategic predominance in the Asia-Pacific region (Silove 2016, p.46). Two important aspects of this new approach were the further development of bilateral security alliances with Japan and South Korea and the engagement with Southeast Asian states (Friedberg 2015; Green 2016). This, together with the more assertive US military presence in Northeast Asia, including its missile defence system and strategic nuclear forces, sparked Chinese fears of encirclement (Xiang 2012).

The dynamic precipitated by the increased US involvement in the Asia-Pacific reactivated latent conflicts, like the one in the South China Sea (Kireeva 2014, p.37). Moscow viewed the intensified US engagement in the region with caution and ambivalence, partly because Russia itself enjoyed limited leverage in East Asia and remained dependent upon China in regional political affairs. Moscow was, however, not as critical of the US presence in East Asia as China. Some Russian scholars even called for the possibility of East Asia becoming an arena for a Russian–US détente (Lukin 2012). Officially, however, the Kremlin in its 2013 Foreign Policy Concept in the section on the Asia-Pacific warned that US attempts at 'preserv[ing] their traditional positions' was causing 'instability in international relations' (Ministry of Foreign Affairs 2013).

Russia's Approach to Multilateralism

East Asia as a region is above all characterized by its advanced economic networks. Russia's engagement has traditionally relied on bilateral relations—with China in particular. By dealing with countries on a bilateral basis, Russia remains outside regional trade agreements and, to some extent, regional networks. This has hampered the political leverage that greater economic engagement and diplomatic investment could otherwise bring (Karaganov 2012; Kuhrt 2014, p.141). And this is why Russia has in recent years increasingly begun to participate in East Asian multilateral forums, signalled above all by Russia's hosting of the 2012 Asia-Pacific Economic Cooperation (APEC) summit in Vladivostok (Koldunova 2016, pp.533–34).

Russia became a member of APEC already in 1997 and had joined the Asian Regional Forum (AFR) even earlier, in 1994. In 2010, Russia joined the Asia–Europe Meeting (ASEM) and, in 2011, the East Asia Summit (EAS), and Moscow had signed several treaties aimed at facilitating cooperation between ASEAN and Russia. In particular, the EAS is relevant for security issues. In 2013 Russia used this forum to call—with the support of China and Brunei—for a new regional security architecture in East Asia (Shestakov 2013). With its emphasis on a non-bloc approach to regional security, the proposal was clearly formulated as a reaction against the US-sponsored 'hub and spokes' system of alliances in the Asia-Pacific region.

However, by the time of the Ukrainian crisis, the success of the various multilateral efforts was still limited: few significant steps towards economic integration had been taken. Although engagement with the region increased, this was still secondary to bilateral engagement. The main strategic direction of Russia's policy in East Asia remained its partnership with China. Russian academics have blamed the Russian Ministry of Foreign Affairs and called for a more comprehensive approach which would include actors from sectors such as private business, academia and civil society

(Koldunova 2016, pp.540–46). There have also been calls for a true willingness to reform, in a manner that could facilitate integration into the East Asian economic networks (Baev 2016, p.94).

THE 2014 CRISIS WITH THE WEST AND RUSSIA'S NORTHEAST ASIAN SECURITY POLICY

Has anything changed in Russia's security policy or actions in East Asia in light of the crisis with the West? Some scholars have indicated that the 2014 crisis and Russia's subsequent relative isolation may have triggered an intensification of the foreign policy 'turn to the East' (Kireeva 2014, p.48; Baev 2016, p.90). We will assess the plausibility of this claim against the baseline established above.

The most tangible effects of the war in Ukraine and subsequent Western sanctions on Russian security policy in East Asia concern the practical consequences for the Russian military in the Far East. As noted, the EMD includes the Pacific Fleet. A significant share of the State Armament Programme 2020 was earmarked for improvement of naval capabilities. And it was precisely this capability development that was hit the hardest by the sanctions and by Ukraine's freeze of military exports to Russia. The two Mistral amphibious assault ships that had been purchased from France, and that fell victim to the sanctions, were meant for the Pacific Fleet. Likewise, construction of several types of vessels has been severely delayed due to the unavailability of parts from Germany and Ukraine (Cooper 2016, p.49).

Other procurements under the armaments programme have proceeded according to plan. For example, the EMD troops have had their firepower significantly strengthened, as they have been re-equipped with new Iskander-M ballistic and cruise missile systems (*RIA Novosti* 2015a). In 2015 and 2016, Russia also deployed S-400 surface-to-air missile defence systems along its eastern coast to 'protect the sky over the main bases of the Pacific Fleet' against US missile systems and aircraft (*RIA Novosti* 2016; see also Plopsky 2016). However, the decision to deploy Iskander-M missile systems in the Far East had been announced already in 2011 (*RIA Novosti* 2011). Thus, their deployment shows that the decision to strengthen Russia's military posture in Northeast Asia had been taken long before the 2014 crisis.

Since 2014, official Russian statements praising the strategic partnership with China have proliferated. In an interview with a Chinese news agency, Putin even stated that bilateral relations had advanced so far that Russian experts 'have had trouble defining today's general state of our common affairs' (*Kremlin.ru* 2016a). The rhetoric of public statements resonates with doctrinal-level statements. The 2013 version of the Russian Foreign Policy Concept was the first to define Russia's perspective on East Asia in direct relation to the dwindling role of the West in world affairs: 'The ability of the West to dominate world economy and politics continues to diminish. The global power and development potential is now more dispersed and is shifting to the East, primarily to the Asia–Pacific region' (Ministry of Foreign Affairs 2013). Similar statements are found in the 2016 version, where the Asia-Pacific enjoys a far more prominent role than in previous versions (Ministry of Foreign Affairs 2016).

That international-level concerns are among the main political drivers behind the Sino-Russian partnership is already well established. In early 2014, Russian Foreign Minister Sergei Lavrov went so far as to state that international cooperation was the most important element of the bilateral relationship (Ministry of Foreign Affairs 2014). To the extent that this holds true, we could expect the breakdown in Russia's relations with the West would lead to further coordination with China on international-level issues. And, indeed, this is what has been happening. The two countries have had an unusually high number of top-level meetings since 2014; according to the Chairman of the Standing Committee of the Chinese National People's Congress Zhang Dejiang, Putin is the state leader with whom the Chinese president has met the most often (*Kremlin. ru* 2016b).

In the UN Security Council (UNSC), the two countries have been said to form a bloc with regard to the search for an international solution to the Syrian conflict: altogether five resolutions have been vetoed by both countries. Still, while both Russia and China refer to concerns related to the territorial sovereignty of the Syrian state, their approaches appear to diverge. In October 2016, China abstained for the first time from voting on a UNSC resolution on Syria that Russia vetoed. Afterwards, China stated that it was important to find a solution to the conflict, but, since key concerns of some Council members had not been taken into consideration, it had to abstain (Permanent Mission of the People's Republic of China to the UN 2016). By contrast, Russian ambassador Vitalii Churkin indicated that Western UNSC members wanted to 'destroy' Syria, as they had done with Libya (United Nations 2016). This seems to validate Aglaya Snetkov and Marc Lanteigne's labelling of Russia as 'the loud dissenter' and China as 'the cautious partner' (Snetkov and Lanteigne 2015).

Chinese dissatisfaction with what it perceives as Russia's exaggerated anti-Western attitudes—aggravated by the 2014 crisis—is precisely one of the reasons why Pavel Baev (2016, p.91) argued that, as of late 2015, attempts to strengthen Sino-Russian ties had failed. Baev is correct in noting that these relations do not make for any 'super-partnership' (Baev 2016, p.91). Indeed, the bilateral relationship does appear rather similar to what it was before 2014: somewhat ambivalent, with setbacks in certain areas and progress in others. What *is* different now compared to the pre-Crimea period is that Russia's room for manoeuvre is more circumscribed, and the need for a flourishing relationship with its Eastern partner has thus become more pressing.

At the regional level we can note certain progress in Russian–Chinese coordination, as regards both security and the economic aspects. The 2013 Russian–Chinese–Bruneian initiative for a new security architecture, which initially appeared to have low priority,[3] has been followed up with five rounds of East Asia Summit meetings. Specifically, Russia and China have, according to Lavrov, agreed to coordinate more closely their 'efforts to advance the initiative for forming a modern security architecture in the Asia-Pacific region' (Ministry of Foreign Affairs 2015). Furthermore, joint military exercises continue to be organized. In particular, the joint naval exercises appear to have become important for bilateral Russian–Chinese military relations. These exercises have been held on a larger scale and include more vessels than in previous years. In 2015, the initial phase of the joint naval exercise was for the first time held in the Mediterranean (Selishchev and Reshetnikov 2016; *TASS* 2016).

There have also been concerted efforts concerning the dual task of developing the Russian Far East and integrating the region into Asia-Pacific economic networks. In 2015, the first Eastern Economic Forum was held in Vladivostok, with the second being held the year after and the third planned for autumn 2017. The forum is attended by high-level political figures as well as business leaders (participants at the second forum included President Putin, Korean President Park Geun-hye and Japanese Prime Minster Abe). As discussed in Helge Blakkisrud's chapter (Chap. 2), various mechanisms have also been established for attracting foreign investment (most importantly the ASEZs and the Free Port of Vladivostok). These measures indicate that the Russian authorities have taken steps towards overcoming the insecurities associated with regional economic integration of the Russian Far East in the wider Asia-Pacific region.

Politically, fears of Chinese influence have not disappeared. Russia is wary of losing autonomy in its foreign policy. A voice close to the Kremlin cautions that, while China has been an important source of support between 2014 and 2016 'making it easier for Russia to uphold its interests', 'with this paradigm still in existence, Russia will never be able to take decisions interfering with the Chinese interests' (Bordachev 2017). The answer is diversification. If Russia is serious about wanting to broaden its circle of Asia-Pacific partners, this could facilitate rapprochement with Japan. One unexpected outcome of the post-Crimea security developments is the continued improvement in relations between Russia and Japan. To some extent, this improvement is the result of a longer-term attempt to reinvigorate ties, but it also reflects Tokyo's concerns regarding the burgeoning Russo-Chinese ties in the Asia-Pacific. Given the overall intractability of the Kuril Island dispute over the past decades, any swift resolution of the territorial issue is unlikely. However, Japan's interests are pragmatic in nature, focused to a large extent on energy. While this focus on energy security may help in defusing territorial tensions, it nevertheless entails its own challenges: 'basing Japan–Russia ties primarily on energy runs the risk that the bilateral relationship will become a prisoner to market forces, such as fluctuations in oil price' (Rinna 2016).

Conclusions

Examining Russia's security policy in the Far Eastern region necessitates a broad approach. As this chapter has shown, there have been several key initiatives in the military sphere and in international relations that matter for the Kremlin's security policy. The strategic partnership with China remains central, also against the background of intensified Russian diplomacy towards Japan: in the context of the overall deterioration in relations with the West, attempts to diversify relations remain difficult. At the same time, some actors—notably Japan—have moved to take advantage of Russia's limited range of options in the economic sphere resulting from its current financial isolation, hereunder concluding new energy agreements. Such agreements do not, however, have the capacity to transform Russia from being a bystander in the Asia-Pacific region nor will they, without a concerted push from the Russian federal authorities to improve investor confidence, boost the development of the Russian Far East.

However, it is important to keep in mind that Russian policy documents and statements clearly identify the underdevelopment of the Russian Far East as a threat to national security. For all the official statements on the primacy of the Russo-Chinese strategic partnership or the growing centrality of the Asia-Pacific region in world affairs, security concerns related to the social and economic underdevelopment of the Russian Far East have delayed any grounding of the 'pivot' in broad regional engagement. The asymmetry between Russia's underdeveloped Far Eastern region and the populous and economically thriving countries of the Asia-Pacific region is recognized as a significant vulnerability for Russia. This leads to the securitization of policies aimed at developing the Russian Far East, integration of Russia into the Asia-Pacific region and a deepening of Russo-Chinese relations.

It might be argued that the Russian approach to the Russian Far East and Asia-Pacific region are marked by an urgency borne out of long-standing security concerns and the increasing awareness of shifts in global economic power, especially after the financial crisis—and China's One Belt, One Road (OBOR) initiative has, if anything, intensified this urgency. However, the 2014 Ukrainian crisis in itself seems to have caused only limited concrete changes; as we have seen, the drivers behind Moscow's various post-2014 activities towards the Russian Far East and the Asia-Pacific region were present already before the 2014 crisis. The major difference lies in the intensified political and diplomatic attention to bilateral relations with China, although this may be more rhetorical than substantial. Moreover, Russia's deteriorating relations with the West also challenge the Sino-Russian bilateral relationship: China generally seeks cooperative relations ('a harmonious world') across the board, whereas for both countries, relations with the West remain a higher priority than relations with each other.

Nevertheless, the real challenge to the strategic partnership lies not at the international level, but at the regional and local levels. The Russian Far East has always relied on massive assistance from the federal authorities. Now that this is cut back due to current economic constraints, the need for foreign investment has become more pressing than ever. The only real investor remains China, and that underlines the longer-term dilemma for Russia: Chinese investment is seen as part and parcel of Chinese economic hegemony not only here but also in Central Asia and further afield, and thus as a major security concern. In 2015, the Heilongjiang Land and Maritime Silk Road Economic Belt, incorporating the Russian Far East, was included in the China–Mongolia–Russia Economic Corridor (Xuefei and Mengxing 2015). Thus, when the OBOR with its Silk Road Economic Belt in Central Asia and the Maritime Silk Road in Asia-Pacific is rolled out in a Chinese grand strategy initiative, both exclusion and inclusion from the OBOR may mean peripheral status for the Russian Far East—as part of a declining Russia, or in relation to a greater China.

Notes

1. Data retrieved from the Federal State Statistic Service's migration data available at http://www.gks.ru/bgd/regl/b11_107 (2010); http://www.gks.ru/bgd/regl/b12_107 (2011) and http://www.gks.ru/bgd/regl/b13_107 (2012). Data on net numbers are not available for the period 2009–13.
2. The Kuril Islands/Northern Territories are located southwest of the Russian Kamchatka Peninsula. The dispute has long historical antecedents; its current iteration stems from Soviet claims to administrative control over the southern Kuril Islands following the Second World War.
3. President Putin was one of few state leaders absent at the summit when Russia had launched this initiative.

References

Akaha, Tsuneo. 2012. 'A distant neighbor: Russia's search to find its place in East Asia', *Global Asia* 7(2): 1–14.

Baev, Pavel. 2016. 'Russia's pivot to China goes astray: the impact on the Asia-Pacific security architecture', *Contemporary Security Policy* 37(1): 89–110.

Blank, Stephen. 2014. 'Russia and Japan: can two-plus-two equal more than four?' *East Asia Bulletin*, 251. http://scholarspace.manoa.hawaii.edu/bitstream/10125/32714/1/APB%20no.%20251.pdf. Accessed on 15 February 2017.

Bolt, Paul J. and Sharyl Cross. 2010. 'The contemporary Sino-Russian strategic partnership: challenges and opportunities for the twenty-first century', *Asian Security* 6(3): 191–213.

Bordachev, Timofei. 2017. 'To Russia's friends in Asia and beyond', *Valdai Discussion Club*, 15 February. http://valdaiclub.com/a/highlights/to-russia-friends-in-asia-and-beyond. Accessed on 30 June 2017.

Carlsson, Märta, Johan Norberg and Fredrik Westerlund. 2013. 'The military capability of Russia's armed forces in 2013', in *Russian military capability in a ten-year perspective – 2013*, edited by Jakob Hedenskog and Carolina Vendil Pallin, 23–70. Stockholm: FOI.

Chotani, Vindu Mai. 2015. 'Can Japan and Russia resolve their territorial dispute?' *The Diplomat*, 5 October. http://thediplomat.com/2015/10/can-japan-and-russia-resolve-their-territorial-dispute. Accessed on 15 January 2017.

Connolly, Richard. 2016. 'The empire strikes back: economic statecraft and the securitisation of political economy in Russia', *Europe-Asia Studies* 68(4): 750–73.

Cooper, Julian. 2016. *Russia's state armament programme to 2020: a quantitative assessment of implementation 2011–2015*. Stockholm: FOI.

Fortescue, Stephen. 2016. 'Russia's "turn to the east": a study in policy making', *Post-Soviet Affairs* 32(5): 423–54.

Friedberg, Aaron L. 2015. 'The debate over US China strategy', *Survival* 57(3): 89–110.

Gabuev, Alexander. 2015. 'A soft alliance? Russia–China relations after Ukraine', *European Council on Foreign Relations Policy Brief*, 10 February. http://www.ecfr.eu/publications/summary/a_soft_alliance_russia_china_relations_after_the_ukraine_crisis331. Accessed on 28 June 2017.

Gelb, Leslie H. and Dimitri K. Simes. 2013. 'Beware Collusion of China, Russia', *The National Interest*, July/August. http://nationalinterest.org/article/beware-collusion-china-russia-8640. Accessed on 26 October 2017.

Goldstein, Lyle. 2017. 'A China–Russia alliance?', *The National Interest*, 25 April. http://nationalinterest.org/feature/china-russia-alliance-20333. Accessed on 29 June 2017.

Green, Mike. 2016. 'The legacy of Obama's 'pivot' to Asia', *Foreign Policy*, 3 September. http://foreignpolicy.com/2016/09/03/the-legacy-of-obamas-pivot-to-asia. Accessed on 15 December 2016.

Hyodo, Shinji. 2014. 'Russia's security policy towards East Asia', in *Russia and East Asia: informal and gradual integration*, edited by Tsuneo Akaha and Anna Vassilieva, 44–55. London: Routledge.

Karaganov, Sergei. 2012. *K velikomu okeanu, ili novaia globalizatsiia Rossii* [*To the great ocean, or the new globalization of Russia*]. Moscow: Valdai Club/RIA Novosti.

Karaganov, Sergei. 2014. 'Strategiia XXI: Povorot na Vostok' [Strategy 21: the pivot to the east], 28 January. http://www.vedomosti.ru/newspaper/articles/2014/01/28/povorot-na-vostok. Accessed on 10 January 2017.

Kireeva, Anna. 2014. 'Regional strategies and military buildup in East Asia and Indo-Pacific: a Russian perspective', *Maritime Affairs* 10(2): 33–51.

Koldunova, Ekaterina. 2016. 'Russia's involvement in regional cooperation in East Asia', *Asian Survey* 56(3): 532–54.

Kremlin.ru. 2013. 'Soveshanie po voprosam sotsial'no-ekonomicheskogo razvitiia Primor'ia' [Meeting on the socioeconomic development of Primorye], 31 August. http://www.kremlin.ru/events/president/news/19112. Accessed on 21 January 2017.

Kremlin.ru. 2016a. 'Interview to the Xinhua News Agency of China', 23 June. http://en.kremlin.ru/events/president/news/52204. Accessed on 27 December 2016.

Kremlin.ru. 2016b. 'Meeting with Chairman of the Standing Committee of the National People's Congress Zhang Dejiang', 25 June. http://en.kremlin.ru/events/president/news/52267. Accessed on 28 December 2016

Kuhrt, Natasha. 2007. *Russian policy towards China and Japan: the El'tsin and Putin periods.* London: Routledge.

Kuhrt, Natasha. 2012. 'The Russian Far East in Russia's Asia policy: dual integration or double periphery?' *Europe-Asia Studies* 64(3): 471–93.

Kuhrt, Natasha. 2014. 'Russia and Asia-Pacific: from "competing" to "complementary" regionalisms?' *Politics* 34(2): 138–48.

Larin, Aleksandr. 2008. *Kitai i zarubezhnye kitaitsy* [*China and the Chinese abroad*]. Moscow: RAN, Institut Dal'nego Vostoka.

Larin, Victor. 2012. 'Perceptions of Chinese migrants in the Russian Far East', in *Chinese Migrants in Russia, Central Asia and Eastern Europe*, edited by Felix B. Chang and Sunnie T. Rucker-Chang, 69–83. London: Routledge.

Lenta.ru. 2015. 'Strashnaia skazka' [A scary fairy tale], 24 November. https://lenta.ru/articles/2015/11/24/mythsaboutchinese. Accessed on 27 December 2017.

Lo, Bobo. 2008. *Axis of convenience: Moscow, Beijing, and the new geopolitics.* London: Chatham House.

Lukianov, Fedor. 2010. 'Povorot na vostok' [The turn to the East], *SVOP*, 15 February. http://old.svop.ru/mm/2010/mm25.htm. Accessed on 10 January 2017.

Lukin, Artyom. 2012. 'Russia and America in the Asia-Pacific: a new entente?' *Asian Politics & Policy* 4(2): 153–71.

Ministry of Foreign Affairs. 2013. *Concept of the Foreign Policy of the Russian Federation.* http://www.mid.ru/en/foreign_policy/official_documents/-/asset_publisher/CptICkB6BZ29/content/id/122186?p_p_id=101_INSTANCE_CptICkB6BZ29&_101_INSTANCE_CptICkB6BZ29_languageId=en_GB. Accessed on 7 December 2016.

Ministry of Foreign Affairs. 2014. 'Interview of the Russian Foreign Minister Sergey Lavrov to China Daily', 15 April. http://www.mid.ru/en/foreign_policy/news/-/asset_publisher/cKNonkJE02Bw/content/id/65422. Accessed on 17 March 2017.

Ministry of Foreign Affairs. 2015. 'Foreign Minister Sergey Lavrov's opening remarks and answers to media questions at a joint news conference following a meeting of the foreign ministers of Russia, India and China (RIC)', 2 February. http://www.mid.ru/en/foreign_policy/news/-/asset_publisher/cKNonkJE02Bw/content/id/947158. Accessed on 15 January 2017.

Ministry of Foreign Affairs. 2016. *Foreign Policy Concept of the Russian Federation*. http://www.mid.ru/foreign_policy/news/-/asset_publisher/cKNonkJE02Bw/content/id/2542248. Accessed on 12 March 2017.

Pajon, Céline. 2013. 'Japan–Russia: toward a strategic partnership?' *Russie.nei. visions* 72. Paris: IFRI.

Permanent Mission of the People's Republic of China to the UN. 2016. 'Statement by Ambassador Liu Jieyi at the Security Council after voting on the draft resolutions on Syria', 8 October. http://www.china-un.org/eng/hyyfy/t1405969.htm. Accessed on 28 December 2016.

Plopsky, Guy. 2016. 'How Russia is bolstering missile defense in its Far East', *The Diplomat*, 2 August. http://thediplomat.com/2016/08/how-russia-is-bolstering-missile-defense-in-its-far-east. Accessed on 16 November 2016.

Pravitel'stvo Rossiiskoi Federatsii. 2013. *Federal'naia tselevaia programma 'Ekonomicheskaia i sotsial'naia razvitiia Dal'nego Vostoka i Baikal'skogo regiona na period do 2018 goda'* [Federal targeted programme 'Economic and Social Development of the Far East and Baikal Region until 2018']. http://assoc.khv.gov.ru/files/docs/2015/0e1559ec080b88029c99.pdf. Accessed on 20 December 2016.

Pulin, Gennadii. 2005. 'Smysly i podteksty "Mirnoi missii-2005"' [The meanings and implications of 'Peace Mission-2005'], *Voenno-promyshlennyi kur'er*, 31 August. http://vpk-news.ru/articles/56. Accessed on 19 December 2016.

RIA Novosti. 2011. 'Tretii polk S-400 budet razmeshchen na Dal'nem Vostoke' [The third S-400 regiment will be deployed in the Far East], 18 February. https://ria.ru/defense_safety/20110218/335524995.html. Accessed on 19 November 2016.

RIA Novosti. 2015a. 'Voennye vo Vladivostoke nachali osvaivat' S-400 "Triumf"' [The military in Vladivostok began to work with S-400 'Triumph'], 25 November. https://ria.ru/defense_safety/20151125/1327872970.html. Accessed on 10 November 2016.

RIA Novosti. 2015b. 'Priamure i KNR: avtomost, kanatnaia doroga i eksport sladostei' [Amur and China: auto-bridge, cable line and export of sweets], 24 December. https://ria.ru/east/20151224/1347999399.html. Accessed on 14 March 2017.

RIA Novosti. 2016. 'Pervoe uchenie na novykh kompleksakh 'Iskander-M' startovalo v Buriatii' [The first exercise with the new Iskander-M complex began in Buriatia],29February.https://ria.ru/defense_safety/20160229/1381755471.html. Accessed on 10 November 2016.

Rinna, Anthony. 2016. 'Japan–Russia relations need more than just energy', *East Asia Forum*, 27 May. http://www.eastasiaforum.org/2016/05/27/japan-russia-relations-need-more-than-just-energy. Accessed on 7 February 2017.

Rossiiskaia gazeta. 2009. 'Ukaz Prezidenta Rossiiskoi Federatsii ot 12 maia 2009 g. N 537 "O Strategii natsional'noi bezopasnosti Rossiiskoi Federatsii do 2020 goda"' [Decree of the President of the Russian Federation of 12 May 2009, N 537 'On the National Security Strategy of the Russian Federation until 2020'], 19 May. https://rg.ru/2009/05/19/strategia-dok.html. Accessed on 30 June 2017.

Selishchev, Aleksei and Dmitrii Reshetnikov. 2016. 'Voenno-morskie uchenia RF i Kitaia nachinaiutsia v Iuzhno-Kitaiskom more' [Naval exercises of Russia and China to begin in the South China Sea], *TASS*, 12 September. http://tass.ru/armiya-i-opk/3612999. Accessed on 16 December 2016.

Shestakov, Evgenii. 2013. 'Stanet li Rossiia liderom v Azii?' [Will Russia become a leader in Asia?], *Rossiiskaia gazeta*, 11 October. https://rg.ru/2013/10/11/atr-site.html. Accessed on 15 January 2017.

Shin, Beom-Shik. 2014. 'Post-Cold War Russian foreign policy and the Korean Peninsula', in *Russia and East Asia: informal and gradual integration*, edited by Tsuneo Akaha and Anna Vassilieva, 130–53. London: Routledge.

Silove, Nina. 2016. 'The pivot before the pivot: U.S. strategy to preserve the power balance in Asia', *International Security* 40(4): 45–88.

Snetkov, Aglaya and Marc Lanteigne. 2015. '"The loud dissenter and its cautious partner" – Russia, China, global governance and humanitarian intervention', *International Relations of the Asia-Pacific* 15(1): 113–46.

Stokes, Jacob. 2017. 'Russia and China's enduring alliance', *Foreign Affairs*, 22 February. https://www.foreignaffairs.com/articles/china/2017-02-22/russia-and-china-s-enduring-alliance. Accessed on 28 June 2017.

Tabata, Shinichiro. 2012. 'The booming Russo-Japanese economic relations: causes and prospects', *Eurasian Geography and Economics*, 53(4): 422–41.

TASS. 2016. 'Rossiisko-kitaiskie uchenia "Morskoe vzaimodeistvie". Dos'e' [Russian-Chinese exercises 'Naval interaction': Dossier], 12 September. http://tass.ru/info/1960969. Accessed on 16 December 2016.

United Nations. 2016. 'Security Council fails to adopt two draft resolutions on Syria, despite appeals for action preventing impending humanitarian catastrophe in Aleppo', *Meetings coverage and Press Releases*, 8 October. https://www.un.org/press/en/2016/sc12545.doc.htm. Accessed on 13 January 2017.

Weitz, Richard. 2012. 'Superpower symbiosis: the Russia–China axis', *World Affairs*, November/December. http://www.worldaffairsjournal.org/article/superpower-symbiosis-russia-china-axis. Accessed on 12 March 2017.

Weitz, Richard. 2015. 'Parsing Chinese–Russian military exercise', *The Letort Papers*. Carlisle, PA: US Army War College.

Wishnick, Elizabeth. 2017. 'In search of the "Other" in Asia: Russia–China relations revisited', *The Pacific Review* 30(1): 114–32.

Xiang, Lanxin. 2012. 'China and the "pivot"', *Survival* 54(5): 113–28.

Xuefei, Tian and Song Mengxing. 2015. 'Economic belt work gets underway', *China Daily*, 17 April. http://www.chinadaily.com.cn/cndy/2015-04/17/content_20453422.htm. Accessed on 28 June 2017.

Open Access This chapter is licensed under the terms of the Creative Commons Attribution 4.0 International License (http://creativecommons.org/licenses/by/4.0/), which permits use, sharing, adaptation, distribution and reproduction in any medium or format, as long as you give appropriate credit to the original author(s) and the source, provide a link to the Creative Commons license and indicate if changes were made.

The images or other third party material in this book are included in the book's Creative Commons license, unless indicated otherwise in a credit line to the material. If material is not included in the book's Creative Commons license and your intended use is not permitted by statutory regulation or exceeds the permitted use, you will need to obtain permission directly from the copyright holder.

CHAPTER 6

Did China Bankroll Russia's Annexation of Crimea? The Role of Sino-Russian Energy Relations

Indra Overland and Gulaikhan Kubayeva

Abstract This chapter analyses bilateral Chinese–Russian energy relations, pre- and post Crimea. The signing of the Power of Siberia megaproject in May 2014, only two months after Russia's annexation of Crimea, created the impression that China bankrolled Russia out of the crisis. To assess the veracity of this impression, the authors draw a longer timeline of Russian–Chinese cooperation, examining general economic data as well as Chinese involvement in four concrete energy projects managed by leading Russian energy companies. They find that, in general, deals made from 2014 onwards are in line with trends that originated well before the current crisis in Russia's relations with the West, and that Chinese financial contributions to the sector are not as large as they sometimes appear.

Keywords Russia • China • Energy • Crimea • Sanctions

I. Overland (✉)
Energy Programme, Norwegian Institute of International Affairs, Oslo, Norway

G. Kubayeva
The Regional Environmental Centre for Central Asia, Almaty, Kazakhstan

© The Author(s) 2018
H. Blakkisrud, E. Wilson Rowe (eds.), *Russia's Turn to the East*,
Global Reordering, https://doi.org/10.1007/978-3-319-69790-1_6

In the years leading up to the conflict over Ukraine, oil prices were high, Western countries open to cooperation and foreign companies eager to invest in Russia—especially in the petroleum sector. Many Russian companies, including state-controlled oil and gas corporations, took on high levels of debt, based on the assumption that oil prices would remain high. After Crimea, Russia faced not only international sanctions but also a collapse in the price of oil. The combination of the lower oil price and sanctions left Russia economically and politically vulnerable, and potentially dependent on its biggest non-Western trading partner: China.

After the introduction of Western sanctions, several major developments took place in Sino-Russian energy cooperation. In May 2014, the two countries reached a deal on the Power of Siberia natural gas pipeline, with an estimated value of USD 400 billion (Overland et al. 2015, p.42). During the same year, imports of oil from Russia to China increased by 36 per cent, reaching 30 million tons (Cunningham 2015b). Oil exports from Russia even displaced other suppliers: in 2014, Chinese oil imports from Saudi Arabia fell by 8 per cent and from Venezuela by 11 per cent (Cunningham 2015a; see Fig. 6.1 for further details). This development was one important motivation behind Saudi Arabia's unexpected decision to raise oil production and lower the price of oil in 2014, despite the negative impact on Saudi revenues and on intra-OPEC solidarity.

These developments create the impression that China was discreetly providing the financial backing for Russia's annexation of Crimea. While

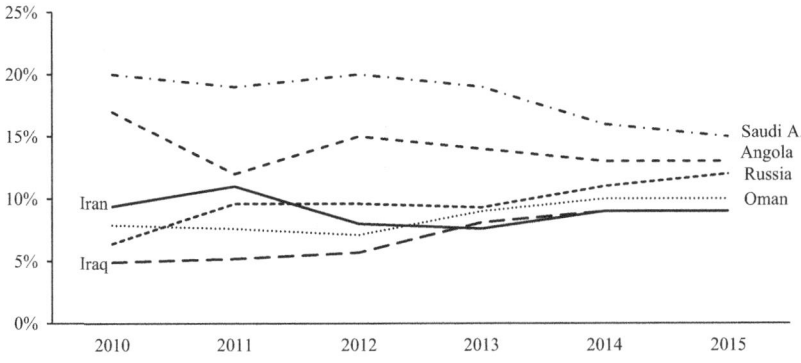

Fig. 6.1 Chinese oil imports, by country of origin, main suppliers (Sources: Observatory of Economic Complexity 2014; Workman 2016)

Western countries were trying to choke Russia's cash supply, China seemed to be stepping in to fill the financial void. As Margarete Klein and Kirsten Westphal wrote: 'After its relations with the West deteriorated massively in the course of the Ukraine crisis, Russia has been aligning itself increasingly with China. This shift is most obvious in the strategic spheres of military and energy cooperation' (Klein and Westphal 2016, p.1; see also Gabuev 2015, p.2; Charap et al. 2017, p.25). Did China in practice bankroll Russia after the annexation of Crimea by injecting capital into the Russian energy sector?

During the pre-Crimea period of rising oil prices (2000–14, with a dip in 2008), it was not clear whether the relationship between China and Russia was doomed to remain a mere 'axis of convenience' (Lo 2008, p.1), or whether the strategic convergence between the two states—complementary assets, common outlook and shared interests—gave the relationship greater potential (Braekhus and Overland 2007; Overland and Braekhus 2009; Røseth 2017, p. 23). The Ukraine crisis and the ensuing Western sanctions would seem to have provided a unique opportunity for realizing whatever potential lies in the relationship.

This chapter approaches the Ukraine crisis as a natural quasi-experiment to which the Sino-Russian relationship has been subjected. If the relationship between the two countries has the potential to grow, the Ukraine crisis should have provided ideal conditions for this potential to be realized. In order to determine whether China really did step in and actively provide the financing to carry Russia through this period, it is necessary to analyse systematically whether the trajectory of Sino-Russian energy cooperation changed in connection with the Crimea crisis.

Throughout the chapter, we seek to provide a systematic and multifaceted empirical basis for the analysis by drawing on the relevant data that are available. In the next section we present the sanctions against Russia and their consequences, and discuss the Chinese approach to the sanctions. We then chart and compare changes in patterns of economic interaction between China and Russia in the years before and after the annexation of Crimea: lending, investments and trade. After discussing those macro-data, we examine Chinese involvement in four specific energy projects managed by some of Russia's main energy companies: Gazprom/Power of Siberia, Novatek/Yamal LNG, Rosneft/Vankor and Transneft/ESPO. Next, we look back on Sino-Russian relations since the collapse of the Soviet Union, in order to relate post-Crimea developments to the long-term trend in relations. In the final section we offer some conclusions and discuss the prospects for a deeper relationship between China and Russia.

Sanctions Against Russia

In response to Russia's annexation of Crimea, the EU, the United States and several other Western countries and allies implemented three types of sanctions: a ban on the provision of technology and equipment for deepwater, Arctic offshore and shale oil and gas exploration; a ban on mid- and long-term credit to Russian oil companies and state banks; and travel bans for prominent Russians considered to be involved in the annexation of Crimea or close to President Vladimir Putin. Our focus is on the economic sanctions. Table 6.1 provides an overview of their main targets. One of the banks included in the sanctions list was Gazprombank, and several of the others were heavily involved in the petroleum sector. In sum, the economic sanctions were largely centred on the Russian oil industry.

The referendum on Crimea's reunification with Russia was held on 16 March 2014, and the first sanctions were implemented the following day. This date is thus a key time-point in our analysis: did Chinese financing for Russian energy projects make a jump around that time?

Table 6.1 Main EU and US economic sanctions against Russia

Ban on equipment for oil industry	*Financial ban on oil and gas companies*	*Financial ban on banks*
Deep water	Gazprom	Bank of Moscow
Offshore Arctic	Gazprom Neft	Gazprombank
Shale oil production	Lukoil	InvestCapital Bank
	Rosneft	JSB Sobinbank
	Sakhatrans	Rosselkhozbank
	SGM Pipeline Construction	Sberbank
	Stroitransgaz	SMP Bank
	Surgutneftegaz	Vneshekonombank
	Transneft	VTB Bank
	Transoil	

Note: This overview is non-exhaustive, as sanctions varied over time and by country
Sources: Dunn and Smith (2014), Fjaertoft and Overland (2015, p.66)

China's Stance on the Sanctions

At first China maintained a neutral position on the Ukraine crisis. The Chinese abstained from voting on a 15 March UN Security Council resolution declaring the results of the Crimean referendum on reunification with Russia invalid—but they did not use their right of veto as one of the Permanent Five (Zhang, Lihua 2015). Chinese banks adhered *de facto* to the Western sanctions, with the exception of the Export-Import Bank of China and China Development Bank (*Pravda.ru* 2016).

This wait-and-see stance made some sense. It offered a precarious balance between, on the one hand, China's traditionally conservative view on interference in the internal affairs of other states and its preoccupation with maintaining its own territorial integrity (Taiwan, Tibet and Xinjiang) and, on the other hand, its growing friendship with Russia and dislike for the Western meddling in Ukrainian politics that had prefaced the conflict (see Lanteigne, Chap. 7, this volume).

Gradually, however, China tilted moderately towards the Russian position on Crimea. On 6 June 2014, the Secretary of the Russian Security Council and former Director of the Federal Security Service, Nikolai Patrushev, stated that China and Russia had arrived at a common understanding of the Ukrainian crisis (*TV Tsentr* 2014); and in February 2015 the Chinese Ambassador to Belgium, Qu Xing, expressed support for the Russian point of view and encouraged the West to end its quarrel with Russia (Boren 2015). However, it is difficult to determine the extent of China's tilt towards the Russian position: it is hard to find clear pro-Russian statements from policymakers in Beijing, and the level of Chinese support was played up by the Russians.

PATTERNS OF ECONOMIC INTERACTION BETWEEN CHINA AND RUSSIA

Data on the Sino-Russian economic relationship give a mixed picture. As shown in Fig. 6.2, borrowing from China by Russian companies and households did rise in 2014 and 2015. However, that trend had started in 2013, before the Ukraine crisis. Thus, it is difficult to know whether the rise in borrowing was simply the continuation of a trend that had begun earlier and was not related to events in Ukraine, or was reinforced by the Ukraine crisis. On the other hand, there was also a spike in Russian borrowing from China in 2008–09, when Russia experienced a severe financial

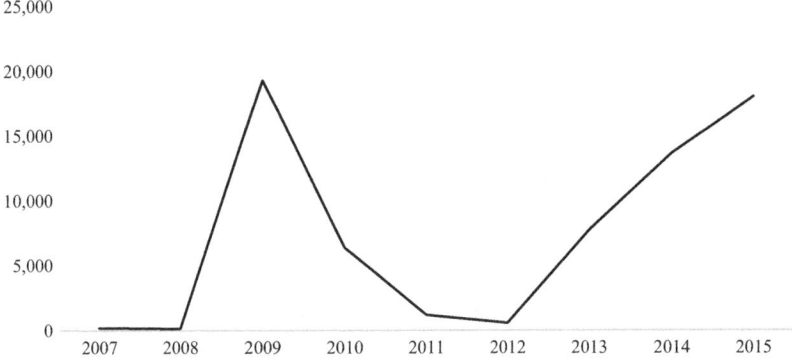

Fig. 6.2 Loans of Russian non-bank entities from China, million USD (Source: Calculated based on data from the Central Bank of Russia, available at http://www.cbr.ru/eng/statistics/?PrtId=svs. Accessed on 26 March 2017)

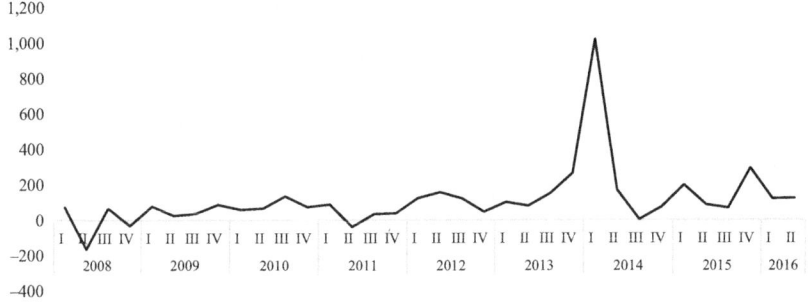

Fig. 6.3 FDI from China to Russia, million USD (Source: Calculated based on data from the Central Bank of Russia, available at https://www.cbr.ru/statistics/credit_statistics/inv_in-country.xlsx. Accessed on 26 March 2017)

crisis. Seen together, these two spikes could indicate that Russia turns to China when cash becomes scarce.

As shown in Fig. 6.3, there was a large jump in Chinese foreign direct investment (FDI) in Russia in early 2014. However, that came in the first quarter of that year, whereas economic sanctions were not introduced until the beginning of the second quarter, in mid-April. Thus the jump in Chinese FDI is not likely to be related to the sanctions regime, although it might have been mobilized in *anticipation* of sanctions. Another possible explanation is that it might be related to the Power of Siberia deal, although this deal was officially announced only in May. In any case, the jump was only to one billion USD. Although that was a significant divergence from the long-term pattern of FDI, it is a relatively small sum for a country such as Russia, and much smaller than the impact of sanctions or the falling oil price.

Finally, it is worth considering whether increased sales of oil and gas to China buoyed the Russian economy during this period. As shown in Fig. 6.4, Russia's income from oil exports to China rose only modestly in 2014, and then actually fell in 2015. Income from the sale of coal to China fell continuously and steeply from 2013 to 2015. The reason for these declines was mainly the lower international prices for energy commodities—which neither China nor Russia controls. But at least it is clear that income from energy exports to China did not rise and save the Russian economy.

Thus, the patterns of lending, investments and energy trade between China and Russia spanning the pre- and post-Crimea years do not point towards a major role for China in keeping Russia's wheels turning during

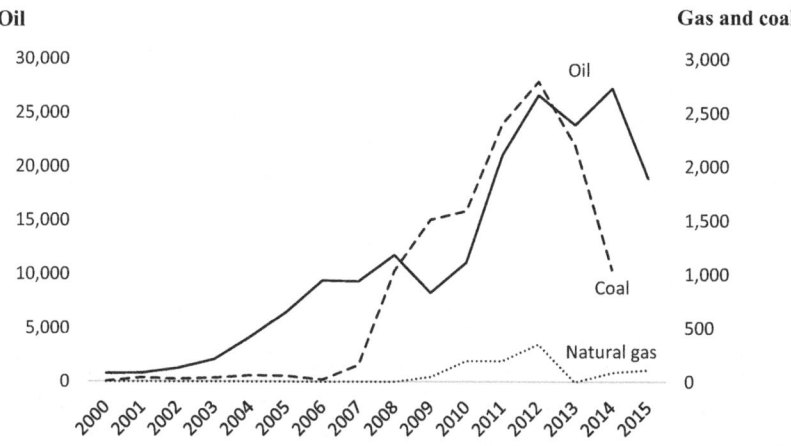

Fig. 6.4 Russian income from the export of oil, gas and coal to China, million USD (Source: Based on data on import of 'coal, coke and briquettes', 'petroleum, petroleum products and related materials', 'gas, natural and manufactured' from Russia to China, retrieved from https://comtrade.un.org/data. Accessed on 10 October 2016)

this period. Although the data on lending and FDI may appear interesting at first glance, and offer some striking graphics, on closer inspection we find little of significance there.

Sino-Russian Energy Projects

We now turn to the petroleum sector and examine four large energy projects in which the Chinese and the Russians have attempted to cooperate. All four involve major Russian oil and gas companies that have been subject to Western sanctions: Transneft, Gazprom, Novatek and Rosneft. Did the role of the Chinese in these projects change after the Ukraine conflict?

Transneft: ESPO Pipeline

The Eastern Siberia–Pacific Ocean (ESPO) oil pipeline was constructed and is managed by Russia's state-owned oil pipeline monopoly Transneft, the world's largest oil pipeline company. The history of Sino-Russian discussions of ESPO goes many years back. The construction of ESPO was first mooted in the 1970s. In 1994, President Boris Yeltsin proposed building a pipeline from Angarsk (Irkutsk Oblast) to China. In 1996, after long negotiations, Beijing and Moscow signed an agreement on energy cooperation, including plans for a pipeline from Eastern Siberia to Daqing in northern China. However, the cooperation moved slowly, partly due to the difficult investment climate in Russia, and partly because China sought concessions from the Russians on pricing.

In 1999, the head of the privately owned oil company Yukos, Mikhail Khodorkovskii, conducted negotiations with China National Petroleum Corporation (CNPC) on the construction of ESPO, and in 2001 Prime Minister Mikhail Kasianov signed an agreement on feasibility studies for the pipeline (*Kommersant* 2006). Russian and Chinese oil companies started technical-economic assessments for the project, and it was expected that the leaders of the two countries would sign an agreement in December 2002. But the negotiations slowed down again, this time because Japan showed interest in paying for a pipeline from East Siberia to the Pacific coast. The Russian government decided to merge the Chinese and Japanese projects into one project that would go to Kozmino on the Pacific coast (Driakin 2014, pp.102–10).

There was also competition between Yukos and the state oil pipeline monopoly Transneft. The government decided that Transneft would be in charge of the pipeline and Yukos would supply the oil (Helmer 2008). In May 2003, China and Russia agreed on the construction of the pipeline (*ChinaDaily.com* 2003), and the work started in April 2006 (Koyama 2010). Meanwhile Khodorkovskii had been arrested and most of Yukos assets confiscated by the state. While various sections of the pipeline were being built, interim arrangements were made to pump oil in reverse through a section of the pipeline and transport it by rail part of the way (Bryanski 2009; Watkins 2009). The second stage of the pipeline was inaugurated in December 2012.

In April 2009, China and Russia agreed to build a spur to Daqing through which Russia would supply China with 15 million tons of oil per year for 20 years in exchange for a USD 25 billion loan to Transneft and Rosneft. Construction of the spur from the Russian side started in April 2009 and was completed by September 2010 (*BBC Monitoring* 2009; Page 2010). On 1 January 2011, Russia announced that oil shipments to China had commenced.

By 2015, ESPO capacity had risen to 58 million tons per year, and the branch line from the Russian town of Skovorodino to Daqing to 15 million tons per year (Platts 2015) (Table 6.2).

Table 6.2 Timeline of Sino-Russian cooperation on ESPO pipeline

Date	Development
July 2001	Russian and Chinese prime ministers sign agreement on feasibility studies for ESPO
May 2003	China and Russia agree on the construction of the pipeline
Dec. 2004	Russian government approves the construction of ESPO
Apr. 2006	Construction of pipeline starts
June 2009	China and Russia agree to build a spur to Daqing in China
Dec. 2009	First stage of the pipeline completed
Sept. 2010	Daqing spur completed
Jan. 2011	Shipments via Daqing commence
Dec. 2012	Second stage of the pipeline completed
June 2016	Work on second pipe of Daqing spur commences, to double spur capacity to 30 mt/year
Oct. 2017	Daqing spur second pipe scheduled for completion

Gazprom: Power of Siberia

The Power of Siberia pipeline will be the largest gas transmission system in eastern Russia, transporting natural gas from Irkutsk and Sakha to the Russian Far East, partly for production of liquefied natural gas (LNG) on the Pacific coast, partly for pipeline export to China. The 4000-kilometre long pipeline will link the Kovykta gas and condensate field in Eastern Siberia and the Chaiandinskoe oil, gas and condensate field in Sakha to the existing Sakhalin–Khabarovsk–Vladivostok pipeline. The fields are scheduled to come on stream in 2021 and 2019, respectively (Gazprom 2016; Sidortsov et al. 2016, pp.54–68).

After a cooperation agreement had been signed between Gazprom and CNPC in 2004, Sino-Russian natural gas negotiations went on for more than ten years. Initially, the parties discussed a pipeline through Altai, linking the rich gas fields of the NadymPurTaz area in West Siberia to the northwestern corner of China. The length of this pipeline would be 2800 rather than 4000 kilometres, and the price of the gas would be lower, because it would initially draw on gas fields already in production. It would also have put China in direct competition with Europe for West Siberian gas. But the Chinese rejected the Altai route because it would take gas to one of the most remote and sparsely populated parts of China, which can be supplied with gas from Turkmenistan and local Chinese fields (Anker et al. 2010; Overland et al. 2010; Klein and Westphal 2016, p.4).

In 2009, China and Russia signed an agreement on major terms and conditions for the supply of gas which detailed the terms of actual implementation. While negotiations with the Chinese continued, Gazprom started preparations for developing the Chaiandinskoe gas field and planning the Power of Siberia pipeline. Even though a deal with the Chinese still had not been finalized, in late October 2012 President Putin instructed Gazprom to start building the pipeline (*Interfax.ru* 2012).

Disagreement on the price of the gas to flow through the pipeline postponed the signing of the final contract from November 2013 to January 2014—and then to the St Petersburg Economic Forum in May 2014. Only then could Putin, who flew in to the forum at the last moment directly from negotiations in Shanghai, present a deal. The signing of the agreement with China was presented as a major geopolitical victory: a narrow escape from dependence on the capricious European market and the

Table 6.3 Timeline of Sino-Russian cooperation on Power of Siberia

Date	Development
Nov. 2004	Gazprom and CNPC sign cooperation agreement
March 2006	CNPC signs MoU with Gazprom on supplying natural gas from Russia to China
Dec. 2009	Gazprom and CNPC sign agreement on major terms and conditions for gas supply to China
May 2014	Gazprom and CNPC sign a contract to supply gas to China via Power of Siberia
June 2014	Gazprom accelerates the construction of infrastructure related to Power of Siberia
Aug. 2014	Gazprom and Chinese leaders enhance the bilateral strategic partnership in the gas sector
Sept. 2014	Power of Siberia construction launched
Oct 2014	Gazprom and CNPC discuss the negotiation schedule for gas supply to China via Altai
Feb. 2015	The parties address the state of the Altai negotiations
June 2015	Further negotiations on gas supply via Altai
Aug. 2015	Further negotiations on gas supply via Altai
Nov. 2015	The parties discuss the progress of the construction of the Power of Siberia gas pipeline.
Dec. 2015	Negotiations on finalization of agreement on cross-border section of Power of Siberia
Dec. 2015	The parties discuss both Power of Siberia and Altai
May 2016	Gazprom and the Chinese review possible joint activities relating to hydrocarbon exploration and production, including LNG
June 2016	Gazprom and CNPC discuss gas supplies via Altai in detail
June 2016	Gazprom and CNPC sign MoU on underground gas storage and gas-fired power generation
July 2016	Gazprom and CNPC agree on roadmaps for implementing MoU on underground gas storage and gas-fired power generation
Aug. 2016	Gazprom and Chinese Ambassador Li Hui make positive statements about Sino-Russian cooperation in gas sector
Sept. 2016	Gazprom and CNPC sign contract on underwater border crossing for Power of Siberia

yoke of Western sanctions. However, the agreement was also criticized. Detractors argued that the price paid by the Chinese would not cover the costs of the project, that Russia's political interests had prevailed over its economic interests, and that China had taken advantage of the situation (Prelovskaia 2014).

On 21 May 2014, the heads of Gazprom and CNPC signed the Power of Siberia contract to supply 1032 trillion cubic metres of gas to China over a 30-year period. The total value of the contract exceeded USD 400 billion. Gazprom estimated that it would need five years to build the pipeline, at a cost of USD 55 billion (Prelovskaia 2014). Construction started on 1 September 2014 in Sakha, in the presence of President Putin and Deputy Chinese Prime Minister Zhang Gaoli (*TASS* 2014).

While the construction of the Power of Siberia is ahead of schedule (Gazprom 2017), negotiations over an additional pipeline via Altai have been slow and no final deal appears to be on the horizon (Astakhova and Kobzeva 2017). Klein and Westphal (2016, p.4) refer to this pipeline as 'a remote prospect at best' (Table 6.3).

Novatek: Yamal LNG

Yamal LNG is a liquefied natural gas plant on the Yamal Peninsula in northwestern Siberia (Yamal LNG 2015). The project has a budget of USD 27 billion and will increase Russia's LNG capacity twofold, with initial production starting in 2017 and full capacity reached by 2021 (Belinski 2015). Discussions about Yamal LNG started in the early 2000s; the project was initially owned by some Russian oligarchs and then the company Novatek, a rising star in Russia's natural gas sector. Novatek brought international companies into the project, with the sale of a 20 per cent stake to French Total in 2011 and a 20 per cent stake to CNPC in 2013 (Bros and Mitrova 2016).

Although the Western sanctions are not supposed to affect Russian natural gas supplies to Europe, Yamal LNG was one of the largest projects to face financial problems after the introduction of sanctions. Novatek has limited access to the pipelines to Europe, and Yamal LNG will export gas to European and above all Asian markets in the form of LNG by tanker. The sanctions applied not only to Novatek but also to its daughter companies, including Yamal LNG, as the owners are seen as being closely connected with President Putin (Lunden et al. 2013, p.668; Overland et al. 2013, p.145). Novatek had planned to borrow USD 20 billion from

Table 6.4 Timeline of Sino-Russian cooperation on Yamal LNG

Date	Development
June 2013	Novatek and CNPC conclude framework agreement on the Yamal LNG project
Sept. 2013	Novatek sells 20 per cent share of Yamal LNG to CNPC
March 2014	Russia and China sign an agreement on cooperation on the Yamal LNG project. The Chinese commit to buying at least three million tons of LNG per year and secure financing for the project from Chinese financial institutions
March 2014	Yamal LNG and Fluxys (Belgium) sign cooperation agreement on LNG trans-shipment
May 2014	Binding contract on LNG from Yamal is concluded with CNPC. China Development Bank, Vneshekonombank, Gazprombank and Yamal LNG sign MoU on project financing
Jan. 2015	Gazprom Singapore and Yamal Trade sign long-term LNG supply agreement
Apr. 2015	Yamal LNG and Fluxys sign contract for LNG shipment services at Zeebrugge LNG
Nov. 2015	Yamal LNG receives second tranche of funding from Russian National Wealth Fund
Apr. 2016	Yamal LNG signs agreements with the Export-Import Bank of China and the China Development Bank on two 15-year loans for a total amount exceeding USD 12 billion
June 2016	Yamal LNG receives first tranche of funds from Chinese banks
Dec. 2016	Yamal LNG gets EUR 200 million credit line from Japan Bank for International Cooperation

US and European banks. After the introduction of sanctions, the Russians lost access to US banks and negotiated with Chinese banks and European export agencies instead. Meanwhile, the shareholders were forced to finance the project independently (Barsukov and Mordiushenko 2016). In 2016, however, Yamal LNG received loans from Chinese and Japanese state banks worth USD 12 billion and EUR 200 million, respectively. Negotiations on loans from Chinese banks had started in 2014, but grew out of deals signed in mid- and late 2013 (Farchy 2016) (Table 6.4).

Rosneft: Vankor

The Vankor cluster of oil and gas fields in Siberia, discovered in 1988, is currently the largest source of oil in Russia, with recoverable reserves of 361 million tons of oil and condensate and 138 billion cubic metres of gas

Table 6.5 Timeline of Sino-Russian cooperation on Vankor field

Date	Development
Apr. 1988	Discovery of Vankor oil field
Feb. 2004	Rosneft subsidiary Vankorneft founded
Aug. 2009	Formal launch ceremony for commercial production at the Vankor field
Jan. 2013	The Vankor field produce their 50-millionth ton of oil
Nov. 2013	Rosneft's Board of Directors approves Vankorneft as the operator of three fields: Lodochnoe, Suzunskoe and Tagulskoe
Dec. 2013	70 million tons of oil produced at the field cumulatively
Sept. 2014	Putin suggests participation in project to Chinese Deputy Prime Minister
June 2016	Oil India, Indian Oil and Bharat PetroResources purchase 23.9 per cent of Vankorneft's shares

(Panteleev 2006; Gan 2015). Rosneft has invested USD 5 billion in Vankor; production started in 2009 (Gan 2015). Vankor will send 70 per cent of its oil through the ESPO pipeline.

There was little discussion of foreign investment in Vankor until September 2014, when Putin suggested during a meeting with Chinese Deputy Prime Minister Zhang Gaoli that the Chinese take part in the project. Two months later, Rosneft and CNPC signed a memorandum of intention on the sale of a 10 per cent share of Vankor. However, the parties were unable to turn the memorandum into an agreement (Motoharu 2016). Instead, in March 2016 Rosneft signed a deal with Indian companies on the sale of 23.9 per cent of Vankor (Rosneft 2016). Through this purchase, the Indian companies gained seats on the Board of Directors, while Rosneft retained a majority stake in the project. During the rest of 2016, Rosneft and the Indian companies negotiated further sale of Vankor shares, potentially bringing the Indian stake up to 49.9 per cent (*Sputnik* 2016) (Table 6.5).

Summing Up the Four Projects

The four major projects examined here do not indicate any significant change in Chinese involvement in the Russian energy sector after the Ukraine crisis. In three of them, discussions on Chinese involvement started well before the crisis. The exception is the Vankor project, but it ultimately did not result in Chinese investment. It may be that finalization of the Power of Siberia deal was accelerated due to the Ukraine crisis, but also this was something that had been planned and negotiated intensively for a long time, so we should take care not to exaggerate the connection with the Ukraine crisis.

The Long-Term Perspective

The previous sections sought to identify the dynamics of Sino-Russian cooperation around the time of the annexation of Crimea. It may also be helpful to examine the longer lines in the relationship between the two countries to determine whether the cooperation from 2014 onwards represented something new triggered by the Ukraine crisis, or was an extension of a more long-term trend that pre-dated the crisis.

Relations between the Chinese and Soviet communist behemoths were rarely warm and frequently tense (Henderson and Mitrova 2016, p.1). Warding off a potential Chinese attack was a main reason for the emphasis that the Soviets put on their tactical nuclear weapons (Trenin 1999, p.41; Yost 2001, p.550). Moreover, during a seven-month period in 1969, there were actually military clashes along the Sino-Soviet border, leaving scores of Chinese and Soviet soldiers dead. During the post-Soviet period, relations improved steadily—upgraded incrementally, first to 'constructive partnership' (1994), then 'strategic partnership of cooperation' (1996) and then 'comprehensive deepening strategic partnership' (2010) (Klein and Westphal 2016, p.1). Another sign of the improvement was the finalization of agreements delimiting the border between the two countries in 1991, 1994, 1998, 1999 and 2004 (Moe et al. 2011, p.153).

In the energy sector, an important part of the long-term picture is the evolution of Chinese demand for Russian energy resources (Aguilera et al. 2013). Energy security became a strategic aspect of Chinese foreign policy when the country became a net importer of oil in 1993 (Overland and Braekhus 2009). Dependence on oil imports continued to grow, from 70 million tons in 2000 to 336 million tons by 2015 (Hsu 2016). The Chinese government took an active approach to energy security, including it in the Tenth Five-Year Plan (2001–2005). Among the measures proposed were the building of pipelines from Kazakhstan and Russia, and increasing Chinese investments in international oil exploration and field operations.

In 2013, China had a natural gas deficit of 6.7 billion cubic metres. The Chinese National Reform and Development Commission has forecast that demand for natural gas in 2020 will be 411 billion cubic metres, whereas domestic production will be only 200 billion—necessitating a steep rise in imports (Prelovskaia 2014). Although the international gas trade is

Table 6.6 Sino-Russian energy deals and developments

	Deal
2001	Russian company Yukos proposes Eastern Siberia–Pacific Ocean (ESPO) oil pipeline
2003	CNPC signs a framework agreement with Sakhalin Energy on exploration and development
2004	Gazprom and CNPC sign cooperation agreement
2005	China lends Russia USD 6 billion to help finance Yukos deal
2005	CNPC signs agreement on long-term cooperation with Rosneft
2006	CNPC signs MOU with Gazprom, Rosneft and Transneft on supplying natural gas
2006	CNPC buys a USD 500 million stake in Rosneft
2006	CNPC signs strategic cooperation agreement with Lukoil
2006	CNPC and Rosneft establish the joint venture Vostok Energy
2007	Vostok Energy wins a bid for oil and gas exploration licences in Irkutsk
2008	CNPC and Transneft sign agreement to build oil pipeline to China
2009	China, Rosneft and Transneft agree to supply 15 million tons annually for 20 years from East Siberia for USD 25 billion
2009	China signs framework agreement with Gazprom on natural gas supply and MoU with Rosneft
2010	Oil pipeline to China officially starts to operate
2011	China agrees to contribute USD 1 billion to China–Russia Investment Fund
2012	27 business deals, worth USD 15 billion, signed at Sino-Russian investment forum
2012	China Development Bank and Sberbank agree to cooperate
2013	Chinese investment in Russian coal worth USD 2 billion
2013	Rosneft deal to supply oil to China, with USD 70 billion prepaid (total value USD 270 billion)
2013	CNPC buys 20 per cent of Novatek's Yamal LNG project
2013	China lends USD 1.9 billion to Russian banks
2014	30-year Power of Siberia natural gas deal signed, worth USD 400 billion
2014	CNOOC gets contract for engineering at Novatek-led Yamal LNG project worth USD 1.6 billion
2016	Yamal LNG signs agreements with the Export-Import Bank of China and the China Development Bank on two 15-year loans for a total amount exceeding USD 12 billion

Sources: Ministry of Foreign Affairs (2001), Gazprom (2004), White and Chazan (2005), Paxton and Soldatkin (2009), Zhang, Chi (2015)

increasingly competitive and there are some alternatives to Russia as supplier, there is little doubt that China will need significant amounts of Russian gas. Table 6.6 provides an overview of Sino-Russian energy deals and developments over time, and shows that the cooperation had gained momentum well before the 2014 Ukraine crisis.

Thus it has long been clear that Russian energy resources are of great interest to the Chinese and the Chinese market is of great interest to the Russians (Locatelli et al. 2017, p.159). The two countries had already been moving two steps forward, one step back on energy cooperation for two decades before the Ukraine crisis. The Chinese deals with Gazprom on Power of Siberia and with Novatek on Yamal LNG were logical continuations of this dance and helped resolve long-standing Chinese energy-security concerns (Overland 2015, p.3532). Russian oil exports to China doubled between 2010 and 2014—*before* the Ukraine crisis (Klein and Westphal 2016, p.5). In this perspective, the energy cooperation from 2014 onwards fits into a longer-term trend towards greater energy trade between the two countries.[1]

CONCLUSIONS

In some respects, Chinese involvement and financing did surge in the aftermath of the Ukraine crisis. After many years of slow negotiations, there was an increased frequency in meetings to discuss major energy projects like Power of Siberia, one of the largest energy deals in world history.

However, in most cases the deals from 2014 onwards fit with trends that had started well before the crisis. The Chinese financial contribution was not as large as it might seem at first sight; and, in some cases, it did not continue beyond 2014 into 2015 and 2016 (Motoharu 2016). The failure to reach an agreement on the Vankor project and the fact that the boom in Chinese FDI did not last beyond the first quarter of 2014 are examples of the slowdown. In sum, we find little basis for arguing that China bankrolled Russia's annexation of Crimea.

Several factors may have hindered a surge in Sino-Russian energy cooperation. First, both sides are often determined to have a controlling role in partnerships, and that makes it difficult to close deals, even when the interests of the two countries are complementary (*Rosbalt.ru* 2016). Second, the Russian oil and gas companies managed to weather the storm better than expected due to the precipitous drop in the value of the Russian ruble: while their income from oil and gas exports fell, also their costs in Russia fell, cancelling out a good part of the foreign earnings loss. Thus Russian companies did not become as dependent on Chinese help as might have been expected. Third, the Russian government maximized the public relations potential of Power of Siberia and other deals with the

Chinese. On the one hand, this means that the role of the Chinese may have been psychologically more important than the financial data show (O'Sullivan 2016, p.23); on the other hand, it also means that the media image of the role of the Chinese was exaggerated.

What then are the implications of our findings for the depth and long-term prospects of the Sino-Russian relationship? To some extent they confirm Bobo Lo's argument that it is an 'axis of convenience' (Lo 2008). When the Russians need financing or markets, they seek out the Chinese—but not more than necessary. When the Chinese need natural resources, they buy them from Russia—but only if the price is right (Simola 2016, p.3; Henderson and Mitrova 2016, p.1). This has not amounted to a deeper relationship where the two countries identify with each other. The fact that even with the Ukraine crisis the surge in Sino-Russian cooperation was modest, indicates that the relationship still has limited potential. Thus, Lo's 'axis of convenience' perspective seems to have weathered the natural quasi-experiment of the Ukraine crisis quite well.

However, the fact that the cooperation from 2014 onwards fits with longer-term trends can also be read the other way around. Although the Ukraine crisis did not lead to a sudden strengthening of Sino-Russian relations, it represents an international context increasingly conducive to cooperation between China and Russia, a relationship that has already been growing for a quarter of a century. If this continues for a long period, the two countries may well grow closer over time. After all, it is not so long since the Russians 'discovered' China in earnest: it was only in 2012 President Putin told Russian gas producers to look east (cited in O'Sullivan 2016, p.22). In the future, the two countries may yet grow closer.

Another way to read the Ukraine crisis and the ensuing jump in economic complementarity between China and Russia is that it shows that, for the relationship to become qualitatively different, things will have to happen not only at the economic level but also at the level of culture, identity and ideology. Otherwise Sino-Russian relations will remain a marriage of convenience in which either partner may lose interest as soon as the economic complementarities fade.

Acknowledgements This chapter is a product of the RusChange research project, which is financed by the PETROSAM II Programme of the Research Council of Norway.

Notes

1. This finding echoes that by Tom Røseth (2017, p.37).

References

Aguilera, Roberto, Julian Inchauspe and Ronald Ripple. 2013. 'The Asia Pacific natural gas market: large enough for all?' *Energy Policy* 65: 1–6.

Anker, Morten, Pavel Baev, Bjørn Brunstad, Indra Overland and Stina Torjesen. 2010. *The Caspian Sea region towards 2025: Caspia Inc., national giants or trade and transit?* Delft: Eburon.

Astakhova, Olesya and Oksana Kobzeva. 2017. 'Russia-China talks over new gas routes stalled: sources', *Reuters*, 7 June. http://www.reuters.com/article/us-russia-china-energy-idUSKBN18Y1TX. Accessed on 3 July 2017.

Barsukov, Iurii and Ol'ga Mordiushenko. 2016. 'S oporoi na sobstvennye sily' [Relying on one's own strength]. *Kommersant*, 30 April. http://kommersant.ru/doc/2978177. Accessed on 30 December 2016.

BBC Monitoring. 2009. 'Chinese envoy to Russia: oil pipeline serves strategic goals of both sides', 11 May. http://downstreamtoday.com/news/article.aspx?a_id=16321&AspxAutoDetectCookieSupport=1. Accessed on 30 December 2016.

Belinski, Scott. 2015. 'Putin may have last laugh over Western sanctions', *Oilprice.com*, 2 April. http://oilprice.com/Energy/Energy-General/Putin-May-Have-Last-Laugh-Over-Western-Sanctions.html. Accessed on 30 December 2016.

Boren, Zackary Davies. 2015. 'Ukraine crisis: top Chinese diplomat backs Putin and says West should "abandon zero-sum mentality"', *The Independent*, 27 February. http://www.independent.co.uk/news/world/europe/ukraine-crisis-top-chinese-diplomat-backs-putin-says-west-should-abandon-zero-sum-mentality-10075762.html. Accessed on 30 December 2016.

Braekhus, Kyrre and Indra Overland. 2007. 'A match made in heaven? Strategic convergence between China and Russia', *China and Eurasia Forum Quarterly* 5(2): 41–61.

Bros, Aurelie and Tatiana Mitrova. 2016. 'Yamal LNG: an economic project under political pressure', *Fondation pour la Recherche Stratégique*. https://www.frstrategie.org/publications/notes/web/documents/2016/201617.pdf. Accessed on 30 December 2016.

Bryanski, Gleb. 2009. 'Russia's Putin launches new Pacific oil terminal', *Reuters*, 28 December. http://uk.reuters.com/article/russia-putin-terminal-idUKLDE5BR00F20091228?sp=true. Accessed on 30 December 2016.

Charap, Samuel, John Drennan and Pierre Noël. 2017. 'Russia and China: a new model of great-power relations', *Survival* 59(1): 25–42.

ChinaDaily.com. 2003. 'China, Russia sign oil pipeline agreement', 29 May. http://www.chinadaily.com.cn/en/doc/2003-05/29/content_166888.htm. Accessed on 30 December 2016.

Cunningham, Nick. 2015a. 'Russia and China's growing energy relationship', *Oilprice.com*, 28 January. http://oilprice.com/Energy/Energy-General/Russia-and-Chinas-Growing-Energy-Relationship.html. Accessed on 30 December 2016.

Cunningham, Nick. 2015b. 'The battle for China's oil market', *Oilprice.com*, 15 July. http://oilprice.com/Energy/Crude-Oil/The-Battle-For-Chinas-Oil-Market.html. Accessed on 30 December 2016.

Driakin, Andrei. 2014. 'Energeticheskaia diplomatiia Rossii v aziatsko-tikhookeanskom regione: osnovnye aspekty i napraveliia' [Russia's energy diplomacy in the Asia-Pacific: key aspects and trends], *Izvestiia vysshikh uchebnykh zavedenii. Povolzhskii region* 4: 102–10.

Dunn, Alan and Jennifer Smith. 2014. 'U.S. added 17 companies and 7 individuals, including Rosneft CEO Sechin, to Russia sanctions list and further restricted exports to certain Russian entities; EU, Canada, and Japan also stepped up sanctions', *Stewart and Stewart*, 1 May. http://www.stewartlaw.com/Article/ViewArticle/1000. Accessed on 27 December 2016.

Farchy, Jack. 2016. 'Chinese lend $12bn for gas plant in Russian Arctic', *Financial Times*, 29 April. https://www.ft.com/content/4ca8886e-0e14-11e6-ad80-67655613c2d6. Accessed on 5 February 2017.

Fjaertoft, Daniel and Indra Overland. 2015. 'Financial sanctions impact Russian oil, equipment export ban's effects limited', *Oil and Gas Journal* 113(8): 66–72.

Gabuev, Alexander. 2015. 'A "soft alliance"? Russia–China relations after the Ukraine crisis', *European Council on Foreign Relations Policy Brief* 126. http://www.ecfr.eu/page/-/ECFR126_-_A_Soft_Alliance_Russia-China_Relations_After_the_Ukraine_Crisis.pdf. Accessed on 9 February 2017.

Gan, U. 2015. 'Spetsial'nyi reportazh: "zhemchuzhina v rossiiskoi korone" – Vankorskoe neftegazovoe mestorozhdenie' [Special report: 'a pearl in the Russian crown' – the Vankor field], *Russian.news.cn*, 31 March. http://russian.news.cn/economic/2015-03/31/c_134113387.htm. Accessed on 30 December 2016.

Gazprom. 2004. 'Gazprom and CNPC signed a cooperation agreement', 14 October. http://www.gazprom.com/press/news/2004/october/article62935. Accessed 30 December 2016.

Gazprom. 2016. 'Power of Siberia', http://www.gazprom.com/about/production/projects/pipelines/built/ykv. Accessed on 30 December 2016.

Gazprom. 2017. 'Over 1,100 kilometers of Power of Siberia gas pipeline to be completed by late 2017', 8 June. http://www.gazprom.com/press/news/2017/june/article335985/. Accessed on 3 June 2017.

Helmer, John. 2008. 'China ties up Russia's crude – again', *Asia Times*, 1 November. http://www.atimes.com/atimes/China_Business/JK01Cb01.html. Accessed on 30 December 2016.
Henderson, James and Tatiana Mitrova. 2016. 'Energy relations between Russia and China: playing chess with the dragon', *OIES Paper* 67. https://www.oxfordenergy.org/wpcms/wp-content/uploads/2016/08/Energy-Relations-between-Russia-and-China-Playing-Chess-with-the-Dragon-WPM-67.pdf. Accessed on 9 February 2017.
Hsu, Jenny W. 2016. 'China's crude oil imports rise 8.8% in 2015', *Marketwatch. com*, 26 January. http://www.marketwatch.com/story/chinas-crude-oil-imports-rise-88-in-2015-2016-01-26. Accessed on 25 December 2016.
Interfax.ru. 2012. '"Gazprom" poluchil impul's dlia osvoeniia Chaiandy' [Gazprom received an impetus to develop Chaianda], 29 October. http://www.interfax.ru/business/273323. Accessed on 30 December 2016.
Klein, Margarete, and Kirsten Westphal. 2016. 'Russia: turn to China?' *SWP Comments* 7. https://www.swp-berlin.org/fileadmin/contents/products/comments/2016C07_kle_wep.pdf. Accessed on 29 December 2016.
Kommersant. 2006. 'Istoriia proekta VSTO' [History of the ESPO project], 27 April. http://kommersant.ru/doc/670339. Accessed on 30 December 2016.
Koyama, Ken. 2010. 'Progress made toward operations of China–Russia crude oil pipeline on completion of Russian portion', *The Institute of Energy Economics*, 3 September. https://eneken.ieej.or.jp/data/3574.pdf. Accessed on 30 December 2016.
Lo, Bobo. 2008. *Axis of convenience: Moscow, Beijing, and the new geopolitics*. Washington, DC: The Brookings Institution.
Locatelli, Catherine, Mehdi Abbas and Sylvain Rossiaud (2017) 'The emerging hydrocarbon interdependence between Russia and China: institutional and systemic implications', *Europe–Asia Studies* 69(1): 157–170.
Lunden, Lars Petter, Daniel Fjaertoft, Indra Overland and Alesia Prachakova. 2013. 'Gazprom vs. other gas producers: friends or foes?' *Energy Policy* 61: 663–70.
Ministry of Foreign Affairs of the People's Republic of China. 2001. 'Joint statement signed by the Chinese and Russian heads of states', 16 July. http://www.fmprc.gov.cn/mfa_eng/wjdt_665385/2649_665393/t15772.shtml. Accessed on 30 December 2016.
Moe, Arild, Daniel Fjærtoft and Indra Overland. 2011. 'Space and timing: why was the Barents Sea delimitation dispute resolved in 2010?' *Polar Geography* 34(2): 145–62.
Motoharu, Ikeda. 2016. 'Razmolvka mezhdu Kitaem i Rossiei, i kak ona povliiaet na rossiisko-iaponskie otnosheniia' [The spat between China and Russia, and how it will affect the Russia–Japan relationship], *Inosmi.ru*, 12 April. http://inosmi.ru/economic/20160412/236092426.html. Accessed on 30 December 2016.

Observatory of Economic Complexity. 2014. 'Where does China import petroleum oils, oils from bituminous minerals, crude from?' http://atlas.media.mit.edu/en/visualize/tree_map/hs92/import/chn/show/270900/2014. Accessed on 9 February 2017.

O'Sullivan, Meghan. 2016. 'Asia: a geopolitical beneficiary of the new energy environment', in *Asia's energy security amid global market change*, edited by Muhamad Izham Abd. Shukor, Clara Gillispie, Antoine Halff, Mikkal E. Herberg, Meghan L. O'Sullivan, Leslie Palti-Guzman and Cecilia Tam, 19–30. Seattle, WA: National Bureau of Asian Research.

Overland, Indra. 2015. 'Future petroleum geopolitics: consequences of climate policy and unconventional oil and gas', *Handbook of Clean Energy Systems*, 3517–44. Chichester: Wiley.

Overland, Indra and Kyrre Braekhus. 2009. 'Chinese perspectives on Russian oil and gas', in *Russian energy power and foreign relations*, edited by Jeronim Perovic, Robert Orttung and Andreas Wenger, 201–21. Abingdon: Routledge.

Overland, Indra, Jakub Godzimirski, Lars Petter Lunden and Daniel Fjaertoft. 2013. 'Rosneft's offshore partnerships: the re-opening of the Russian petroleum frontier?' *Polar Record* 49(2): 140–53.

Overland, Indra, Nodari Simonia, Sergey Vasiliev and Elana Wilson Rowe. 2015. 'The international context for Barents oil and gas: Asia's double impact', in *International Arctic petroleum cooperation: Barents Sea scenarios*, edited by Anatolii Bourmistrov, Frode Mellemvik, Alexei Bambulyak, Ove Gudmestad, Indra Overland and Anatoly Zolotukhin, 35–51. Abingdon: Routledge.

Overland, Indra, Stina Torjesen and Heidi Kjaernet. 2010. 'China and Russia: partners or firewalls for the Caspian petro-states?' in *Caspian energy politics: Azerbaijan, Kazakhstan and Turkmenistan*, edited by Indra Overland, Heidi Kjaernet and Andrea Kendall-Taylor, 93–100. Abingdon: Routledge.

Page, Jeremy. 2010. 'Russian oil route will open to China', *The Wall Street Journal*, 26 September. http://www.wsj.com/articles/SB10001424052748704082104575515543164948682. Accessed on 30 December 2016.

Panteleev, Vladimir. 2006. 'Ot Kuiumby do Vankora' [From Kuiumba to Vankor], *Krasnoiarskii rabochii*, 2 September. http://www.krasrab.com/archive/2006/09/02/07/view_article. Accessed on 30 December 2016.

Paxton, Robin and Vladimir Soldatkin. 2009. 'China lends Russia $25 billion to get 20 years of oil', *Reuters*, 17 February. http://uk.reuters.com/article/uk-russia-china-oil-sb-idUKTRE51G3S620090217. Accessed on 22 December 2016.

Platts. 2015. 'China to double Russia ESPO pipeline imports to 30 mil mt/year in Oct 2017', 17 September. https://www.platts.com/latest-news/oil/singapore/china-to-double-russia-espo-pipeline-imports-27812989. Accessed on 3 July 2017.

Pravda.ru. 2016. 'China to join anti-Russian sanctions?' 9 February. http://www.pravdareport.com/news/world/09-02-2016/133287-china_russia_sanctions-0. Accessed on 30 December 2016.

Prelovskaia, Vera. 2014. 'Glavnye voprosy i otvety o "samom krupnom stroitel'nom proekte v mire"' [Highlights on 'the biggest construction project in the world'], *RBK*, 27 November. http://www.rbc.ru/magazine/2014/11/56bc7e8c9a794701b81d2ba3. Accessed on 30 December 2016.

Rosbalt.ru. 2016. 'SMI: Kitai podderzhal sanktsii protiv Rossii' [Media: China supported sanctions against Russia], 8 February. http://www.rosbalt.ru/world/2016/02/08/1487611.html. Accessed on 29 December 2016.

Røseth, Tom. 2017. 'Russia's energy relations with China: passing the strategic threshold?', *Eurasian Geography and Economics*, 58(1): 23–55.

Rosneft. 2016. '"Rosneft" i konsortsium indiiskikh investorov podpisali soglasheniia o vkhozhdenii v Vankorskii proekt' [Rosneft and consortium of Indian investors signed contract on joining Vankor project], 17 June. https://www.rosneft.ru/press/releases/item/182655. Accessed on 30 December 2016.

Sidortsov, Roman, Aytalina Ivanova and Florian Stammler. 2016. 'Localizing governance of systemic risks: a case study of the Power of Siberia pipeline in Russia', *Energy Research and Social Science* 16: 54–68.

Simola, Heli. 2016. 'Economic relations between Russia and China: increasing inter-dependency?' *BOFIT Policy Brief* 6. Helsinki: Bank of Finland.

Sputnik. 2016 'Vying for more: India to acquire stake in Russia's Vankor cluster', 13 October. https://sputniknews.com/business/201610131046295545-india-vankor-oil. Accessed on 21 February 2017.

TASS. 2014. 'Putin gives start to Power of Siberia gas pipeline construction', 1 September. http://tass.com/economy/747552. Accessed on 30 December 2016.

Trenin, Dmitry. 1999. *Russia's China problem*. Moscow: Carnegie Endowment for International Peace.

TV Tsentr. 2014. 'Patrushev: Rossiia i Kitai solidarny v svoikh vzgliadakh na ukrainskii krizis' [Patrushev: Russia and China hold similar views on Ukrainian crisis], 6 June. http://tvc.moscow/news/show/id/41593. Accessed on 30 December 2016.

Watkins, Eric. 2009. 'China, Russia agree on loans for ESPO pipeline spur', *Oil&Gas Journal*, 17 February. http://www.ogj.com/articles/2009/02/china-russia-agree-on-loans-for-espo-pipeline-spur.html. Accessed 30 December 2016.

White, Gregory L. and Guy Chazan. 2005. 'China lends Russia $6 billion to help finance Yukos deal', *The Wall Street Journal*, 2 February. http://www.wsj.com/articles/SB110728599279442584. Accessed on 22 December 2016.

Workman, Daniel. 2016. 'Crude oil imports by country', *World's Top Experts*, 10 September. http://www.worldstopexports.com/crude-oil-imports-by-country. Accessed on 9 February 2017.

Yamal LNG. 2015. 'About the project'. http://yamallng.ru/en/project/about. Accessed on 30 December 2016.

Yost, David. 2001. 'Russia's non-strategic nuclear forces', *International Affairs* 77(3): 531–51.

Zhang, Chi. 2015. *The domestic dynamics of China's energy diplomacy*. Singapore: World Scientific.

Zhang, Lihua. 2015. 'Explaining China's position on the Crimea referendum', *Carnegie-Tsinghua Center for Global Policy*, 1 April. http://carnegietsinghua. org/2015/04/01/explaining-china-s-position-on-crimea-referendum-pub-59600. Accessed on 30 December 2016.

Open Access This chapter is licensed under the terms of the Creative Commons Attribution 4.0 International License (http://creativecommons.org/licenses/by/4.0/), which permits use, sharing, adaptation, distribution and reproduction in any medium or format, as long as you give appropriate credit to the original author(s) and the source, provide a link to the Creative Commons license and indicate if changes were made.

The images or other third party material in this book are included in the book's Creative Commons license, unless indicated otherwise in a credit line to the material. If material is not included in the book's Creative Commons license and your intended use is not permitted by statutory regulation or exceeds the permitted use, you will need to obtain permission directly from the copyright holder.

CHAPTER 7

Russia, China and the Shanghai Cooperation Organization: Diverging Security Interests and the 'Crimea Effect'

Marc Lanteigne

Abstract The Shanghai Cooperation Organization (SCO) is an emerging security community created in 2001 to address looming threats, including terrorism and separatism, in the Central Asian region. China and Russia remain the major shapers of the SCO; but in recent years, differences over how the organization should evolve have begun to drive a subtle yet growing wedge between the two powers. Impending challenges related to expansion (India and Pakistan became full members in 2017), deepening Sino-Russian rifts (with China pushing for a stronger economic role for the organization, and Russia being more interested in hard security) and the 'shadow of Crimea' are likely to impede any Sino-Russian alliance in the foreseeable future.

Keywords Shanghai Cooperation Organization • Security • Russia • China • Multilateralism

M. Lanteigne (✉)
Centre for Defence and Security Studies, Massey University, Auckland, New Zealand

© The Author(s) 2018
H. Blakkisrud, E. Wilson Rowe (eds.), *Russia's Turn to the East*, Global Reordering, https://doi.org/10.1007/978-3-319-69790-1_7

After a long period of isolation and, at times, open hostility, the end of the Cold War resulted in far more cordial diplomatic and strategic relations between Russia and China. Since the 1990s, there have been numerous examples of improved bilateral communication and cooperation, greater alignment of policies on regional security affairs, and sharing of mutual concerns about US-led security orders, including those in Asia and the Middle East. With the ascension to power of Xi Jinping in 2012 as President of China and the diplomatic and economic isolation of Russia in the wake of the 2014 annexation of Crimea, what has changed is the more pronounced shift in position in global hierarchies between these two great powers. China continues to move towards global power status in political, economic and strategic terms. By contrast, with the worsened relations between Moscow and the West, Russia is grappling with its own international status. While the Putin administration has experienced considerable ostracism over Ukraine, Beijing has continued to enhance its relations with Russia—but significant differences remain in the interests and viewpoints of the Kremlin and Beijing.

This chapter uses the case of the Shanghai Cooperation Organization (SCO) as a multilateral organization to argue that the 2014 Crimea crisis and the subsequent conflict in eastern Ukraine have further underscored the divergence in regional Eurasia policies between the SCO's two largest member states, Russia and China. Not only have the geopolitical and geostrategic aspects of the Ukraine crisis affected direct bilateral relations, they have also affected Sino-Russian behaviour within the SCO. While Russia continues to view the organization as a security regime with strong military dimensions, Beijing has pursued a more holistic and varied approach, accentuating the regime's security benefits while also seeking to develop a more expansive economic and diplomatic identity for the SCO. This chapter will also assert that it remains in Beijing's interest to keep the murky security situation in eastern Ukraine at arm's length, while maintaining its approach to Russia as a valuable, if often problematic, regional partner.

A Troubled Pivot: Russia's Turn to East Asia Under Putin

Around the time of the Crimea crisis, China and Russia reached significant agreements in the areas of economic cooperation, as exemplified by the May 2014 natural gas agreement reportedly worth USD 400 billion (*RT*

2014; Savic 2016), as well as in strategic areas. Moreover, even before the Crimea crisis, the Putin regime announced that, in view of the economic growth in the Asia-Pacific, East Asia would be a priority for Russian foreign policy. This proposed 'pivot to Asia' (Hill and Lo 2013; Storey and Tsvetov 2016) was an updated manifestation of the traditional 'West versus East'-debate, the two-headed eagle ideological alignment question which had beset Russia since the times of the Empire (Westwood 1988; Neumann 1996). However, the diplomatic isolation and economic sanctions imposed on Russia after 2014 prompted an intensified policy of engaging East Asia, and especially China, in a search for alternative economic partners.

Due to the differing power trajectories of Beijing and Moscow, and their divergent views of regional and global security priorities, the possibility of a formal alliance between the two remains remote. Despite China's growth as a great power, Beijing has maintained a 'neo-Westphalian' policy stance, reflecting the idea that hegemonic power should not be overtly sought, and that great-power intervention in the domestic affairs of other states, especially developing ones, should be eschewed (Harris 2014, pp.1–23; Lanteigne 2016, p.9; Zhang 2016, pp.245–66). Such interventions should be undertaken only as a method of last resort, optimally through multilateral channels such as the UN Security Council. These concerns stem from China's long and difficult history of being subjected to colonialism in the pre-Maoist era, as well as China's status as a developing state sandwiched between two ambitious superpowers for much of the twentieth century (Wang 2012, pp.17–69).

For a long time, Moscow also advanced ideas about non-intervention, and expressed reservations about US activist foreign and security policy. These concepts, and the sanctity of state sovereignty, were constant themes in official Russian discourse during the crises in Kosovo in 1999 and later in Iraq, Libya and Syria (Wilhelmsen 2014). As Russian Foreign Minister Sergei Lavrov argued during a UN General Assembly session in September 2014—incidentally some six months *after* Russia's own formal annexation of Crimea—'Shouldn't the General Assembly adopt a declaration on the inadmissibility of interference into domestic affairs of sovereign states and non-recognition of *coups d'état* as a method of the change of power?' (quoted in Gladstone 2014).

However, these views were being expressed while Russia under Putin was beginning to resist what was seen as ongoing US-led encroachment into the post-Soviet space that had been considered the Russian 'near abroad' since the breakup of the USSR. The Kremlin's unease over the 'colour revolutions'—the Georgian 'Rose Revolution' in 2003, the 2004 'Orange Revolution' in Ukraine and the 'Tulip Revolution' in Kyrgyzstan in 2005—was followed by the Russian intervention in Georgia in 2008, a warning that Moscow was reaching the end of its patience with what it saw as its rapidly declining sphere of influence in Eurasia (Allison 2008; Way 2008; Pallin and Westerlund 2009). The 2013–2014 'Euromaidan' protests in Kiev, the Russian annexation of Crimea and the ongoing low-intensity conflict in eastern Ukraine can therefore be considered a culmination of Kremlin concerns about lost power and a shift towards a more *realpolitik* approach to the question of non-intervention. The increase in Russian military support for the Bashar al-Assad regime in the Syrian civil war is another manifestation of this view (Bagdonas 2012; Charap 2013).[1]

The divergent standings in international relations/hierarchies and views on sovereignty and non-intervention are key factors in understanding the evolving Sino-Russian relationship, especially in the security realm. Despite ongoing agreements and cordiality between the Putin and Xi governments, Russia after Crimea has begun to deviate more sharply from Chinese strategic thinking. In addition to the bilateral relationship, the policies of China and Russia within the SCO, the most mature security regime in Eurasia since its creation in 2001, provide stark evidence of these differing views. While the two great powers continue to seek ways of strengthening their relationship, including within the SCO, the possibility of a Sino-Russian alliance and the transformation of the SCO as a platform for such a pact is a non-starter. This was evident even before the events of 2014, but the post-Crimea crises have driven a sharper wedge between China and Russia over the trajectory of the SCO as well as the organization's developing identity.

The Shanghai Cooperation Organization: An Overview

Since the 1990s, Chinese policies on multilateral security have indicated greater acceptance of the need for regional-level problem solving. This view supports Russia's concerns about maintaining security in its 'near abroad', especially among the still-fragile states in Central Asia. Both great powers have also been wary of the Cold-War-era hierarchical and alliance-based forms of cooperation (such as the North Atlantic Treaty Organization

[NATO]) favoured by the West, arguing that modern security problems necessitate new thinking on more effective cooperation in addressing threats above the state level. It was also during the 1990s that Beijing decided to depart from its traditional reluctance to shape regional security norms and organizations directly, and to assume a more active role in developing new tools to address security problems—especially on its periphery.

The most visible example of converging Sino-Russian policies has been the founding of the SCO, which grew out of the 'Shanghai Five' dialogues on ensuring peaceful regional development and settling leftover border disputes from the Soviet era (for more on the 'Shanghai Five' and the roots of the SCO, see the next section). The SCO brings together China, Russia and most of Central Asia, along with four observers, and six 'dialogue partners'. The membership was extended further outwards with a 2016 agreement welcoming former SCO observer states India and Pakistan as full members in 2017 (Ministry of Foreign Affairs of the Republic of Uzbekistan 2016). Turkmenistan, the only former Soviet Central Asian republic which is not a SCO member, periodically sends representatives to its meetings as 'guests', but remains outside the organization due to the country's commitment to 'permanent' or 'endless' neutrality (Polese and Horák 2015). Guest delegations have also been sent by the Association of Southeast Asian Nations (ASEAN) and the Moscow-led Commonwealth of Independent States (CIS). In November 2016, Turkish President Recep Tayyip Erdoğan announced Turkey's imminent application for full SCO membership as his government continued to distance itself from the West (Hasanova 2016) (Table 7.1).

Table 7.1 From the Shanghai Five to the SCO

Shanghai Five 1996–2001	Shanghai Cooperation Organization 2001–present		
Members	Members	Observers	Dialogue partners
China	China	Afghanistan	Armenia
Kazakhstan	India	Belarus	Azerbaijan
Kyrgyzstan	Kazakhstan	Iran	Cambodia
Russian Federation	Kyrgyzstan	Mongolia	Nepal
Tajikistan	Pakistan		Sri Lanka
	Russian Federation		Turkey
	Tajikistan		
	Uzbekistan		

The SCO's initial mandate was to promote regional security and to protect its members from non-state security threats—especially terrorist organizations, ranging from local groups to more globalized entities such as al-Qaeda. The creation of the SCO could also be considered proof of the old axiom of nature abhorring a vacuum, as security cooperation in the region had previously been weak and untethered. SCO policymakers have frequently stressed that the organization is not an alliance, and is not balancing against the West or any other state-actor adversary; indeed, this position is codified in the organization's 2002 Charter (SCO 2002).

Moscow still acts as a 'big brother' in much of Eurasian politics and security; but in recent years, China has become a key economic partner for Central Asia, especially with the development (since 2013) of the 'Belt and Road' trade routes, featuring extensive participation by the states of Central Asia and Caucasus—as well as Russia—as conduits for overland trade between China and Europe (*China Daily* 2013; Putz 2016). The United States, by contrast, began to disengage from the region under the Obama administration. Although there were signs by the incoming Trump administration that US forces would remain in Afghanistan, US forces continue to be withdrawn from Afghanistan, albeit more slowly than predicted. The last US base in Central Asia, at Manas in Kyrgyzstan, was closed in 2014 (Pillalamarri 2014; Roberts 2016).

The decision to extend SCO membership to India and Pakistan significantly expands the geographic reach of the organization, and adds the considerable security problems of South Asia, such as the Kashmir conflict, to the SCO's already extensive agenda. The inclusion of India was a divisive issue, since Beijing was concerned about a dilution of its own role in the SCO, while Moscow viewed Indian membership as a way of checking Beijing's formidable influence within the group. Unlike the cordial India–Russia relations under the governments of Putin and Indian Prime Minister Narendra Modi, Sino-Indian relations have been quite cool during the past decade. This is due not least to periodic incursions by Chinese military forces into the two countries' border regions, including the April 2013 incident when a detachment of People's Liberation Army (PLA) forces camped for over a week in the disputed Daulat Beg Oldi area of Ladakh (Misra 2013, p.66). For its part, New Delhi remains concerned that China's economic diplomacy in South Asia—especially with Myanmar, Pakistan, Seychelles and Sri Lanka—may amount to a *de facto* containment plan against India's regional strategic interests. In this context, the India–Iran Chabahar development project agreed to in May 2016 can be a seen as a move countering China's ambitious port projects in the Indian Ocean (Hantke 2016; *The Hindu* 2016). The question remains whether the 2017 expansion of the SCO might diminish its decision-making power while unwittingly creating an arena for tacit China–India–Russia strategic competition.

The Putin regime has also supported Iran's interest in membership status—possibly further complicating the SCO's agenda, given ongoing questions about Teheran's nuclear development, and perhaps further diluting Beijing's status within the group. Given the Iranian nuclear question, Iranian admission could raise Western suspicions of the SCO, especially given the Trump administration's hostility towards Iran and opposition to the 2015 Iranian nuclear deal, and might significantly affect the SCO's official stance, supported by China, of non-alignment. Nonetheless, in June 2017, the Chinese Foreign Ministry publicly expressed its support for Teheran to become a member (Yang 2017). On the plus side for Beijing, Iranian membership may serve to bring China closer to Middle East affairs and markets, a region of growing importance for Beijing.

Sino-Russian Relations and the Evolution of the SCO

The SCO was a product of the 'Shanghai Five' border dialogues in the late 1990s. In April 1996, China, Kazakhstan, Kyrgyzstan, Russia and Tajikistan signed a Five-Power Agreement in Shanghai. In addition to settling outstanding Soviet-era border concerns, the agreement regulated military activity in the frontier regions, prohibited provocative military exercises in those areas and called for strategic information-sharing, the conduct of joint exercises and increased military contacts among signatory states (Allen 2001, p.235).

In the bilateral Sino-Russian context, the agreement paved the way for more frequent meetings between military officials, more inspections and additional Chinese purchases of Russian weaponry. It also served to reduce tensions on a previously very tense borderland and provided another conduit for Sino-Russian cooperation. The final rounds of bilateral Sino-Russian border negotiations were completed in 2004, further improving the strategic relationship and the climate for bilateral trade discussions (Wilhelmsen and Flikke 2011, pp.872–73)—not least on sales of fossil fuels, necessary to China because of its rapidly expanding economy.

All five signatories agreed to maintain coordination of shared security concerns; the Shanghai Five thus became an important mechanism for Russia, China and Central Asia to address their strategic interests. By the end of the 1990s, the Taliban movement occupied most of Afghanistan, and nearby states became increasingly worried about the potential for spillover from that conflict into greater Eurasia. As a result, the region's 'three evils'—terrorism, extremism and 'splittism'/separatism—overtook border security concerns as the primary concern of the Shanghai Five (Chung 2004, pp.990–91). In addition to the Taliban, other regional terrorist threats included the Islamic Movement of Uzbekistan (IMU), a group dedicated to the overthrow of the Uzbek government and the establishment of a unified Islamic state in Central Asia, and the *Hizb-ut Tahrir al-Islami*, or Party of Islamic Liberation, which, despite its advocacy of non-violent struggle, was also viewed as a security risk, given its stated goal of establishing an Islamic caliphate in Central Asia (ICG 2002).

Beijing for its part had ongoing concerns about extremist activities in its Far West seeking to destabilize Chinese rule. The most prominent of these groups was the East Turkestan Independence Movement (ETIM), now known as the Turkistan Islamic Party (TIP) (Reed and Raschke 2010, pp.46–67). Since first being identified by Beijing in 2002, ETIM/TIP has been blamed for fomenting instability in China's Xinjiang region through bombings and attacks. Beijing has also linked the group to the larger al-Qaeda network (Sheives 2006, pp.209–10). For its part, TIP has claimed responsibility for a terrorist bombing in Beijing's Tiananmen Square in October 2013 and a knife attack at the Kunming train station in March 2014 (Buckley 2014; Kaiman 2013; Holdstock 2015).

The Shanghai Five assumed greater formalization and international visibility in 2001 when, on the occasion of welcoming Uzbekistan into the group, a declaration was signed which formed the genesis of the SCO. Shortly thereafter, the 9/11 terrorist attacks occurred in the United States, further globalizing terrorism and highlighting the danger of extremism in Central Asia. The newly created SCO faced the challenges of deepening its security agenda, trying to balance strategic and non-strategic cooperation, and ensuring cooperation between Russia and China.

The organization's official charter, unveiled at its second conference in St Petersburg in June 2002, described the SCO's mandate as building 'mutual trust, friendship and good neighbourliness' while encouraging 'comprehensive cooperation' in security and related areas (SCO 2002).

The document also introduced a Regional Anti-Terrorism Structure (RATS) to act as an information nexus for regional security. Based in Tashkent, RATS is currently the only such centre operating in Central Asia (Gill 2007, pp.130–31). Two years later, in 2004, a permanent SCO Secretariat was established in Beijing, with former Chinese Ambassador to Russia, Zhang Deguang, appointed as the organization's first secretary-general.[2]

The SCO has sought to coordinate joint military operations to improve confidence among members while creating a coordinated policy against potential threats. The first such exercises were held by China and Kyrgyzstan in October 2002, but were expanded to include all members except Uzbekistan in August of the following year (Chung 2006, p.10). The 2005 Peace Mission manoeuvres, conducted in the vicinity of Vladivostok, Russia, and in Weifang, Shandong Province, China, included joint strategic planning and a simulated offshore blockade and amphibious landing (Cohen 2006, p.56). Despite the apparent hard-security dimensions of the simulation, it was officially described as an anti-terror exercise. This pattern has continued: For example, the 2016 Peace Mission, held for the first time in Kyrgyzstan, included exercises involving the deployment of heavy weaponry as well as practice drills with air-to-air missiles (Kucera 2016).

Despite the regularity of the Peace Missions, there has not always been agreement between China and Russia as to their planning. For example, Beijing was unwilling to conduct the 2007 Peace Mission exercises in tandem with the Russia-dominated Collective Security Treaty Organization (CSTO) (Deng 2007). The latter includes all SCO members except for China and Uzbekistan, and the staunch Russian allies Armenia and Belarus.

Security Debates Within the SCO

The omnipresent military dimension of the SCO has led to debate over whether the organization is acting as the genesis of an eventual alliance or a possibly stronger anti-Western axis. However, these concerns are tempered by geopolitical realities that influence the differing security viewpoints of the two great powers; Sino-Russian policy differences have called into question the SCO's degree of leverage versus the West (Fels 2009, pp.23–28).

The relationship between the SCO and the CSTO remains a subject of debate. Beijing was not pleased about the recommendation introduced at the 2014 SCO Dushanbe summit of a merger between the two organizations (Salimov 2014). As the SCO has evolved, China has been comparatively much more enthusiastic than Russia about promoting the organization as a multifaceted entity with a strong economic and developmental dimension to match its security identity. Russia, by contrast, has been more supportive of the SCO as a regional power nexus to counter the West. For example, in 2008, Leonid Ivashov, General-Colonel and President of the Academy of Geopolitical Problems, made the now-notorious suggestion that the SCO should develop into 'the world's second pole' (Ivashov 2008).

Beijing has shared Moscow's unease about the 'colour revolutions' in the former Soviet space, with both powers tending to view those events as external interference designed to promote alternative pro-Western regimes (Shambaugh 2008, pp.87–92). Since the creation of the People's Republic in 1949, Beijing has been wary of Western attempts to undermine the legitimacy of the communist government, a process frequently denigrated as 'peaceful evolution' in Chinese policy circles. The Tulip Revolution in Kyrgyzstan prompted considerable internal debate in Beijing about regional security, leading to promises made by the government of Hu Jintao to fight a 'smokeless war' against 'liberal elements' seeking to destabilize China as they were apparently seeking to do in Central Asia (Kahn 2005). However, Beijing has been less enthusiastic than Moscow about using hard military means. During the July 2015 SCO Summit in Ufa, Russia, a recommendation by Russian Defence Minister Sergei Shoigu that the organization consider a more formal alliance which could serve to block any future 'colour revolutions' in Eurasia received a cold response from Beijing (Blank 2015).

The SCO has enabled Chinese policymakers to enhance regional friendship policies, adding weight to Beijing's policies of 'peaceful development' and becoming a 'responsible great power' via deeper engagement with regional economic and strategic organizations well beyond Eurasia or the Asia-Pacific (Glaser and Medeiros 2007; Johnston 2008, pp.148–49). In a 2013 speech at Nazarbayev University in Astana, Kazakhstan, Chinese President Xi Jinping described the fundamentals of a new 'Twenty-First-Century Silk Road' trade network, which later became a main component of the Chinese Belt and Road initiative (*China Daily* 2013). Xi also commented on the possibility of several regional organizations aligning more closely, specifically focusing on the potential for greater cooperation between the SCO and the Eurasian Economic Community (EAEC)

(Xi 2014, p.317). In January 2015, the latter organization became the Eurasian Economic Union (EAEU), an organization dedicated to improving economic integration policies in the post-Soviet space.

Another example of differences between Beijing and Moscow over the 'non-security' identity of the SCO emerged in November 2016, when Chinese Premier Li Keqiang, in an attempt to further the economic dimension of the organization, recommended the creation of an SCO free trade zone, a long-standing interest in Beijing ever since the establishment of the SCO. However, Russian Prime Minister Medvedev responded by noting that such a regime would be a 'complicated matter given that any preferential regime always requires renunciation of internal decisions of one kind or another' (Russian Government 2016). Li also proposed the creation of an SCO-sponsored bank and development fund—another idea which was met with Russian misgivings.[3]

Despite statements stressing organizational unity following major SCO meetings, the separate policy directions favoured by the two great powers have become an open secret. In the wake of Russia's interventionist regional policies and the increasingly globalist foreign policies of Xi, evidence that Sino-Russian policies within the SCO are divaricating has mounted.

Georgia and Ukraine: The Cracks Get Wider?

China's powerful position in Central Asia enabled the SCO to construct the most visible model of Beijing's 'New Security Concept' policies, developed at the end of the Cold War and stressing the widespread use of informal strategic cooperation and community-building rather than hierarchical alliances such as NATO (Foot 2006, p.85). With the Kremlin assuming a more assertive role in the post-Soviet space, China, despite unease with Russia's turn towards unilateral intervention (in Georgia and then in Crimea/eastern Ukraine), attempted to maintain its commitments to Russian ties and the development of the SCO.

Russia's August 2008 military intervention in the disputed Georgian territories of Abkhazia and South Ossetia, under the aegis of 'peace enforcement', was not well received by Beijing or the other SCO members. Although they recognized Russia's peacekeeping roles in the Caucasus, there was no SCO endorsement of the intervention despite Moscow's attempts to obtain the organization's formal backing. Chinese concerns about the Russia–Georgia conflict were numerous, including what was perceived as the circumvention of core Chinese views on the sanctity of borders and non-intervention policies, which Beijing hoped would be highlighted by the SCO. Concerns about a 'demonstration effect', especially after Russia called for the recognition of Abkhazia and South Ossetia as independent entities following the conflict, prompted China's relative silence on the crisis, save for a suggestion by a Foreign Ministry spokesperson that the conflict could be referred to the United Nations (Barriaux 2008; Liu 2016, p.151; Ministry of Foreign Affairs of the People's Republic of China 2008). The fact that military action began on the eve of the Beijing Summer Olympic Games, intended as a 'coming-out party' for China on the global stage, did not help to mollify concerns in Beijing.

Difficult relations between Russia and Georgia since 2008 (Georgia withdrew from the CIS in August 2008 in protest at the Russian military actions) provided an opening for China to improve its own ties with Tbilisi. Beijing has declined to grant official recognition to the two breakaway republics, maintaining its diplomatic relations with Georgia and commencing bilateral free trade agreement (FTA) talks with Tbilisi in December 2015. The agreement, signed in May 2017, is the first FTA Beijing has concluded with a former Soviet republic.[4] Georgia is also expected to be a component of the Silk Road overland trade routes, given its location, the potential for infrastructure development and the opportunity for Beijing to balance Russian interests in the Caucasus (Topuria 2016; *Xinhua* 2016). However, Chinese shipping through Georgia remains underdeveloped compared to the primary routes through Kazakhstan and Russia.

Russia's annexation of Crimea and the Russia-backed establishment in 2014 of 'people's republics' in Donetsk and Luhansk in eastern Ukraine were also challenges for Chinese diplomacy and its ability to juggle its Russian and Ukrainian interests. Russian involvement in the fighting in eastern Ukraine, and the July 2014 downing of a Malaysian civilian jetliner over rebel-held territories, allegedly by pro-Russian separatist forces, created a toxic diplomatic atmosphere between Russia and Europe and the United States. Beijing responded to these events by seeking to reconcile its Russian diplomacy with its stance on non-intervention in sovereign state affairs. At the 2014 SCO Summit in Dushanbe, Putin failed to secure formal support for Russia's interpretation of the Ukraine crisis:

The summit declaration simply called for the restoration of peace through negotiations in war-torn eastern Ukraine (Lillis 2014).

Official statements from the Chinese government reiterated the country's long-standing policy that the territorial sovereignty of states be maintained, but stopped short of criticizing Russian actions. China did not support economic sanctions introduced by the United States and Europe. In March 2014, a Chinese Foreign Ministry spokesperson stated that while Beijing recognized and respected the role of non-interference and international law, 'we take into account the historical facts and realistic complexity of the Ukrainian issue' (Ministry of Foreign Affairs of the People's Republic of China 2014). During a May 2014 UN Security Council vote on non-recognition of the referendum on Crimean 'independence', China chose to abstain rather than join Russia in exercising a veto. Despite its hesitancy to align overtly against Russia, Beijing was anxious to avoid being labelled a 'spoiler' in this conflict. China has proceeded to promote a non-aligned approach to the question of Crimean sovereignty, and has maintained that the conflict in eastern Ukraine is best settled through negotiation (*Reuters* 2015).

This 'double game' being played out in bilateral relations between Beijing and Moscow is likely to dominate discussion on the future of the SCO as a security community and as a strategic actor. The cases of Georgia and Crimea provide insights into the divergence of ideas between China and Russia in regard to Eurasian diplomacy and the evolution of the organization. Moreover, within the SCO, these issues indicate growing unease on the part of Beijing over Russia's longer-term security interests in Eurasia, as well as Moscow's overall political health in light of its post-2014 diplomatic ostracism. During World War I, a German general was said to have bitterly commented about his country's main ally, the peremptory but decaying Austro-Hungarian Empire: 'we are shackled to a corpse' (Taylor 2013, p.9). China very much wants to avoid that type of scenario, especially should power levels between the two great powers continue to diverge as China continues to grow to potential global power status. A likely wild card is the difficult relationship between the United States under Trump and the Putin regime (MacFarquar 2016), but also the differences between Trump and President Xi over economic and strategic issues. Beijing continues to view Russia as a close friend, but retains its interest in balancing hawkish Russian policies within the SCO, and eschewing the possibility of a formal alliance either bilaterally or within the SCO itself.

Conclusions: Same Bed, Different Dreams?

Concerning intervention, it has been argued that Russia has taken on the role of a 'loud dissenter', repelling perceived unfair Western norms, while China has assumed the persona of a 'cautious partner', affiliating informally with Russia but stopping well short of formal alignment with Moscow, including within the confines of the SCO (Snetkov and Lanteigne 2015). Although it can be argued that policy divergence between China and Russia regarding SCO policy and identity existed long before the post-2014 Ukraine crisis, the annexation of Crimea and conflict in eastern Ukraine, like the Georgia conflict before it, have illustrated the widening of policy trajectories of the two great powers. Within the SCO, there remain fundamental differences regarding both the ideal security identity of the organization and the degree to which non-security issues such as economic cooperation should be incorporated within its framework.

Although military cooperation and coordination continue, including the Peace Mission exercises, Beijing remains wary of the SCO becoming a formal alliance as well as potentially affecting vital economic relations with the United States and its allies. At the May 2014 summit of the Conference on Interaction and Confidence Building Measures in Asia (CICA), the Xi government called for a new 'Asian' security concept (*Xinhua* 2014). Beijing has, however, compared with Moscow, preferred more comprehensive approaches to security cooperation. The Belt and Road agreements, potentially enhancing Chinese economic relations across Eurasia as well as with Europe, show that China sees security in these regions as important, but also as part of a larger diplomatic process that includes development, transportation and communication. The 2017 expansion of the SCO may pose challenges for Beijing as it seeks to prevent its voice being muted because of the inclusion of big powers India and Pakistan. However, there are also opportunities for China to better utilize an expanded SCO to further its Belt and Road economic and strategic interests, especially if further expansion to include Iran and Turkey takes place.

With China politically and economically developing a more independent and activist foreign policy, Beijing considers itself the alternative major power in Eurasian development. The SCO, a security organization still establishing its identity, has been at the forefront of Beijing's efforts to expand its strategic interests in Eurasia and solidify its security and, increasingly, its economic interests in this pivotal region. However, the case of the SCO further underscores Beijing's interests in retaining Russia as a valuable strategic partner, while also maintaining a discreet 'agree to disagree' stance on Moscow's post-Crimea Eurasian strategic policies.

Notes

1. The Bashar al-Assad government in Syria is one of Moscow's few remaining friends in the Middle East. Russia maintains a naval base at Tartus and, starting in September 2015, Russia has been active in military operations against the Islamic State.
2. The current SCO Secretary-General is Tajikistani diplomat Rashid Olimov, who assumed the position in January 2016 and who is expected to oversee the organization and its expansion until 2018 (*Global Times* 2016).
3. Under Xi, China was the driving force behind the establishment of a range of new financial institutions, including the Asian Infrastructure Investment Bank (AIIB) and the New Development Bank (NDB), in addition to the Silk Road Fund attached to the Belt and Road initiatives. Russia was a founding member of both the AIIB and the NDB.
4. Moldova, another ex-Soviet state experiencing erratic relations with Moscow, agreed in September 2016 to commence FTA talks in 2017 (*TASS* 2016; *Xinhua* 2017).

References

Allen, Kenneth W. 2001. 'Confidence-building measures and the People's Liberation Army', in *Remaking the Chinese state: strategies, society and security*, edited by Chien-min Chao and Bruce J. Dickson, 228–56. London: Routledge.

Allison, Roy. 2008. 'Moscow's campaign to "coerce Georgia to peace"', *International Affairs* 84(6): 1145–71.

Bagdonas, Azuolas. 2012. 'Russia's interests in the Syrian conflict: power, prestige, and profit', *European Journal of Economic and Political Studies* 5(2): 55–77.

Barriaux, Marianne. 2008. 'China cannot back Russia in Georgia crisis: analysts', *AFP*, 30 August. http://macaudailytimes.com.mo/archive-2007-2009/china-cannot-back-russia-in-georgia-crisis-analysts.html. Accessed on 18 February 2017.

Blank, Stephen. 2015. 'Was the SCO Summit in Ufa a breakthrough?' *CACI Analyst*, 19 August. https://www.cacianalyst.org/publications/analytical-articles/item/13261-was-the-sco-summit-in-ufa-a-breakthrough?.html. Accessed on 18 February 2017.

Buckley, Chris. 2014. 'Attackers with knives kill 29 at Chinese rail station', *The New York Times*, 1 March. https://www.nytimes.com/2014/03/02/world/asia/china.html. Accessed on 18 February 2017.

Charap, Samuel. 2013. 'Russia, Syria and the doctrine of intervention', *Survival* 55(1): 35–41.
China Daily. 2013. 'President Xi proposes Silk Road economic belt', 7 September. http://www.chinadaily.com.cn/china/2013xivisitcenterasia/2013-09/07/content_16951811.htm. Accessed on 18 February 2017.
Chung, Chien-peng. 2004. 'The Shanghai Cooperation Organization: China's changing influence in Central Asia', *The China Quarterly* 180 (December): 989–1009.
Chung, Chien-peng. 2006. 'China and the institutionalization of the Shanghai Cooperation Organization', *Problems of Post-Communism* 53(5): 3–14.
Cohen, Ariel. 2006. 'After the G-8 summit: China and the Shanghai Cooperation Organization', *China and Eurasia Forum Quarterly* 4(3): 51–64.
Deng, Yong. 2007. 'Remoulding great power politics: China's strategic partnerships with Russia, the European Union, and India', *Journal of Strategic Studies* 30(4–5): 863–903.
Fels, Enrico. 2009. *Assessing Eurasia's powerhouse: an inquiry into the nature of the Shanghai Cooperation Organisation.* Bochum: Verlag Dr. Dieter Winkler.
Foot, Rosemary. 2006. 'Chinese strategies in a US-hegemonic global order: accommodating and hedging', *International Affairs* 82(1): 77–94.
Gill, Bates. 2007. *Rising star: China's new security diplomacy.* Washington, DC: Brookings Institution Press.
Gladstone, Rick. 2014. 'Russian diplomat's speech depicts the West as hypocritical', *The New York Times,* 28 September. https://www.nytimes.com/2014/09/28/world/russian-diplomats-speech-depicts-the-west-as-hypocritical.html?_r=0. Accessed on 18 February 2017.
Glaser, Bonnie S. and Evan S. Medeiros. 2007. 'The changing ecology of foreign policy-making in China: the ascension and demise of the theory of "peaceful rise"', *The China Quarterly* 190 (June): 291–310.
Global Times. 2016. 'China stresses security cooperation as new SCO Secretary-General takes office', 27 January. http://www.globaltimes.cn/content/965922.shtml. Accessed on 18 February 2017.
Hantke, André. 2016. 'Will India and Pakistan cripple the SCO?' *The Diplomat,* 9 November. http://thediplomat.com/2016/11/will-india-and-pakistan-cripple-the-sco. Accessed on 18 February 2017.
Harris, Stuart. 2014. *China's foreign policy.* Cambridge: Polity Press.
Hasanova, Gunay. 2016. 'Turkey eyes joining SCO', *Azernews,* 21 November. http://www.azernews.az/region/105405.html. Accessed on 18 February 2017.
Hill, Fiona and Bobo Lo. 2013. 'Putin's pivot: why Russia is looking east', *Foreign Affairs,* 31 July. https://www.foreignaffairs.com/articles/russian-federation/2013-07-31/putins-pivot. Accessed on 18 February 2017.

The Hindu. 2016. 'India to develop Iran's Chabahar port', 24 May. http://www.thehindu.com/news/national/India-to-develop-Irans-Chabahar-port/article14336893.ece. Accessed on 18 February 2017.

Holdstock, Nick. 2015. *China's forgotten people: Xinjiang, terror and the Chinese state.* London: I.B. Tauris.

ICG. 2002. 'The IMU and the Hizb-ut Tahrir: implications of the Afghanistan campaign', 30 January. https://www.crisisgroup.org/europe-central-asia/central-asia/uzbekistan/imu-and-hizb-ut-tahrir-implications-afghanistan-campaign. Accessed on 18 February 2017.

Ivashov, Leonid. 2008. 'Heartland expanding, or the Shanghai Cooperation Organization', 8 January. http://pocombelles.over-blog.com/article-24832397.html. Accessed on 18 February 2017.

Johnston, Alastair Iain. 2008. *Social states: China in international institutions, 1980–2000.* Princeton, NJ: Princeton University Press.

Kahn, Joseph. 2005. 'China's leader, ex-rival at side, solidifies power', *The New York Times*, 25 September. http://www.nytimes.com/2005/09/25/world/asia/chinas-leader-exrival-at-side-solidifies-power.html. Accessed on 18 February 2017.

Kaiman, Jonathan. 2013. 'Islamist group claims responsibility for attack on China's Tiananmen Square', *The Guardian*, 25 November. https://www.theguardian.com/world/2013/nov/25/islamist-china-tiananmen-beijing-attack. Accessed on 18 February 2017.

Kucera, Joshua. 2016. 'SCO starts first-ever military exercises in Kyrgyzstan', *Eurasianet.org*, 19 September. http://www.eurasianet.org/node/80566. Accessed on 18 February 2017.

Lanteigne, Marc. 2016. *Chinese foreign policy: an introduction.* 3rd ed. New York: Routledge.

Lillis, Joanna. 2014. 'Putin fails to win Ukraine consensus at SCO Summit', *Eurasianet.org*, 12 September. http://www.eurasianet.org/node/69961. Accessed on 18 February 2017.

Liu, Guoli. 2016. *China rising: Chinese foreign policy in a changing world.* New York: Palgrave.

MacFarquar, Neil. 2016. 'With Trump, Russia goes from Thursday's foe of U.S. to Friday's friend', *The New York Times*, 31 December. https://www.nytimes.com/2016/12/31/world/europe/trump-russia-us-foe-to-friend.html?_r=0. Accessed on 18 February 2017.

Ministry of Foreign Affairs of the People's Republic of China. 2008. 'Foreign Ministry spokesperson Jiang Yu's regular press conference on September 4, 2008', http://houston.china-consulate.org/eng/nv/fyrth/t513362.htm. Accessed on 18 February 2017.

Ministry of Foreign Affairs of the People's Republic of China. 2014. 'Foreign Ministry spokesperson Qin Gang's regular press conference on March 4, 2014'.

http://www.china-un.org/eng/fyrth/t1134077.htm. Accessed on 18 February 2017.
Ministry of Foreign Affairs of the Republic of Uzbekistan. 2016. 'The Tashkent Declaration of the Fifteenth Anniversary of the Shanghai Cooperation Organization'. 26 June. http://www.mfa.uz/en/press/sco-uzbekistan/2016/06/7780. Accessed on 18 February 2017.
Misra, Ashutosh. 2013. 'Will the emerging India ever arrive?' *Griffith Asia Journal* 1(1): 53–78.
Neumann, Iver B. 1996. *Russia and the idea of Europe: a study in identity and international relations*. London: Routledge.
Pallin, Carolina Vendil and Fredrik Westerlund. 2009. 'Russia's war in Georgia: lessons and consequences', *Small Wars and Insurgencies* 20(2): 400–24.
Pillalamarri, Akhilesh. 2014. 'The United States just closed its last base in Central Asia', *The Diplomat*, 10 June. http://thediplomat.com/2014/06/the-united-states-just-closed-its-last-base-in-central-asia. Accessed on 18 February 2017.
Polese, Abel and Slavomir Horák. 2015. 'A tale of two presidents: personality cult and symbolic nation-building in Turkmenistan', *Nationalities Papers* 43(3): 457–78.
Putz, Catherine. 2016. 'China pushes One Belt, One Road in Central Asia', *The Diplomat*, 24 May. http://thediplomat.com/2016/05/china-pushes-one-belt-one-road-in-central-asia. Accessed on 18 February 2017.
Reed, J. Todd and Diana Raschke. 2010. *The ETIM: China's Islamic militants and the global terrorist threat*. Santa Barbara, CA: Praeger.
Reuters. 2015. 'China premier says respects Ukraine integrity, won't be drawn on Crimea', 15 March. http://www.reuters.com/article/us-china-parliament-ukraine idUSKBN0MB05220150315. Accessed on 18 February 2017.
Roberts, Dan. 2016. 'Obama delays US troop withdrawal from "precarious" Afghanistan', *The Guardian*, 6 July. https://www.theguardian.com/us-news/2016/jul/06/obama-delays-us-troop-withdrawal-afghanistan-al-qaida. Accessed on 18 February 2017.
RT. 2014. 'Russia and China seal historic $400bn gas deal', 21 May. https://www.rt.com/business/160068-china-russia-gas-deal. Accessed on 18 February 2017.
Russian Government. 2016. 'Meeting of the SCO Council of Heads of Government', 3 November. http://government.ru/en/news/25170. Accessed on 18 February 2017.
Salimov, Oleg. 2014. 'SCO-CSTO merger raised at Dushanbe Conference', *CACI Analyst*, 4 June. https://www.cacianalyst.org/publications/field-reports/item/12983-sco-csto-merger-raised-at-dushanbe-conference.html. Accessed on 18 February 2017.
Savic, Bob. 2016. 'Behind China and Russia's "special relationship"', *The Diplomat*, 7 December. http://thediplomat.com/2016/12/behind-china-and-russias-special-relationship. Accessed on 18 February 2017.

SCO. 2002. 'Shanghai Cooperation Organisation Charter'. http://www.soi.org.br/upload/34b4f65564132e7702726ee2521839c790b895453b6de5509cf1f997e9e50405.pdf. Accessed on 18 February 2017.
Shambaugh, David. 2008. *China's Communist Party: atrophy and adaptation*. Berkeley, CA: University of California Press.
Sheives, Kevin. 2006. 'China turns West: Beijing's contemporary strategy towards Central Asia', *Pacific Affairs* 79(2): 205–24.
Snetkov, Aglaya and Marc Lanteigne. 2015. '"The loud dissenter and its cautious partner" – Russia, China, global governance and humanitarian intervention', *International Relations of the Asia-Pacific* 15(1): 113–46.
Storey, Ian and Anton Tsvetov. 2016. 'The limits to Russia's pivot to Asia', *Wall Street Journal*, 18 May.
TASS. 2016. 'Moldova plans to sign free trade agreement with China', 14 September. http://tass.com/economy/899656. Accessed on 18 February 2017.
Taylor, Frederick. 2013. *The downfall of money: Germany's hyperinflation and the destruction of the middle class*. London: Bloomsbury.
Topuria, Rivaz. 2016. 'Georgia: the key to China's "Belt and Road"', *The Diplomat*, 28 April. http://thediplomat.com/2016/04/georgia-the-key-to-chinas-belt-and-road. Accessed on 18 February 2017.
Wang, Zheng. 2012. *Never forget national humiliation: historical memory in Chinese politics and international relations*. New York: Columbia University Press.
Way, Lucien. 2008. 'The real causes of colour revolutions', *Journal of Democracy* 19(3): 55–69.
Westwood, John N. 1988. *Endurance and endeavour: Russian history 1812–1986*. 3rd ed. Oxford: Oxford University Press.
Wilhelmsen, Julie. 2014. 'Russland, folkeretten og militær intervensjon: selektiv prinsippfasthet' [Russia, international law and military intervention: selective firmness of principles]. *Internasjonal Politikk* 72(1): 135–46.
Wilhelmsen, Julie and Geir Flikke. 2011. 'Chinese–Russian convergence and Central Asia', *Geopolitics* 16(4): 865–901.
Xi, Jinping. 2014. *The governance of China*. Beijing: Foreign Languages Press.
Xinhua. 2014. 'China focus: China's Xi proposes security concept for Asia', 21 May. http://news.xinhuanet.com/english/china/2014-05/21/c_133351210.htm. Accessed on 18 February 2017.
Xinhua. 2016. 'China, Georgia eye greater cooperation on Silk Road Economic Belt Initiative', 4 June. http://news.xinhuanet.com/english/2016-06/04/c_135411583.htm. Accessed on 18 February 2017.
Xinhua. 2017. 'China, Georgia ink free trade agreement', 14 May. http://news.xinhuanet.com/english/2017-05/14/c_136280144.htm. Accessed on 24 June 2017.

Yang, Sheng. 'SCO to expand as Xi attends summit', 6 June. http://www.globaltimes.cn/content/1050352.shtml. Accessed on 24 June 2017.

Zhang, Yunling. 2016. 'China and its neighbourhood: transformation, challenges and grand strategy', *International Affairs* 92(4): 245–66.

Open Access This chapter is licensed under the terms of the Creative Commons Attribution 4.0 International License (http://creativecommons.org/licenses/by/4.0/), which permits use, sharing, adaptation, distribution and reproduction in any medium or format, as long as you give appropriate credit to the original author(s) and the source, provide a link to the Creative Commons license and indicate if changes were made.

The images or other third party material in this book are included in the book's Creative Commons license, unless indicated otherwise in a credit line to the material. If material is not included in the book's Creative Commons license and your intended use is not permitted by statutory regulation or exceeds the permitted use, you will need to obtain permission directly from the copyright holder.

CHAPTER 8

Russia's New Asian Tilt: How Much Does Economy Matter?

Roman Vakulchuk

Abstract The economic development of Russia's Far East has been proclaimed a policy priority, to be facilitated by an ambitious turn or 'pivot' to Asia. This chapter assesses Russia's economic reorientation towards Asia, offering an overview of the Far Eastern dimension of Russia's economic relations with its major Asian partners in 2010–16, based on analysis of the dynamics of investment, trade relations and business climate development. Since 2014, trade with Asian partners has stagnated, while foreign investment (except for Chinese) has remained negligible. Moreover, trade is still mainly oriented towards markets in European Russia. The chapter concludes that Russia's pivot to Asia has not yet become an economic pivot—and that such a turn would be more easily attainable under a non-sanctions regime.

Keywords Russian Far East • Trade • Foreign direct investment • Sanctions • Business climate

---

R. Vakulchuk (✉)
Research Group on Russia, Eurasia and the Arctic, Norwegian Institute of International Affairs, Oslo, Norway

The economic development of Russia's Far East has been announced as a policy priority, to be facilitated by an ambitious pivot to Asia. In 2015, speaking at the first Eastern Economic Forum in Vladivostok, President Vladimir Putin pointed out that the Russian Far East is a key region for Russia's development and 'a region that should be effectively integrated into the developing Asia-Pacific region as a whole' (*Kremlin.ru* 2015). At the second Forum, in September 2016, ideas about developing an 'Energy Super Ring' (to involve China, Japan, Mongolia, Russia and South Korea) and turning Vladivostok into Russia's 'San Francisco' were discussed (*Russia Direct* 2016a; Zubacheva 2016). Russian officials have also repeatedly declared that the government hopes to strengthen economic ties with China, Japan and South Korea. But how credible is Russia's commitment to reorient itself economically towards Asia?

The first official announcements about an imminent Russian pivot to Asia were made in connection with the adoption of the 2009 'Strategy for the Socioeconomic Development of the Far East and Baikal Region until 2025' (*Vl.ru* 2010; Sakai 2015). Since 2014, this policy has been further stimulated by such factors as the Western economic sanctions, falling oil prices and domestic economic decline in Russia. The sanctions introduced by the USA and the European Union in connection with the Ukraine crisis have served to separate Russia from the West, accelerating a reorientation of economic and foreign policy, as well as diplomatic relations, towards the East (Dave 2016; Gabuev 2016a).

After nearly three years of Western sanctions and Russian efforts to redirect trade, we can conclude that Moscow has only partly succeeded in this endeavour. As will be shown below, Moscow's attempts to turn eastwards have led to the emergence of new complexities and contradictions related to economic governance in the Russian Far East as well as in Russia's relations with its Asian neighbours. Moreover, China has not lived up to Moscow's expectations regarding investment (*Russia Today* 2016).

In this chapter I assess the Russian participation—or lack thereof—in the growing Asia-Pacific economies, and offer an overview of the Far Eastern dimension of Russia's economic relations with its major Asian partners in 2010–16.[1] I discuss the dynamics of investment and trade relations and also reflect on Russia's changing economic priorities before and after 'Crimea', with a focus on implications for Russia–Asia relations in the Russian Far East. The analysis draws on secondary data, supplemented by ten expert interviews conducted in order to identify nascent trends and possible future trajectories.[2]

My main argument is that Russia's pivot to Asia has not yet become an *economic* one. Further, I hold that pivoting would have been easier and more attainable earlier: the Ukraine crisis and the subsequent international sanctions regime have complicated, rather than facilitated, Russia's economic turn to the East.

Context Does Matter

The Russian Far East has for decades been recognized as a region of unfulfilled promise and potential (Bradshaw 2012). The region has continued to project largely the same overall trends throughout the period under scrutiny here. Natural population growth has remained negative and out-migration high, and demographic decline continues to slow economic development (Belenets 2016). Other factors with negative impacts on the region's economic development are geography (huge uninhabited territories), harsh weather conditions (making investments more costly), lack of infrastructure (poorly developed road network, etc.), the limited capacity of Russia's railways (the main east–west transport artery) and insufficient labour resources (Sakai 2015, p.128; *East Russia Magazine* 2015).

Five main factors shape the context of the Russian Far East's integration into Asian markets: the international sanctions regime, Russia's prioritization of economic openness versus import substitution, economic infrastructure, continued reliance on energy as the major driver of economic development and the business climate. Taken together, these factors create a complicated environment for domestic and foreign investors to engage economically with the region on a scale in line with the ambitious goals and objectives set by the Kremlin.

First, the impact of sanctions on the development of the Russian Far East has been significant, not least because the USA and other Western countries were active investors in the region prior to 2014. And yet, despite the sanctions, Western countries continue to be important players in terms of foreign direct investment (FDI). In fact, the size of Western investment in the Russian Far East in 2014–15 was comparable to that of all East Asian countries taken together (see Fig. 8.3).

Second, Russia's countersanction measures and the introduction of import substitution policies have negatively affected the Russian Far East. Since 2014, import substitution has constituted an integral part of Russian industrial policy (WTO 2016). Moscow's import substitution plan foresees the implementation of no less than 2059 projects across 19 sectors of the economy between 2016 and 2020 (Edovina and Shapovalov 2015). State incentives for import substitution—such as infrastructure grants, tax breaks and preferential domestic treatment in government procurement contracts—are held to have a perverting effect on the economy:

> This [import substitution] has concretely translated into the subsidization of many sectors of economic activity ... These policies ... have not brought more trade or growth to Russia. Neither have they increase [sic] product quality or lowered prices to Russian consumers. Far from it, they have introduced an economic and trade environment distant from the principles and spirit underpinning the WTO and global economic cooperation. (European Union External Action 2016)

In their assessment of Russia's import substitution policy, Richard Connolly and Philip Hanson characterize the plan as 'Soviet style'—which in their view 'raises doubts about the reality that lies behind it' (Connolly and Hanson 2016, p.2). In any case, Moscow's attempts to open up the Russian Far East to foreign investment, including turning Vladivostok into Russia's 'San Francisco', are undermined by the simultaneous introduction of import substitution policies, which in practice means pursuing greater economic isolation.

Russian economist Sergei Guriev (2015) has argued that import substitution is part of Russia's ongoing 'de-globalization'. However, while import substitution complicates access for foreign investors in the Russian Far East, it does not rule out inward FDI. What it does imply is that foreign firms that plan to invest in the 19 affected sectors are now required to 'localize' their production instead of simply exporting their products to Russia (Connolly and Hanson 2016, p.21). This inherent tension between openness and import substitution complicates economic governance in the Russian Far East and has negative implications for policy coordination among various ministries and public agencies, as we shall see.

Third, the challenges related to integrating the Russian economy in the Asia-Pacific markets are in many ways insurmountable (*Russia Direct* 2016b). If the sanctions were to be lifted, it would be much easier for Russia to reintegrate economically with Western markets than to achieve substantial progress in the Asia-Pacific markets. The combination of underdeveloped infrastructure, demographic challenges and lack of skilled labour in the Russian Far East as compared to in the western part of Russia all speak in favour of reintegrating with the West rather than pivoting to the East. Moreover, after the Ukraine crisis, the Russian government has prioritized boosting infrastructure development in Crimea (Jeh et al. 2015, p.6). This has put substantial pressure on the federal budget. For instance, the construction of a bridge that would connect the Russian mainland with the Crimean Peninsula is estimated to cost USD 3.2–4.3 billion (Choi 2016). With the economy struggling and the shift in priorities, the budget for the development of the Russian Far East has had to take cuts—and that undermines the chances for successful realization of the eastward pivot.

Fourth, energy remains the main attraction for foreign investors in the Russian Far East (Zubacheva 2016). Also domestic energy actors such as Rosneft, Gazprom, Transneft and RusHydro have become increasingly interested in developing the region. As one local expert explained, 'in Russia, state investment follows large energy companies and this places constraints on significant investment in other, non-energy industries'.[3]

The fifth factor, the development of the business climate in the Russian Far East, requires special attention. To this I return in the next section.

Overall, the Russian Far East serves as a clear example of how Russia's external economic constraints and limited domestic policy options have hindered regional economic development. While Moscow stresses the goal of becoming economically self-sufficient through import substitution policies, it cannot deny the fact that foreign investors will have to play an important role in the process of developing the Russian Far East. As shown in the next section, however, realization of the ambitious goal of transforming the Russian Far East into an attractive destination for foreign investors has yet to materialize.

ATTEMPTS TO IMPROVE BUSINESS CLIMATE IN THE FAR EAST: NEW EFFORTS, OLD STORY?

Improving the business climate plays an important role in facilitating Russia's turn to Asia. At the 2016 Eastern Economic Forum in Vladivostok, Iurii Trutnev, Presidential Plenipotentiary to the Far Eastern Federal Okrug, announced that economic development would be spurred with the help of preferential tariffs and administrative procedures aimed at attracting foreign investors.

Assessing the progress in business climate development after 2014, we should note that much has been done in developing hard infrastructure for attracting FDI. Most importantly, the government has introduced a special investment regime, the 'advanced special economic zones' (ASEZs) (*territorii operezhaiushchego razvitiia*). As of December 2016, 14 such ASEZs had been established in the region. Each ASEZ specializes in one or two sectors.[4] The goal is to introduce one or two ASEZs in each of the nine federal subjects in the Russian Far East, to ensure balanced distribution of economic activities (see Min and Kang, Chap. 4, this volume).[5]

The process of developing ASEZs is closely linked to the parallel introduction of the Free Port of Vladivostok. The latter project, adopted in 2015, brings together 15 municipalities in the southern part of Primorskii Krai that will enjoy special tax and customs privileges (*East Russia Magazine* 2015; see also Troyakova, Chap. 3, this volume).

To control and supervise the work of the ASEZs and the Free Port, Moscow has created a series of new administrative bodies (*East Russia Magazine* 2015):

- the Department for Advanced Special Economic Zones and Free Port of Vladivostok under the Ministry for the Development of the Far East (the Ministry itself was established in 2012)
- the Far East Human Capital Development Agency (aimed at attracting skilled labour and facilitating relocation to the Far East)
- the Far East Investment and Export Agency (responsible for drafting investor proposals and identifying new ASEZ residents)
- regional investment development agencies in every region of the Far East

However, most of the experts interviewed for this study held that this new bureaucratic mechanism was bulky and with a multi-layered management structure, complicating the coordination of the ASEZs. Vaguely defined and overlapping responsibilities and decision-making power among the various agencies add to the problem. These challenges spring out of the more fundamental problem of the absence of a unified strategy for the economic development of the Russian Far East and what role the Asian factor is intended to play in this (*Russia Direct* 2016b).

Despite attempts to make the Russian Far East, and Vladivostok in particular, an attractive place for investment, thus far, there seems to have been little significant improvement, let alone a breakthrough, in the business climate. A 2012 World Bank study ranked Vladivostok as 15 among 30 major Russian cities in terms of ease of doing business.[6] Khabarovsk and Yakutsk were ranked even lower, 23rd and 28th, respectively. In a 2014 survey of the investment climate in 21 Russian regions, Khabarovsk and Sakha received the second-lowest rating and Primorye the lowest (Lee and Lukin 2015, p.50). The situation has not changed dramatically since then. To the contrary, according to Igor Makarov, general perceptions of the business climate have worsened since 2014 due to the overall economic stagnation and Russia's 'precarious international political standing' (Makarov 2017, p.92). This sends a signal to domestic and foreign investors that, despite the introduction of numerous measures aimed at making the Russian Far East an attractive business destination, realities on the ground have not changed much.[7]

Interestingly, up to 2014, Russia compared itself mainly to Western countries as regards business climate and ease of doing business: now Moscow has begun looking towards its Asian neighbours and trade partners (China, Japan, Singapore and South Korea) (Ministry for the Development of the Far East 2016). This shift could be seen as a signal to Asian governments and investors that Russia is genuinely interested in learning from Asian experiences. However, several experts interviewed for this study share the view that the federal and local authorities have failed to communicate effectively to potential investors the changes introduced in the regulatory regime. For instance, the website of the Ministry for the Development of the Far East devoted to advanced special economic zones is all in Russian, with no translations provided.[8] Moreover, the government has not involved international organizations such as the World Bank in independent, external assessments of the measures undertaken to improve the investment climate. Federal and regional public agencies remain the main source of information for potential foreign investors; there are no impartial sources to consult.

The interviews conducted for this study revealed two major obstacles to attracting FDI after 2014. First, several interviewees held that, although Russia has placed considerable focus on developing hard infrastructure (building roads, establishing special economic zones, etc.), the authorities have largely disregarded the soft infrastructure needs in the Russian Far East. For instance, in order to serve an ASEZ, officials and bureaucrats, local businesspeople and service providers need to know and understand the new rules and regulations. However, they receive little training, and still lack capacity to manage the newly established institutions.

Second, prior to developing the ASEZs, little analysis was undertaken to explore what sectors or products would be relevant for Asian markets.

Thus, ASEZs are largely oriented towards domestic economic needs that are of little interest to foreign investors. As noted by one local expert, 'the structure of ASEZs is a clone of previous initiatives having no or little value to regional markets and global value chains'.[9] Furthermore, current trends in Asian markets for goods and services indicate decreasing demand for Russian exports of raw materials (Makarov 2017, p.92). Instead, they point to the development of consumer- and service-oriented economies—sectors where the Russian Far East, and Russia in general, have limited potential for exports at present. Thus, the business climate and the ASEZ regime have remained largely inward oriented, limiting the attractiveness for foreign investors and, accordingly, the flow of FDI into the Russian Far East.

Trade: Who Is at the Helm?

China, Japan and South Korea are the main trade partners of the Russian Far East, with 80 per cent of the region's total trade in 2014 (Turovskii 2015). However, since 2014, exports and imports between the Russian Far East and China, Japan and South Korea have stagnated in volume and declined significantly in value (see Fig. 8.1 for imports and Fig. 8.2 for exports). In terms of trade, China, Japan and South Korea are clearly

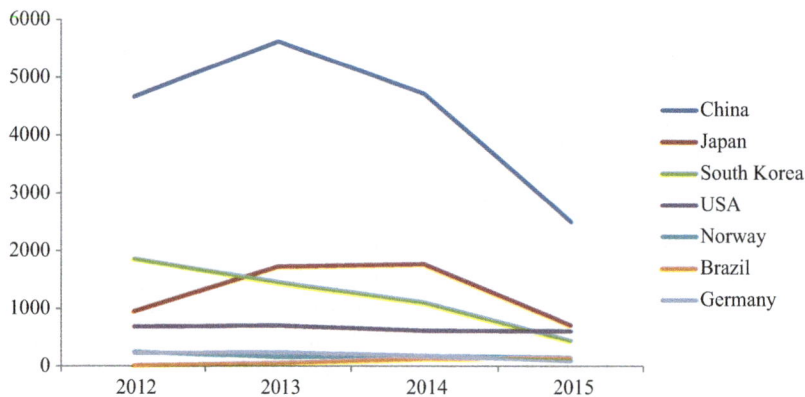

Fig. 8.1 Imports to the Russian Far East from main Asian and non-Asian trade partners (million USD) (Source: Federal State Statistics Service 2016)

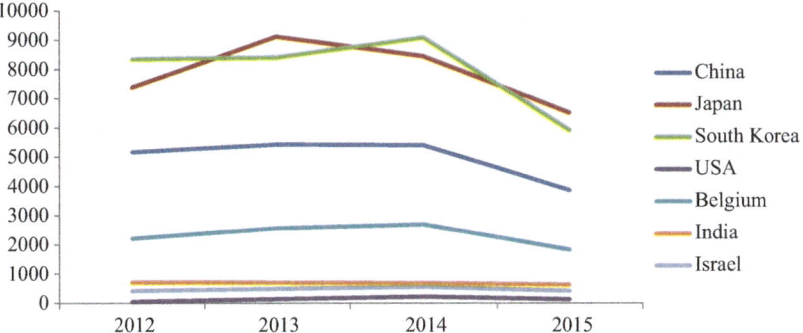

Fig. 8.2 Exports from the Russian Far East to main Asian and non-Asian trade partners (million USD) (Source: Federal State Statistics Service 2016)

ahead of the West, both before and after 2014. The biggest Western exporter is the USA, followed by Norway, Brazil and Germany, while Belgium is by far the biggest Western importer from the region. Interestingly, in terms of value, Far Eastern imports from the West remained stable across 2014—it is the main Asian trade partners that have suffered the most in the Far East.

On the national level, China remains Moscow's biggest trade partner. In 2015, its share in Russia's total foreign trade amounted to 11 per cent (Dave 2016). However, several of the experts interviewed for this study noted that the Russian political elite is concerned about China's current relatively passive position on trade, FDI and cross-border economic collaboration. In practice, they argue, China was more active in developing economic ties before the Western sanctions were introduced.

In 2015, total Chinese exports to Russia decreased by 34.4 per cent, as compared to a 6.8 per cent increase in 2014 (*The Moscow Times* 2016). The ambitious goal adopted in 2011 by the Chinese and Russian governments, of achieving an annual total trade turnover of USD 100 billion by 2015, proved unrealistic—in fact, turnover in the latter year amounted to USD 64.2 billion. A foreseen double increase by 2020 today seems even more out of reach, given the current stagnation in trade relations between the two countries, the struggling Russian economy and slower economic growth in China.[10]

FDI in the Russian Far East

FDI trends in the Russian Far East largely reflect the FDI situation in Russia as a whole. However, as pointed out by Rensselaer Lee and Artyom Lukin (2015), it is sometimes difficult to determine the exact level of regional FDI: the general picture may be distorted due to transactions being counted as central, not regional. In addition, the Federal State Statistics Service publishes data for FDI at the regional level, hereunder the Russian Far East, with a time lag, as compared to its statistics for the total FDI in Russia by individual countries. This further complicates analysis of post-Crimea FDI.

In general, FDI does not exceed 10 per cent of total investments in the Russian Far East: around 90 per cent of investments continue to stem from domestic investors (Labykin 2014). The volume of FDI has, however, been less affected by the international sanctions and the economic slump than is the case with trade: while total trade since 2014 has declined dramatically, total FDI in the region appears to have taken less of a hit. Figure 8.3 shows FDI trends by country over time. We see that total FDI after 2014 from the main Western investors (the Netherlands, Germany and Austria) decreased somewhat, whereas FDI from Japan and South

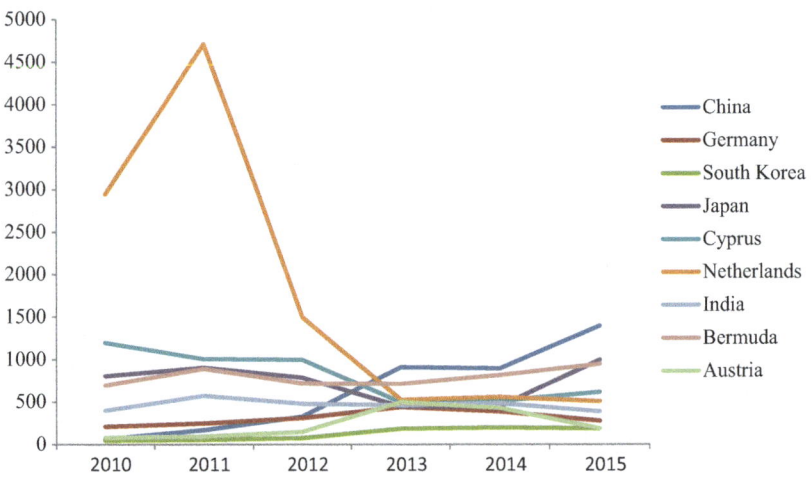

Fig. 8.3 FDI in the Russian Far East by main Asian and non-Asian partners (million USD) (Federal State Statistics Service 2016)

Korea showed modest growth. Only China breaks this pattern with a clear upward trend across the period in question. In 2015–16, according to Aleksandr Galushka, Minister for the Development of the Far East, Beijing invested USD 2.6 billion in the region (*Russia Today* 2016). However, Chinese FDI in 2014–15 was significantly lower than the Dutch FDI in 2010–11, which came in connection with Shell's investment in the Sakhalin oil and gas fields.

Bermuda and Cyprus were among the main investors in the Russian Far East in 2014–15 (Kriuchkova et al. 2016). This investment, however, is predominantly of Russian origin: many Russian state corporations and private firms use offshore accounts, registering in various tax havens in order to reduce the tax burden. Whereas this investment is technically classified as foreign, in practice, it is domestic. For 2017, the Far East Investment and Export Agency under the Ministry for the Development of the Far East announced a goal of attracting USD 1.6 billion—again mainly from domestic investors (Fingar 2016).

As seen in Fig. 8.3, China has in recent years been the single biggest investor in the Russian Far East. According to Galushka, Chinese investments have been 'a result of new Far East development mechanisms', such as the ASEZs, the Free Port of Vladivostok, the Far East Development Fund and targeted infrastructural project support, mechanisms 'popular with Chinese businesses' (*Russia Today* 2016). However, many of the investment projects promised by China after 2014 have never materialized. This is at least partly related to the international sanctions regime and related Chinese apprehensions (Rozman 2016). On the other hand, Moscow and Beijing have been working on developing parallel financial infrastructure 'that will be immune to sanctions' (Gabuev 2016b).

Russia and China have a shared interest in developing the sparsely populated but resource-rich territory of the Russian Far East. The energy sector has been the main driver (see Overland and Kubayeva, Chap. 6, this volume). In 2014, the conclusion of a USD 400 billion contract to build the Power of Siberia pipeline from Irkutsk and Sakha to China was intended to send a message to the West: Russia had alternatives to the European gas market (Dave 2016). The following year, Rosneft signed contracts with China worth over USD 30 billion to supply oil to the Chinese market (*Sputnik International* 2015). However, economic recession and infrastructure gaps in the two countries have complicated implementation of these huge energy projects (Dave 2016), and negotiations over implementation of both are currently stalled.

In other sectors, we find some noticeable success stories. For example, over USD 109 million has been invested in a timber plant in Khabarovsk. The Russian–Chinese Fund for Agro-Industrial Development has set a goal of disbursing USD 1.2 billion to the agricultural sector over the three-year period of 2016–18. Further, Chinese firms have invested in a cement plant in Amur Oblast and have expanded their activities in the Sakha Republic and Primorskii Krai (see Min and Kang, Chap. 4, this volume). Finally, although slow progress on the Russian section has raised concerns, the Amur Bridge, connecting Russia's Blagoveshchensk with China's Heihe in Heilongjiang province, is expected to be completed by 2019.

In general, however, it has proven difficult to attract FDI as well as domestic investment in sectors beyond natural resource extraction. While the idea behind introducing the ASEZs was to promote the production and export of more processed goods, the region has few comparative advantages as regards China; these relate mainly to exports of unprocessed raw materials, including energy.

To balance China's dominance in the Russian Far East, Russia has continued cultivating other partners to add more competition for investment in the region's resources. South Korea and especially Japan are viewed as the most promising potential partners here. For South Korea, integration with the Russian Far East is deemed attractive, as it will strengthen connectivity between Eurasia and the Korean Peninsula. For the Korean ambitions to be fulfilled, however, hard infrastructure will need to be put in place in the Russian Far East (Jeh 2015, p.160).

As for Japan, President Putin, addressing the second Eastern Economic Forum in 2016, spoke of this country as Russia's 'natural' economic partner (*Sputnik International* 2016). According to the Ministry for the Development of the Far East, the volume of Japanese FDI may easily exceed that of China in the near future (*Gazeta.ru* 2016). If Moscow and Tokyo manage to sign a deal on the Kuril Islands/Northern Territories, it would undoubtedly boost economic cooperation between the two countries. Japan has already sought to expand bilateral economic ties as a tool for reaching a solution to the territorial dispute (*The Japan Times* 2016). However, as Gilbert Rozman notes, 'a breakthrough with Japan would hint at multipolarity at China's expense, but it likely would not be transformative' (Rozman 2016). Japan will not be able to satisfy Russia's enormous needs in terms of regional FDI. Still, Russia can use Japan as a wild card in its negotiations with China: increased competition between Beijing and Tokyo over resources and influence might lead to increased FDI in the Russian Far East. This is not an easy task, though: Japanese investors tend to expect higher standards than their Chinese counterparts when it comes to business climate. According to Satoshi Sakai (2015, p.128), Russia will need to improve its business climate significantly before it can become an attractive destination for Japanese investors.

Concluding Discussion: The Swan, the Pike and the Crawfish

Moscow's approach to the economic development of the Russian Far East is reminiscent of Ivan Krylov's well-known fable 'The Swan, the Pike and the Crawfish', where the three protagonists all try to pull a cart in a different direction. This is reflected in the government's economic development policies, where different agencies promote divergent agendas and Moscow largely lacks a unified strategy, but also in the contradictory policies of promoting import substitution policies while trying to open up the Russian Far East to foreign investment.

Assessing the development of trade and FDI in the Russian Far East before and after 2014, we find hardly any positive substantial change, except for the increase in Chinese FDI. On the contrary, trade with Russia's main Asian partners has stagnated in volume and declined in value, and FDI remains negligible compared to domestic capital investment. Implementing the ambitious plans for developing the Russian Far East will require substantial foreign investment, but, as noted by Sung Hoon Jeh et al. (2015, p.6), pivoting to Asia is, paradoxically enough, hardly attainable without investment from Western countries. And as long as the sanctions regime remains in place, large-scale Western investment will not be forthcoming. Moreover, the Ukraine crisis has led to reallocations in the Russian federal budget, and the Russian Far East has had to take cuts in order for Moscow to push forward with expensive infrastructure projects in Crimea. Instead of unequivocally facilitating an eastward pivot, the Ukraine conflict has complicated the reorientation to the East—domestically in Russia as well as internationally.

As to the larger picture, there has hardly been a Russian economic turn to Asia. The Russian Far East remains a small regional actor and cannot be considered yet an internationally important region in terms of its integration in Asian and global markets. Its trade is still mainly oriented towards markets in European Russia; and in economic matters, the Russian

Far East's double-headed eagle continues to look more to Moscow than to the Pacific.

To a large extent, developments in the Russian Far East reflect the overall economic situation in Russia, which has worsened since 2014. This downturn has been caused partly by external factors (most importantly, the collapse of the global oil price and the international sanctions), and partly by internal factors (hereunder the adoption of import substitution policies). The existence of contradictory regulatory regimes and the lack of a unified Russian Far East economic development strategy exacerbate the situation. Attaining a level of economic cooperation with Asian partners in line with the economic ties that Russia had with the West prior to 2014 is unlikely in the near future.

Russia's efforts to improve the hard infrastructure to facilitate foreign investment in the region have brought some results. Although the overall investment climate in the Far Eastern Federal Okrug has not improved significantly since 2014, the region has become more diversified, with new infrastructure introduced in order to attract investment beyond the industries connected with natural resource extraction. The increase in Russian offshore capital being reinvested in the Russian Far East is a good sign; several new initiatives, such as the creation of the Free Port of Vladivostok and state support for new private projects through the Far East Development Fund, have also contributed to this diversification effect. However, the external benefits are yet to be seen in practice.

Acknowledgements This chapter is based on data gathered for the TIGER (Trade Integration, Geopolitics and the Economy of Russia) research project, financed by the NORRUSS Programme of the Research Council of Norway.

Notes

1. The year 2010 has been chosen as a starting point for this study because that was the first full year of implementation of the above-mentioned strategy for the development of the Russian Far East.
2. Interviews were conducted with Russia-based experts (partly based in Moscow, partly in Vladivostok). Their fields of expertise cover economy, business climate, transport, infrastructure and other areas related to the economic development of the Russian Far East. Seven experts were interviewed as part of the 'Trade Integration, Geopolitics and the Economy of Russia (TIGER)' project, funded by the Research Council of Norway. Three interviews were conducted in conjunction with the third 'Developing

Asia-Pacific's Last Frontier' conference in Shanghai. All interviews took place in August–September 2016, under conditions of anonymity.
3. Interview with expert on the Russian Far East, Moscow, 2 September 2016.
4. The following industries have been identified as targets for ASEZs: construction materials, timber processing, fish processing, tourism, metallurgy, the agro-industrial complex, auto parts, logistics, oil and gas, chemistry, and infrastructure (Ministry for the Development of the Far East 2016).
5. The Ministry of Economic Development has, however, been sceptical about the idea of establishing ASEZs, pointing out that previous attempts to promote special economic zones proved unsuccessful and had no impact on economic growth (Lossan 2014).
6. Data retrieved from the World Bank's 'Ease of doing business' webpage for Russia, under section 'Subnational city'—see http://www.doingbusiness.org/data/exploreeconomies/russia. Accessed on 21 February 2017.
7. It is indicative that in 2015, only one foreign investor was registered with an ASEZ (Gabuev 2015).
8. See http://minvr.ru/activities/toser.php. Accessed on 20 February 2017. The Far East Investment and Export Agency has, however, developed easily accessible instructions and infographics in English—see http://www.investvostok.ru/en/why/#territorii-operezhayushchego-razvitiya. Accessed on 20 February 2017.
9. Interview with expert from the Russian Far East, Shanghai, 27 September 2016.
10. Russia had been among China's top 15 trade partners from 2010 to 2014, but in 2015, it fell to 16th position (Fedorinova et al. 2015).

References

Belenets, Patricia. 2016. 'Demographic potential of the Far East: problems and trends', *Problems of Economic Transition* 58(7–9): 587–97.

Bradshaw, Michael J. 2012. *The Russian Far East and Pacific Asia: unfulfilled potential*. London: Routledge.

Choi, David. 2016. '"Putin's Bridge" connecting Russia to Crimea might be having issues', *Business Insider*, 26 September. http://www.businessinsider.com/putins-bridge-russia-crimea-problems-2016-9?r=US&IR=T&IR=T. Accessed on 18 February 2017.

Connolly, Richard and Philip Hanson. 2016. 'Import substitution and economic sovereignty in Russia', *Research Paper*. London: The Royal Institute of International Affairs.

Dave, Bhavna. 2016. 'Russia's Asia pivot: engaging the Russian Far East, China and Southeast Asia', *RSIS Working Paper* 297. Singapore: S. Rajaratnam School of International Studies.

East Russia Magazine. 2015. 'Far East being proactive', September. www.eastrussia.ru/upload/EastRussia_vef.pdf. Accessed on 20 February 2017.

Edovina, Tat'iana and Aleksei Shapovalov. 2015. 'Gossovet sobral plody importozameshcheniia' [The State Council has gathered the fruits of import substitution], *Kommersant*, 26 November. http://kommersant.ru/doc/2862090. Accessed on 18 February 2017.

European Union External Action. 2016. 'WTO review: EU calls on Russia to abandon import substitution measures', 28 September. https://eeas.europa.eu/topics/water-diplomacy/10713/wto-review--eu-calls-on-russia-to-abandon-import-substitution-measures_en. Accessed on 18 February 2017.

Federal State Statistics Service. 2016. 'Main indicators'. http://www.gks.ru/wps/wcm/connect/rosstat_main/rosstat/en/main. Accessed on 18 February 2017.

Fedorinova, Yuliya, Elena Mazneva and Anna Baraulina. 2015. 'Putin's got a new problem with China', *Bloomberg*, 1 September. https://www.bloomberg.com/news/articles/2015-09-01/putin-s-china-turn-hits-potholes-as-trade-drops-markets-slide. Accessed on 18 February 2017.

Fingar, Courtney. 2016. 'A distant dream: Putin plans to revitalise Russian Far East', *FDI Intelligence*, 13 October. http://www.fdiintelligence.com/Locations/Europe/Russia/A-distant-dream-Putin-plans-to-revitalise-Russian-Far-East. Accessed on 18 February 2017.

Gabuev, Alexander. 2015. 'Povorot v nikuda: itogi aziatskoi politiki Rossii v 2015' [Turn to nowhere: results of Russia's Asian policy in 2015], *Moscow Carnegie Center*, 29 December. http://carnegie.ru/commentary/2015/12/29/ru-62369/ioe2. Accessed on 18 February 2017.

Gabuev, Alexander. 2016a. 'Did Western sanctions affect Sino-Russian economic ties?' *Moscow Carnegie Center*, 26 April. http://carnegie.ru/2016/04/26/did-western-sanctions-affect-sino-russian-economic-ties-pub-63461. Accessed on 18 February 2017.

Gabuev, Alexander. 2016b. 'Russian–Chinese relations after the Ukraine crisis', *Moscow Carnegie Center*, 29 June. http://carnegie.ru/2016/06/29/friends-with-benefits-russian-chinese-relations-after-ukraine-crisis-pub-63953. Accessed on 18 February 2017.

Gazeta.ru. 2016. 'Minvostokrazvitiia: ob"em iaponskih investitsii mozhet prevysit' kitaiskie' [Ministry for the Development of the Far East: the volume of Japanese investment may exceed the Chinese], 30 December. https://www.gazeta.ru/business/news/2016/12/30/n_9519971.shtml. Accessed on 18 February 2017.

Guriev, Sergei. 2015. 'Deglobalizing Russia', *Moscow Carnegie Center*, 16 December. http://carnegie.ru/2015/12/16/deglobalizing-russia-pub-62294. Accessed on 18 February 2017.

The Japan Times. 2016. 'Russia, Japan agree to promote economic cooperation in Russian Far East', 5 November. http://www.japantimes.co.jp/news/2016/11/05/business/russia-japan-agree-promote-economic-cooperation-russian-far-east/#.WECOVH0rTbU. Accessed on 18 February 2017.

Jeh, Sung Hoon. 2015. 'Russian Far East development and directions for improvement in Korean–Russian cooperation: Korea's perspective', in *International cooperation in the development of Russia's Far East and Siberia*, edited by Jing Huang and Alexander Korolev, 144–63. Basingstoke: Palgrave Macmillan.

Jeh, Sung Hoon, Jiyoung Min, Boogyun Kang and Sergey Lukonin. 2015. 'Recent development in the Russian Far East–Baikal Region and its implication', *KIEP World Economy Update* 5(17): 1–6.

Kremlin.ru. 2015. 'First Eastern Economic Forum', 4 September. http://en.kremlin.ru/events/president/news/50232. Accessed on 18 February 2017.

Kriuchkova, Evgeniia, Oleg Sapozhkov and Tat'iana Edovina. 2016. 'Dal'nii Vostok razmenial rubl' na dvenadtsat'' [Far East exchanged one ruble for twelve], *Kommersant*, 5 May. http://www.kommersant.ru/doc/2979487. Accessed on 21 February 2017.

Labykin, Aleksandr. 2014. 'Dal'nii Vostok gotov k prihodu investorov' [Far East is ready for the arrival of investors], *Ekspert Online*. http://expert.ru/2014/06/23/aziatskie-kompanii-rvutsya-na-dalnij-vostok. Accessed on 21 February 2017.

Lee, Rensselaer and Artyom Lukin. 2015. *Russia's Far East: new dynamics in Asia Pacific & beyond*. Boulder, CO: Lynne Rienner.

Lossan, Alexei. 2014. 'Seven large foreign investors are to come to Russian Far East', *Russia Beyond the Headlines*, 20 September. http://rbth.com/business/2014/09/20/seven_large_foreign_investors_are_to_come_to_russian_far_east_39979.html. Accessed on 20 February 2017.

Makarov, Igor. 2017. 'Transformation of the economic model in Asia-Pacific region: implications for Russia's Far East and Siberia', in *The political economy of Pacific Russia: regional developments in East Asia*, edited by Jing Huang and Alexander Korolev, 77–101. Basingstoke: Palgrave Macmillan.

Ministry for the Development of the Far East. 2016. 'Plans and objectives', http://minvr.ru/upload/Ministry%20%20Russian%20Far%20East%201.pptx. Accessed on 18 February 2017.

The Moscow Times. 2016. 'Russian–Chinese trade plummets in 2015', 13 January. http://www.themoscowtimes.com/business/article/russian-chinese-trade-plummets-in-2015/555632.html. Accessed on 18 February 2017.

Rozman, Gilbert. 2016. 'Russian dissatisfaction with China and its limits', *China Policy Institute: Analysis*. https://cpianalysis.org/2016/04/07/russian-dissatisfaction-with-china-and-its-limits. Accessed on 18 February 2017.

Russia Direct. 2016a. 'The bold plan to turn Vladivostok into a Russian San Francisco', 2 September. http://www.russia-direct.org/analysis/bold-plan-turn-vladivostok-russian-san-francisco. Accessed on 18 February 2017.

Russia Direct. 2016b. 'Crossing the bridge to the Far East', Moscow: Russia Direct.

Russia Today. 2016. 'China invests $2.4bn in Russian Far East', 5 July. https://www.rt.com/business/349524-china-russian-region-investments. Accessed on 18 February 2017.

Sakai, Satoshi. 2015. 'Economic relations between Japan and the Russian Far East', in *International cooperation in the development of Russia's Far East and Siberia*, edited by Jing Huang and Alexander Korolev, 123–43. Basingstoke: Palgrave Macmillan.

Sputnik International. 2015. 'Rosneft signs contracts with China worth over $30 bln', 3 September. http://sputniknews.com/business/20150903/1026542805.html. Accessed on 18 February 2017.

Sputnik International. 2016. 'Putin's speech at Eastern Economic Forum in Vladivostok', 3 September. http://sputniknews.com/politics/20160903/1044918709/putin-eastern-economic-forum.html. Accessed on 18 February 2017.

Turovskii, Rostislav. 2015. 'Delovoi portret Dal'nego Vostoka' [Business portrait of the Far East], *EastRussia*, 17 September. http://www.eastrussia.ru/material/delovoy-portret-dalnego-vostoka/. Accessed on 21 February 2017.

Vl.ru. 2010. 'Nadezhda Mikheeva: na Dal'nem Vostoke Primor'e poluchaet bol'she vsego investitsii' [Nadezhda Mikheeva: Primorye receives the greatest amount of investment in the Far East], 7 December. http://www.newsvl.ru/biznes/2010/12/07/investprim. Accessed on 18 February 2017.

WTO. 2016. 'Trade policy review: Russian Federation'. https://www.wto.org/english/tratop_e/tpr_e/s345_e.pdf. Accessed on 18 February 2017.

Zubacheva, Kseniia. 2016. 'Next stage in Russian economic development is in the Far East', *Russia Direct*, 30 September. http://www.russia-direct.org/company-news/moscow-vladivostok-next-stage-russian-economic-development. Accessed on 18 February 2017.

Open Access This chapter is licensed under the terms of the Creative Commons Attribution 4.0 International License (http://creativecommons.org/licenses/by/4.0/), which permits use, sharing, adaptation, distribution and reproduction in any medium or format, as long as you give appropriate credit to the original author(s) and the source, provide a link to the Creative Commons license and indicate if changes were made.

The images or other third party material in this book are included in the book's Creative Commons license, unless indicated otherwise in a credit line to the material. If material is not included in the book's Creative Commons license and your intended use is not permitted by statutory regulation or exceeds the permitted use, you will need to obtain permission directly from the copyright holder.

CHAPTER 9

Afterword: 6400 Kilometres Away—But Not a Policy World Apart

Elana Wilson Rowe and Helge Blakkisrud

Abstract The Afterword presents two key findings from this volume. First, while numerous new strategy documents and instruments have been adopted in recent years, contributing authors voice concern about the steps Moscow has taken to translate lofty ideas into practical policies. Second, the key initiatives were formulated well before the current crisis in Russia's relations with the West. While a certain rebalancing of the Western and Eastern vectors is taking place, there is still a long way to go before Russia's 'window to the East' can match its 'window to the West'. Only long-term commitment on the part of Moscow can transform the Russian Far East from a neglected periphery and military outpost into a viable gateway to the Asia-Pacific.

Keywords Russia • Russian Far East • Crimean conflict • Asia-Pacific region • Policymaking

E.W. Rowe (✉)
Research Group on Emerging Powers and Global Development, Norwegian Institute of International Affairs, Oslo, Norway

H. Blakkisrud
Research Group on Russia, Eurasia and the Arctic, Norwegian Institute of International Affairs, Oslo, Norway

© The Author(s) 2018 159
H. Blakkisrud, E. Wilson Rowe (eds.), *Russia's Turn to the East*, Global Reordering, https://doi.org/10.1007/978-3-319-69790-1_9

More than 6400 kilometres separate Vladivostok from Moscow. As the contributions to this volume have demonstrated, being located in a different part of the world from Moscow does matter for how the Russian Far East is developing, and how Russia's connections to the broader Asia-Pacific region are evolving. With its status as a potential 'bridge to Asia', the Russian Far East attracts important federal-level attention—together with a specific set of security concerns.

And yet, some challenges are shared across this geographical vastness. For example, the Russian economy's overwhelming reliance on international natural resource markets remains a challenge for all parts of the country. The collapse of the oil price in 2014, exacerbated by the international sanctions regime imposed after Russia's annexation of Crimea, has brought worsened economic outlooks. In general, growth—or lack thereof—in the Russian Far East tallies with the average of the Russian economy overall. However, as pointed out in Chap. 4, compared to the economic powerhouse regions around Moscow and St Petersburg, the Russian Far East has been lagging far behind and the Far Eastern Federal Okrug remains the second smallest economy among Russia's eight federal okrugs.

In this brief Afterword, we return to two key sets of findings from the preceding chapters. These findings concern the nature of Russia's 'turn to the East' thus far and the prospects for tackling the political and economic challenges that have long hampered regional development.

Pivoting, Turning or Leaning? A Growing Suite of Measures and Institutions

The chapters in this volume have presented the new policy documents and instruments designed to accelerate the economic development of the Russian Far East and strengthen diplomatic connections and trade relations in the broader Asia-Pacific region. A significant point of variation across these efforts and policies is the extent to which they have realized—or seem suitable for realizing—the stated policy aims. While noting that it is still too early to judge what the ultimate outcome of Russia's greater emphasis on its Far East will be, many contributing authors voice concern about some of the first steps Moscow has taken towards translating lofty policy ideas into practical policies.

Concerning the institutional level, Helge Blakkisrud (Chap. 2) notes that a new development model centred around the institutionally innovative, partially decentralized Ministry for the Development of the Far East has been anchored in federal–regional politics. The question remains, however, whether this new model will be capable of generating and implementing policy solutions to the challenges the Russian Far East is facing. Old habits of top-down approaches seem to persist, and bureaucracy has multiplied in overlapping fashion around the newly created regional development instruments.

As regards the economy, it is probably more fruitful to think of Russia's economic growth plans and policy stimuli for the Russian Far East as efforts to realize the untapped potential of the region, rather than as alternatives to relations with Europe (although diversifying may be a very real and economically healthy goal). A series of economic incentives—most importantly, the advanced special economic zones (ASEZs) and the free port regime—have been adopted in order to stimulate regional growth, introducing new framework conditions for local and regional development. These changes include new patterns of governance, favourable tax regimes and special financing available for infrastructure development. However, as pointed out by Jiyoung Min and Boogyun Kang (Chap. 4), the ASEZs are in some ways too blunt an instrument: The plans for economic development zones would have benefitted from being more closely connected to or targeted towards potential markets and investors in East Asia. Similarly, Roman Vakulchuk (Chap. 8) notes that the Russian Far East has failed to develop a business climate attractive to foreign investors—90 per cent of investment in the region still comes from Russian domestic sources. Tamara Troyakova (Chap. 3) voices concern about the lack of coordination among various branches of the government and the new institutions they have set up to facilitate economic development.

Efforts at economic development in the Russian Far East have yet to bear fruit. Several contributing authors argue that it will still take some time before we can see the full potential of the upgrade of the regional infrastructure that is underway. An important consideration here is the broader economic picture: How might federal budgetary constraints play a role? There is already concern about the level of financing that will be available to the newly established regional economic development mechanisms. Non-state contributions, foreign direct investment in particular, have remained negligible; and the number of potential investors has been limited by the European- and North American-supported sanctions regime in place at the time of writing.

As regards international diplomacy, many chapters discuss whether China and Russia will succeed in deepening their bilateral relations, with their shared positioning in the Asia-Pacific region as an anchor point. In Chap. 7, Marc Lanteigne, analysing Sino-Russian relations through the prism of the Shanghai Cooperation Organization (SCO), argues that the China–Russia relationship is constrained by diverging viewpoints on several key issues, especially relating to global politics, and different status positions within international relations (China as a major rising power, Russia as a declining one). Looking more specifically at energy relations, Indra Overland and Gulaikhan Kubayeva (Chap. 6) argue that the relationship remains a marriage of convenience, primarily around energy interests, that could either deepen or fade with time. Malin Østevik and Natasha Kuhrt (Chap. 5) link diplomatic ambitions to security thinking and classify Russia as a 'bystander' in the Asia-Pacific region. They argue that the underdevelopment of the Russian Far East has caused the region to be seen as a security risk, generating a securitized approach that has hindered Russia's aspirations for domestic economic development in the Russian Far East and effective regional diplomacy.

Turning as Turning Away? Europe or Asia in a Post-Crimea Period

Contributing authors have also considered whether the diplomatic and economic consequences of Russia's annexation of Crimea and involvement in Eastern Ukraine in 2014 have affected policies and practices towards the Russian Far East and the broader Asia-Pacific region. We bring together some of those observations here, with the cautionary note that simultaneity should not, of course, automatically be taken to imply causality.

Post 2014, Vakulchuk notes that the Russian Far East's trade with Asian partners has contracted, and suggests that expanding these relations would be easier in a non-sanctions scenario. Likewise, Min and Kang note that it has been challenging for Russia to balance openness to the East Asian region against its politically driven import substitution policy.

Looking at energy projects, Overland and Kubayeva argue that, by and large, post-Crimea cooperation with China on such projects has generally been a continuation of already established trends. Moscow presented the May 2014 deal on the construction of the Power of

Siberia gas pipeline as a major success of diplomacy and a sign of the strong Sino-Russian bilateral relationship. In this specific instance, the authors note, talks were expedited and intensified in 2014. That same year, exports of oil from Russia to China increased by 36 per cent. However, the failure to reach agreement on the Vankor project, where the Chinese were replaced by new Indian partners in 2016, shows the limits of the political willingness to develop bilateral relations with China at any cost.

Østevik and Kuhrt find little concrete change in Russian security policy towards the wider region, with important driving forces for security thinking and engagement in the Russian Far East and broader Asia-Pacific region being established long before 2014 and pursued with few interruptions. A key difference, however, has been the intensified high-political and diplomatic attention to the Sino-Russian bilateral relationship. Still, as also noted by Lanteigne in his chapter on the SCO, Russia's deteriorating relations with the West have made the Sino-Russian bilateral relationship complex. Lanteigne argues that China has resisted Russia's interest in expanding the security/military aspects of the SCO, seeking instead to broaden the portfolio by including economic development questions and new investment opportunities for Chinese capital in Central Asia. On the specific topic of Russia's annexation of Crimea, China has avoided making any statement of support or condemnation, and in the UN Security Council, China chose to abstain rather than joining Russia in exercising its veto power.

* * *

The main conclusion to be derived from these chapters is that the key policy initiatives aimed at developing the Russian Far East were formulated well before the onset of the current crisis in Russia's relations with the West. However, the post-2014 breakdown seems to have added an element of urgency to Russia's 'turn to Asia', as witnessed in the heightened level of diplomatic celebrations around successfully concluded cooperation with the countries of the Asia-Pacific region.

When it comes to realizing Moscow's ambitious plans, however, perhaps the most urgent element is financial. As both Blakkisrud and Troyakova point out, despite the public fanfare, the post-Crimea period has been marked by a steady decline in the scope of state involvement in the Russian Far East. From the peak that accompanied the adoption of

Minister of Far Eastern Development Viktor Ishaev's grandiose state programme in 2013, state funding and promises have been cut back, year after year. These budget cuts may be the product of heavy pressure on limited resources—the fall in the oil price and the effects of the sanctions regime have forced the government to introduce austerity measures. However, even if the cuts do not reflect an actual de-prioritization of Moscow's pivot to the East, they might serve to undermine and obstruct realization of the policy aims that inspired the pivot in the first place.

While a certain rebalancing of the Western and Eastern vectors is clearly taking place, there is still a long way to go before Russia's 'window to the East' can match its 'window to the West'. Only long-term commitment on the part of Moscow can transform the Russian Far East from a neglected periphery and military outpost into a viable gateway to the Asia-Pacific.

Open Access This chapter is licensed under the terms of the Creative Commons Attribution 4.0 International License (http://creativecommons.org/licenses/by/4.0/), which permits use, sharing, adaptation, distribution and reproduction in any medium or format, as long as you give appropriate credit to the original author(s) and the source, provide a link to the Creative Commons license and indicate if changes were made.

The images or other third party material in this book are included in the book's Creative Commons license, unless indicated otherwise in a credit line to the material. If material is not included in the book's Creative Commons license and your intended use is not permitted by statutory regulation or exceeds the permitted use, you will need to obtain permission directly from the copyright holder.

Index[1]

A

Advanced special economic zone (ASEZ), 4, 5, 18–21, 24, 35–38, 44, 45, 51–70, 86, 144–146, 149, 150, 153n4, 153n5, 153n7, 161

Amur Oblast, 65, 80, 150

B

Business climate, 141, 143–146, 151, 152n2, 161

C

Chukotka Autonomous Okrug, 2, 65

Crisis
  East–West relations, 5, 6, 24, 32, 68, 78, 84–88, 97, 121, 140, 141, 143, 151, 159, 163
  economic, 14, 15, 78, 121
  Ukraine, 32, 97, 99, 108–112, 120, 130, 132, 140, 141, 143, 151

D

Diplomacy, 43, 44, 87, 124, 130, 131, 162, 163

E

Eastern Economic Forum (EEF), 26n11, 36, 39, 43, 44, 69, 86, 140, 143, 150

Eastern Military District (EMD), 81, 84

Eastern Siberia–Pacific Ocean (ESPO) pipeline, 6, 53, 97, 102, 103, 108

Energy, 6, 15, 42, 52, 53, 65, 87, 95–113, 141, 143, 149, 150, 162

F

Far East Development Fund, 34, 149, 152

Far Eastern Federal Okrug, 2–5, 7, 12, 13, 16, 17, 19–22, 24, 25, 26n12, 32–37, 40, 41, 43, 44, 52, 53, 55–60, 65, 77, 143, 152, 160

---

[1] Note: Page numbers followed by 'n' refer to notes.

Far Eastern Hectare, 20, 27n13, 40, 41
Far East Human Capital Development Agency, 18, 20, 34, 40, 63, 144
Far East Investment and Export Agency, 18, 34, 144, 149, 153n8
Foreign direct investment (FDI), 7, 43, 100–102, 110, 141, 142, 144–151, 161
Free Port of Vladivostok, 4, 18, 20, 37–40, 42, 44, 45, 62, 86, 144, 149, 152

G
Galushka, Aleksandr, 17, 22, 23, 33, 34, 61, 149
Gas, 6, 96, 98, 101, 102, 104–107, 109–112, 120, 149, 153n4, 163

I
Income, 56, 58, 101, 111
Infrastructure, 3, 7, 15, 31, 32, 34, 35, 37, 41–43, 52, 56, 58–60, 62–65, 68, 82, 130, 133, 141–143, 145, 149–152, 152n2, 153n4, 161
Investment, 3–5, 7, 19, 20, 23–25, 27, 33–35, 38–40, 42–45, 52, 53, 59–62, 64–69, 80, 81, 83, 86, 88, 97, 101, 102, 108, 109, 140–145, 148–152, 153n8, 161, 163
Ishaev, Viktor, 16, 17, 19, 21, 22, 25, 33, 34, 77, 78, 164

J
Japan, 15, 37, 43, 44, 54, 60, 65, 66, 70, 76–78, 81, 82, 87, 102, 140, 145, 146, 148, 150
Jewish Autonomous Oblast, 2, 65

K
Kamchatka Krai, 26n1, 65
Khabarovsk Krai, 16, 77, 78

L
Labour, 18, 34, 35, 54, 57, 60, 141, 142, 144
Liquefied natural gas (LNG), 97, 104–106, 110

M
Magadan Oblast, 2, 16, 66
Medvedev, Dmitrii, 19, 22, 23, 35, 59, 69n4, 82, 129
Migration, 14, 18, 20, 25, 35, 89n1
Military, 78, 79, 81, 82, 84, 86, 87, 97, 109, 120, 122, 124, 125, 127–130, 132, 133n1, 163, 164
Ministry for Regional Development, 13, 16, 21
Ministry for the Development of the Far East, 4, 5, 13, 15–17, 20–26, 27n15, 33, 35–37, 52, 59, 62, 64, 77, 144, 145, 149, 150, 160

N
North Korea, 38

O
Oil, 6, 52–54, 70n6, 87, 96–98, 101–104, 107–111, 140, 149, 152, 153n4, 160, 163, 164
One Belt, One Road (OBOR), 88, 89

P
Pipeline

Eastern Siberia–Pacific Ocean (ESPO), 6, 53, 97, 102–104, 108, 110
Power of Siberia, 6, 96, 97, 104–106, 149, 162
Power of Siberia pipeline, 6, 96, 97, 104–106, 149, 162
Presidential Plenipotentiary to the Far Eastern Federal Okrug, 4, 13, 16, 21, 33, 34, 40, 41, 77, 143
Primorskii Krai (Primorye), 2, 4, 20, 23, 27n17, 31–46, 54, 56, 63–65, 144, 145, 150
Putin, Vladimir, 12, 13, 15–17, 21–23, 33, 36, 38, 52, 59, 61, 77, 82, 85, 86, 89n3, 98, 104, 106, 108, 112, 120–122, 124, 125, 130, 131, 140, 150

S
Sakhalin Oblast, 65
Sakha Republic, 2, 65, 150
Sanctions, 6, 7, 24, 32, 52, 53, 59, 68, 84, 96–102, 106, 107, 121, 131, 140–142, 147–149, 151, 152, 160, 161, 164
Shanghai Cooperation Organization (SCO), 6, 79, 119–133, 162, 163
South Korea, 15, 36, 37, 42, 43, 54, 60, 70n7, 82, 140, 145, 146, 150

Special economic zone (SEZ), 4, 20, 21, 32, 35, 36, 61–65, 145, 153n5
State Commission on the Socioeconomic Development of the Far East, 21, 23
Strategy for the Socioeconomic Development of the Far East and the Baikal Region, 15, 34, 140

T
Taxes, 14, 19, 20, 25, 37, 38, 60, 62, 64, 68, 142, 144, 149, 161
Trutnev, Iurii, 17, 21–23, 27n15, 33, 34, 40, 41, 44, 143

U
United Nations (UN), 85, 86, 130
United States (US), 78, 82–84, 98, 107, 121, 124, 126, 130–132

V
Vankor, 6, 97, 107, 108, 111, 163

Y
Yamal LNG, 6, 97, 106, 107, 111

The manufacturer's authorised representative in the EU is Springer Nature Customer Service Centre GmbH, Europaplatz 3, 69115 Heidelberg, Germany. If you have any concerns regarding our products, please contact ProductSafety@springernature.com

Printed and bound by CPI Group (UK) Ltd, Croydon, CR0 4YY

26/03/2026

02078711-0003